T0413931

The World Trade Organization: Another Round

THE WORLD TRADE ORGANIZATION: ANOTHER ROUND

HAROLD B. WHITIKER
EDITOR

Nova Science Publishers, Inc.
New York

Copyright © 2007 by Nova Science Publishers, Inc.

All rights reserved. No part of this book may be reproduced, stored in a retrieval system or transmitted in any form or by any means: electronic, electrostatic, magnetic, tape, mechanical photocopying, recording or otherwise without the written permission of the Publisher.

For permission to use material from this book please contact us:
Telephone 631-231-7269; Fax 631-231-8175
Web Site: http://www.novapublishers.com

NOTICE TO THE READER

The Publisher has taken reasonable care in the preparation of this book, but makes no expressed or implied warranty of any kind and assumes no responsibility for any errors or omissions. No liability is assumed for incidental or consequential damages in connection with or arising out of information contained in this book. The Publisher shall not be liable for any special, consequential, or exemplary damages resulting, in whole or in part, from the readers' use of, or reliance upon, this material.

Independent verification should be sought for any data, advice or recommendations contained in this book. In addition, no responsibility is assumed by the publisher for any injury and/or damage to persons or property arising from any methods, products, instructions, ideas or otherwise contained in this publication.

This publication is designed to provide accurate and authoritative information with regard to the subject matter covered herein. It is sold with the clear understanding that the Publisher is not engaged in rendering legal or any other professional services. If legal or any other expert assistance is required, the services of a competent person should be sought. FROM A DECLARATION OF PARTICIPANTS JOINTLY ADOPTED BY A COMMITTEE OF THE AMERICAN BAR ASSOCIATION AND A COMMITTEE OF PUBLISHERS.

LIBRARY OF CONGRESS CATALOGING-IN-PUBLICATION DATA
The World Trade Organization : another round / Harold B. Whitiker (editor).
    p. cm.
Includes bibliographical references and index.
ISBN-13: 978-1-60021-816-3 (hbk.)
ISBN-10: 1-60021-816-4 (hbk.)
1. World Trade Organization. 2. International trade agencies. 3. International trade. 4. Commercial policy. I. Whitiker, Harold B.
HF1385.W667   2007
382'.92--dc22   2007028952

Published by Nova Science Publishers, Inc. ✢ New York

CONTENTS

Preface		vii
Chapter 1	Limited Progress at Hong Kong Ministerial Clouds Prospects for Doha Agreement *Government Accountability Office*	1
Chapter 2	Potential Challenges to U.S. Farm Subsidies in the WTO *Randy Schnepf and Jasper Womach*	33
Chapter 3	WTO Doha Round: The Agricultural Negotiations *Charles E. Hanrahan and Randy Schnepf*	87
Chapter 4	U.S. Agricultural Policy Response to WTO Cotton Decision *Randy Schnepf*	121
Chapter 5	Russia's Accession to the WTO *William H. Cooper*	129
Chapter 6	WTO: Antidumping Issues in the Doha Development Agenda *Vivian C. Jones*	153
Chapter 7	Dispute Settlement in the World Trade Organization: An Overview *Jeanne J. Grimmett*	173
Chapter 8	Trade Preferences for Developing Countries and the WTO *Jeanne J. Grimmett*	181
Index		189

PREFACE

The World Trade Organization (WTO) is the only global international organization dealing with the rules of trade between nations. At its heart are the WTO agreements, negotiated and signed by the bulk of the world's trading nations and ratified in their parliaments. The goal is to help producers of goods and services, exporters, and importers conduct their business. Although this is no doubt true, the goal is clouded by the political fog created by both current members and wanabees. This new books tries to shed a ray of light on the current set of imbroglios.

Chapter 1 - U.S. officials often call the World Trade Organization's (WTO) Doha Development Agenda or "Round" of global trade talks, launched in Doha, Qatar, in November 2001, a "once in a generation opportunity" to expand trade. President Bush has identified their success as his administration's top trade priority. Due to various U.S. notification and consultation requirements, concluding the negotiations in 2006 is essential for a Doha agreement to qualify for congressional consideration under U.S. Trade Promotion Authority (TPA), which expires July 1, 2007. A ministerial meeting among the WTO's 149 members was held on December 13-18, 2005, in Hong Kong, China, to make decisions needed to advance the talks.

Given the importance of the WTO Doha Round to the United States, GAO was asked to provide an update on the status of the negotiations. In this report, the latest in a series on the negotiations, we (1) provide the status of the Doha negotiations on the eve of the Hong Kong ministerial, (2) review the outcome of the Hong Kong ministerial, and (3) discuss the prospects for concluding the Doha Round before TPA expires in July 2007.

Chapter 2 - Prior to its expiration on January 1, 2004, the World Trade Organization's (WTO's) Peace Clause (Article 13 of the Agreement on Agriculture) provided protection from trade remedy consideration and WTO dispute settlement for domestic farm subsidies provided they met certain compliance conditions. Absent the Peace Clause, challenges to U.S. farm subsidies now appear to confront a lower threshold for success, that of establishing "serious prejudice" under Articles 5(c) and 6.3 of the Agreement on Subsidies and Countervailing Measures (SCM). In particular, the criteria for establishing serious prejudice claims include demonstrating (1) the magnitude of a commodity's subsidies either as a share of returns or as an important determinant in covering production costs; (2) the relevance of the subsidized commodity to world markets as a share of either world production or world trade; and (3) a causal relationship between the subsidy and the adverse effect in the relevant market. Evidence of these criteria favors a successful challenge ruling by a WTO panel, as demonstrated by Brazil's successful WTO challenge of the U.S. cotton program.

A review of current U.S. farm programs measured against these criteria suggests that all major U.S. program crops are potentially vulnerable to WTO challenges. In addition, a review of recent economic analyses suggests that a partial policy reform of the nature suggested by the U.S. Doha-Round Proposal would do little to diminish the causal relationship between U.S. crop subsidies and adverse effects in international markets. Instead, the most clear method for decreasing exposure to WTO legal challenges is through extensive decoupling of U.S. programs — i.e., removing the linkage between payments and producer or consumer behavior. Such decoupling would sever the causality linkage necessary to consummate a successful WTO challenge.

The potential success of WTO challenges against U.S. farm programs is of concern to the U.S. Congress. If such challenges occur and are successful, the WTO remedy likely would imply either the elimination, alteration, or amendment by Congress of the programs in question to remove their adverse effects. Since most governing provisions over U.S. farm programs are statutory, new legislation could be required to implement even minor changes to achieve compliance. Alternately, in light of an adverse ruling the United States could choose to make compensatory payments (under agreement with the challenging country) to offset the alleged injury.

This chapter provides background regarding the vulnerability of U.S. agricultural support programs to potential WTO dispute settlement challenges. It does not predict which WTO members might challenge U.S. commodity subsidies, nor the likelihood that such challenges will be brought. Instead, this report reviews the general criteria for successfully challenging a farm subsidy program, and then uses available data and published economic analyses to weigh U.S. farm programs against these criteria

Chapter 3 - On July 24, 2006, the WTO's Director General announced the indefinite suspension of further negotiations in the Doha Development Agenda or Doha Round of multilateral trade negotiations. The principal cause of the suspension was that a core group of WTO member countries — the United States, the European Union (EU), Brazil, India, Australia, and Japan — known as the G-6 had reached an impasse over specific methods to achieve the broad aims of the round for agricultural trade: substantial reductions in trade-distorting domestic subsidies, elimination of export subsidies, and substantially increased market access for agricultural products.

The WTO is unique among the various fora of international trade negotiations in that it brings together its entire 149-country membership to negotiate a common set of rules to govern international trade in agricultural products, industrial goods, and services. Agreement across such a large assemblage of participating nations and range of issues contributes significantly to consistency and harmonization of trade rules across countries. Regarding agriculture, because policy reform is addressed across three broadly inclusive fronts — export competition, domestic support, and market access — WTO negotiations provide a framework for give and take to help foster mutual agreement. As a result, the Doha Round represents an unusual opportunity for addressing most policy-induced distortions in international agricultural markets.

Doha Round negotiators were operating under a deadline effectively imposed by the expiration of U.S. Trade Promotion Authority (TPA), which permits the President to negotiate trade deals and present them to Congress for expedited consideration. To meet congressional notification requirements under TPA, an agreement would have to have been completed by the end of 2006. That now appears unlikely. TPA expires on June 30, 2007, and most trade experts and officials think that the authority would not be renewed.

As a result of the suspension of the negotiations, a major source of pressure for U.S. farm policy change will have dissipated. The current farm bill expires in 2007, and many were looking to a Doha Round agreement to require changes in U.S. farm subsidies to make them more compatible with world trade rules. The option of extending the current farm law appears strengthened by the indefinite suspension of the Doha talks. The United States must still meet obligations under existing WTO agricultural agreements, which limit trade-distorting spending to $19.1 billion annually. Some trade analysts think that, now that the Round has been suspended, there could be an increase in litigation by WTO member countries that allege they are harmed by U.S. farm subsidies.

This chapter assesses the current status of agricultural negotiations in the Doha Round; traces the developments leading up to the December 2005 Hong Kong Ministerial; examines the major agricultural negotiating proposals; discusses the potential effects of a successful Doha Round agreement on global trade, income, U.S. farm policy, and U.S. agriculture; and provides background on the WTO, the Doha Round, the key negotiating groups, and a chronology of key events relevant to the agricultural negotiations.

Chapter 4 - In a dispute settlement case (DS267) brought by Brazil against certain aspects of the U.S. cotton program, a WTO Appellate Body (AB) recommended in March 2005 that the United States remove certain "prohibited subsidies" by July 21, 2005, and remove the adverse effects resulting from certain "actionable subsidies" by September 21, 2005. When the United States failed to meet these deadlines, Brazil claimed the right to retaliate against $3 billion in U.S. exports to Brazil based on the prohibited subsidies, and proposed $1 billion in retaliation based on the actionable subsidies. The United States objected to these retaliation amounts and requested WTO arbitration on the matter. However, in mid-2005 the United States and Brazil reached a procedural agreement to temporarily suspend retaliation proceedings.

On August 21, 2006, Brazil submitted a request for a WTO compliance panel to review whether the United States has fully complied with panel and AB rulings. The United States blocked the WTO's Dispute Settlement Body (DSB) from approving Brazil's request on August 31, 2006; however, Brazil is expected to make a second request (which the United States will be unable to block) at the DSB meeting set for September 28, 2006. If a compliance panel finds that the United States has not fully complied with the AB rulings, Brazil could ask the WTO arbitration panel to resume its work. Although the United States has already complied with a portion of the AB's recommendation by eliminating the Step 2 program (August 1, 2006), additional permanent modifications to U.S. farm programs may still be needed to fully comply with the WTO ruling on "actionable subsidies."

Chapter 5 - In 1993, Russia formally applied for accession to the General Agreement on Tariffs and Trade (GATT). Its application was taken up by the World Trade Organization (WTO) in 1995, the successor organization of the GATT. Russia's application has entered into its most significant phase as Russia negotiates with WTO members on the conditions for accession.

Accession to the WTO is critical to Russia and its political leadership. President Vladimir Putin has made it a top priority. He views accession as an important step in integrating the Russian economy with the rest of the world and in fostering economic growth and development by attracting foreign investment and by lowering trade barriers. For the United States, the European Union (EU) and other trading partners, Russia's accession to the WTO could increase stability and predictability in Russia's foreign trade and investment regime.

The Russian accession process is moving forward, but differences over some critical issues remain, making the time for Russian accession to the WTO uncertain. The European Union and the United States have raised concerns about Russian energy pricing policies which allow natural gas, oil, and electricity to be sold domestically far below world prices providing, they argue, a subsidy to domestic producers of fertilizers, steel, and other energy-intensive goods. Russia counters that the subsidies are not illegal under the WTO. Concerns regarding Russian trade barriers in the services sector, high tariffs for civil aircraft and autos, and intellectual property rights have slowed down the process and made the original target of completion in 2003 unattainable. There were indications that Russia and its trading partners, including the United States, wanted to see the process completed in time for the July 15-17, 2006, G-8 summit meeting in St. Petersburg chaired by Russian President Putin. Russia and the United States could not reach agreement in the final bilateral negotiations.

Congressional interest in Russia's accession to the WTO is multifaceted. Members of Congress are concerned that Russia enters the WTO under terms and conditions in line with U.S. economic interests, especially gaining access to Russian markets as well as safeguards to protect U.S. import-sensitive industries. Some Members also assert that Congress should have a formal role in approving the conditions under which Russia accedes to the WTO, a role it does not have at this time. A number of Members of Congress and members of the U.S. business community have advised the Bush Administration not to agree too quickly to Russia's accession to the WTO and to ensure that U.S. concerns are met. The Congress has a direct role in determining whether Russia receives permanent normal trade relations (NTR) status which has implications for Russia's membership in the WTO and U.S.-Russian trade relations. Without granting permanent NTR (PNTR) to Russia, the United States would not benefit from the concessions that Russia makes upon accession. Issues regarding Russia's accession to the WTO may arise during the second session of the 109th Congress.

In 1993, Russia formally applied for accession to the General Agreement on Tariffs and Trade (GATT). Its application was taken up by the World Trade Organization (WTO) in 1995, the successor organization of the GATT.[1] Russia's application has entered into its most significant phase as Russia negotiates with WTO members on the conditions for accession. The process is moving forward, but differences over some critical issues remain, making the time for Russian accession to the WTO uncertain.

Accession to the WTO is critical to Russia and its political leadership. President Vladimir Putin has made it a top priority. He views accession as an important step in integrating the Russian economy with the rest of the world and in fostering economic growth and development by attracting foreign investment and by lowering trade barriers. For the United States, the European Union (EU) and other trading partners, Russia's accession to the WTO could increase stability and predictability in Russia's foreign trade and investment regime. Presidents Bush and Putin have discussed Russia's accession to the WTO at their various bilateral meetings. At a September 2005 meeting in Washington, President Bush told the Russian leader that he was "very interested" in seeing Russia's negotiations for WTO accession completed by the end of the year, a deadline that went unmet.[2]

The United States remains the only WTO member out of 58 members that has not reached a bilateral agreement on Russia's accession. The two countries reportedly wanted to have the U.S.-Russian negotiations completed by the July 15-17, 2006 G-8 summit hosted by President Putin in St. Petersburg. Negotiators for the two sides were reportedly very close to reaching agreement. They conducted three days of intense negotiations led by United States Trade Representative Susan Schwab and Russian Economic Development and Trade Minister German Gref, but to no avail. Although the two sides made progress on key issues, the negotiations stopped short of completion because Russia insisted that its inspectors be able to audit U.S. facilities for beef and pork before those products are exported to Russia. Both countries indicated that they could reach an agreement by the end of October 2006.

Congressional interest in Russia's accession to the WTO is multifaceted. Members of Congress are concerned that Russia enters the WTO under terms and conditions in line with U.S. economic interests, especially gaining access to Russian markets as well as safeguards to protect U.S. import-sensitive industries. Some Members also assert that Congress should have a formal role in approving the conditions under which Russia accedes to the WTO, a role it does not have at this time. The Congress has a direct role in determining whether Russia receive permanent normal trade relations (NTR) status which has implications for Russia's membership in the WTO and U.S.-Russian trade relations. Without granting PNTR to Russia, the United States would not benefit from the concessions that Russia makes upon accession.

This chapter examines the issue of Russia's accession to the WTO, focusing on the implications for Russia, the United States, and the WTO. It begins with a short overview of the WTO accession process and reviews the history of the Soviet Union's relationship with the GATT/WTO. It provides a brief discussion of Russian economic conditions and the status of economic reforms as they are a major impetus for Russia's application to join the WTO. The focus of the chapter is the status of Russia's accession application and the outstanding issues. The report concludes with an analysis of the implications of Russia's accession to the WTO for Russia, the United States, the other WTO members and for the WTO itself and an analysis of the outlook for the Russia's application.

Chapter 6 - At the November 2001 Ministerial meeting of the World Trade Organization (WTO) in Doha, Qatar, WTO member countries launched a new round of trade talks known as the Doha Development Agenda (DDA). One of the negotiating objectives called for "clarifying and improving disciplines" under the WTO Antidumping and Subsidies Agreements. Since antidumping is the most frequently used trade remedy action worldwide, most of the discussion focused on changing ways that WTO members administer antidumping (AD) actions.

WTO negotiations in the DDA directly involve Congress since any trade agreement made by the United States must be implemented by legislation. In addition, Congress has an important oversight role in trade negotiations as provided in legislation granting presidential Trade Promotion Authority in the Trade Act of 2002 (P.L. 107-210).

The frequent use of antidumping actions by the United States and other developed nations has come under criticism by other WTO members as being protectionist. Many Members of Congress defend the use of U.S. antidumping actions brought as necessary to protect U.S. firms and workers from unfair competition. However, because the United States is also a leading target of antidumping actions by other countries, some U.S. export-oriented firms may support changes to the Antidumping Agreement.

The positions of major players in trade remedy talks are well-documented by position papers circulated through the WTO Negotiating Group on Rules. At the December 2005

WTO Ministerial in Hong Kong, rules negotiators were called upon to further "intensify and accelerate the negotiating process."

Most of the proposals on trade remedies focus on changing the Antidumping Agreement, currently a somewhat ambiguous document that gives broad guidelines for conducting AD investigations, in order to provide more specific definitions and stricter procedures. The goal of many of the WTO members seems to be to lower the level of antidumping duties provided per investigation and/or to provide more restrictions on the ability of officials to grant relief to domestic industries. The gap between the U.S. position, where there is strong support in Congress to preserve the rights of WTO members to provide AD relief to domestic industries, and the viewpoints of other countries appears to be wide and may be difficult to narrow, but some countries see revision of the Antidumping Agreement and other WTO disciplines on trade remedies as a "make or break" issue if the DDA is to succeed.

This chapter examines antidumping issues in DDA negotiations by analyzing the issue in three parts. The first provides background information and contextual analysis for understanding why the issue is so controversial. The second section focuses on how antidumping issues fit into the DDA, and the third section provides a more specific overview of major reform proposals that are being considered.

Chapter 7 - Dispute resolution in the World Trade Organization (WTO) is carried out under the WTO Dispute Settlement Understanding (DSU), whose rules and procedures apply to virtually all WTO agreements. The DSU provides for consultations between disputing parties, panels and appeals, and possible compensation or retaliation if a defending party does not comply with an adverse WTO decision by a given date. Automatic establishment of panels, adoption of reports, and authorization of requests to retaliate, along with deadlines for various stages of the dispute process and improved multilateral surveillance and enforcement of WTO obligations, are aimed at producing a more expeditious and effective system than that which existed under the GATT. To date, 349 WTO complaints have been filed, slightly more than half of which involve the United States as a complaining party or defendant. Expressing dissatisfaction with WTO dispute settlement results in the trade remedy area, Congress directed the executive branch to address dispute settlement issues in WTO negotiations in its grant of trade promotion authority to the President in 2002 (P.L. 107-210). WTO Members had been negotiating DSU revisions in the now-suspended WTO Doha Round, though a draft agreement was not produced. S. 817 (Stabenow), S. 1542 (Stabenow), S. 2317 (Baucus), and H.R. 4186 (Camp) would each establish a new position in the Office of the United States Trade Representative (USTR) to help the USTR investigate and prosecute WTO disputes. S. 2467 (Grassley) would make the USTR General Counsel a confirmable position expressly responsible for WTO dispute settlement. H.R. 4733 (Rangel) and H.R. 5043 (Cardin) would create new congressional entities with functions related to WTO disputes.

Chapter 8 - World Trade Organization (WTO) Members must grant immediate and unconditional most-favored-nation (MFN) treatment to the products of other Members with respect to tariffs and other trade-related measures. Programs such as the Generalized System of Preferences (GSP), under which developed countries grant preferential tariff rates to developing country products, are facially inconsistent with this obligation because they accord goods of some countries more favorable tariff treatment than that accorded to goods of other WTO Members. Because such programs have been viewed as trade-expanding, however, Contracting Parties to the General Agreement on Tariffs and Trade (GATT) provided a legal basis for one-way tariff preferences and certain other preferential arrangements in a 1979 decision known as the Enabling Clause. In 2004, the WTO Appellate Body ruled that the Clause allows developed countries to offer different treatment to developing countries, but only if identical treatment is available to all similarly situated GSP beneficiaries. Where WTO Members' preference programs have provided expanded benefits, the WTO has on occasion waived Members' WTO obligations. A number of trade preference bills have been introduced in the 109th Congress, including proposed extensions of the GSP and Andean preference programs, each of which is set to expire in 2006. Among these are H.R. 5070, which would extend the GSP and Andean preferences for one year and expand and extend textile benefits under the African Growth and Opportunity Act (AGOA); H.R. 6076 and S. 3904, which would extend until 2008 the GSP, Andean preferences, and a third-country fabric provision for lesser-developed beneficiaries expiring in 2007; and H.R. 6142, which would extend the GSP and the AGOA third-country fabric provision until 2008 and expand textile and apparel benefits for Haiti.

In: The World Trade Organization: Another Round
Editor: Harold B. Whitiker, pp. 1-32
ISBN: 978-1-60021-816-3
© 2007 Nova Science Publishers, Inc.

Chapter 1

LIMITED PROGRESS AT HONG KONG MINISTERIAL CLOUDS PROSPECTS FOR DOHA AGREEMENT[*]

Government Accountability Office

WHY GAO DID THIS STUDY

U.S. officials often call the World Trade Organization's (WTO) Doha Development Agenda or "Round" of global trade talks, launched in Doha, Qatar, in November 2001, a "once in a generation opportunity" to expand trade. President Bush has identified their success as his administration's top trade priority. Due to various U.S. notification and consultation requirements, concluding the negotiations in 2006 is essential for a Doha agreement to qualify for congressional consideration under U.S. Trade Promotion Authority (TPA), which expires July 1, 2007. A ministerial meeting among the WTO's 149 members was held on December 13-18, 2005, in Hong Kong, China, to make decisions needed to advance the talks.

Given the importance of the WTO Doha Round to the United States, GAO was asked to provide an update on the status of the negotiations. In this report, the latest in a series on the negotiations, we (1) provide the status of the Doha negotiations on the eve of the Hong Kong ministerial, (2) review the outcome of the Hong Kong ministerial, and (3) discuss the prospects for concluding the Doha Round before TPA expires in July 2007.

WHAT GAO FOUND

WTO members made little progress in 2005 toward their goal of completing the steps needed to set the stage for finalizing the Doha Round of global trade talks. The key milestones for progress through July were missed. Despite new proposals on agricultural subsidy and tariff cuts submitted in October 2005, it was clear by November that key players

---

[*] Excerpted from GAO-06-596

were too far apart to achieve the major decisions planned for the December ministerial. To avoid a failure, members agreed to lower expectations for the meeting.

The Hong Kong ministerial resulted in modest agreements on a narrow range of agricultural and development issues. Ministers made little progress on the broader Doha negotiating agenda, including two other U.S. priorities—services and nonagricultural market access. Nevertheless, WTO members renewed their resolve to successfully conclude the Doha Round by the end of 2006 and set new interim deadlines under a compressed schedule to meet that goal. Critical decisions that will determine each member's cuts in tariffs and other barriers were due April 30 and July 31, 2006, but the April 30 deadline will be missed.

WTO members continue to profess commitment to accomplish the ambitious agenda set at Doha. However, with nearly all tough decisions put off, the tension between members' original high ambitions and the U.S. TPA timeframe has become acute. Since the Hong Kong ministerial, members have taken concrete steps to help build consensus. Yet, the ongoing impasse on core areas such as agriculture, and the difficult political decisions needed to resolve it, cause many experts to be skeptical. As illustrated below, numerous time-consuming steps still must be completed in the little more than a year left before TPA expires. While holding out hope for an agreement that lives up to Doha's promise, experts say outright collapse, substantial delay, or modest results are all possible outcomes.

Key Selected Deadlines in 2006 for Doha Negotiations

NAMA: Nonagricultural market access
Source: GAO, based on WTO documents.

ABBREVIATIONS

ACP	African, Caribbean, and Pacific Group of States
C-4	Cotton Four countries
EU	European Union
GATT	General Agreement on Tariffs and Trade
G-4	Group of 4
G-5	Group of 5
G-6	Group of 6
G-10	Group of 10

G-20	Group of 20
G-90	Group of 90
ITC	International Trade Commission
LDC	Least developed countries
NAMA	Nonagricultural market access
TPA	Trade Promotion Authority
USTR	Office of the United States Trade Representative
WTO	World Trade Organization

This is a work of the U.S. government and is not subject to copyright protection in the United States. It may be reproduced and distributed in its entirety without further permission from GAO. However, because this work may contain copyrighted images or other material, permission from the copyright holder may be necessary if you wish to reproduce this material separately.

April 26, 2006   The Honorable William M. ThomasChairmanCommittee on Ways and MeansHouse of RepresentativesTrade ministers from members of the World Trade Organization (WTO) gathered in Hong Kong, China, in December 2005, for a meeting that was originally expected to yield agreements considered critical for concluding the Doha Round negotiations by the end of 2006.[1] Launched in November 2001 in Doha, Qatar, these negotiations involve 149 nations and encompass a far-reaching, ambitious agenda for liberalizing trade ranging from reducing tariffs and eliminating subsidies, to bolstering economic development in poor countries. Because the Doha Round is considered a "package deal"—or single undertaking in WTO parlance—simultaneous agreement by all members on all issues is required to finalize an agreement. U.S. and WTO officials acknowledge that concluding the negotiations in 2006 is essential for a Doha agreement to qualify for the streamlined congressional approval procedures of the U.S. Trade Promotion Authority (TPA), which expires July 1, 2007.[2] President Bush has identified the success of the Doha Round negotiations as his administration's top trade priority.Given the importance of the WTO Doha Round to the United States, you asked us to provide an update on the status of these negotiations. In this report, the latest in a series,[3] we (1) provide the status of the Doha negotiations on the eve of the Hong Kong ministerial, (2) review the outcome of the Hong Kong ministerial, and (3) discuss the prospects for concluding the Doha Round before TPA expires in July 2007.To address these objectives, we met with, and reviewed documents from a range of WTO, U.S., and foreign government officials, as well as academic experts and private sector groups (including business associations, law firms, and civil society groups) in Washington, D.C.; Geneva, Switzerland; and Brussels, Belgium. We also attended the sixth WTO ministerial conference in Hong Kong, China. To assess the prospects for success, we relied on the views of selected participants and experts representing a range of institutional perspectives (government, academia, "think tanks," nongovernmental organizations, business groups, and other trade policy observers), as well as our own analysis. We conducted our work from May 2005 through March 2006 in accordance with generally accepted government auditing standards.

RESULTS IN BRIEF

Between mid-2004 and the eve of the WTO's Hong Kong ministerial conference in December 2005, WTO members made little progress toward their goal of making the major decisions in six core areas that would be needed to set the stage for final negotiations in 2006: (1) agriculture, (2) nonagricultural (or industrial) market access, (3) services, (4) trade facilitation (simplification of customs procedures), (5) development issues, and (6) WTO rules (including antidumping and subsidies). During this period, trade facilitation negotiations got off to a good start and some progress on technical issues was achieved in most other areas of the negotiations, although this generally took longer and proved more contentious than expected. Key milestones were missed, including the May 2005 deadline for submitting new and revised offers in the services negotiations, which was not met by most members. Despite significant proposals on cutting agricultural subsidies and tariffs submitted in October 2005, it was clear to members by November that the negotiating positions of key players were too far apart to achieve major agreements at the December ministerial. To avoid a potentially disastrous collapse at Hong Kong, the new WTO Director-General steered members toward lowered expectations for the meeting. As a result, they shifted the focus to narrower initiatives primarily intended to lock in progress to date and benefit least-developed country members.

The Hong Kong ministerial resulted in modest agreements on a narrow range of agricultural and development issues, but postponed decisions on how much to cut tariffs and other barriers. Notably, WTO members conditionally agreed to eliminate agricultural export subsidies by 2013 and to provide least-developed countries duty-free and quota-free access to developed-country markets for at least 97 percent of their products. However, little progress was made on other core areas of the broader Doha negotiating agenda, including two of the United States' priorities—services and nonagricultural market access. Despite its modest achievements, the Hong Kong ministerial declaration formally committed members to conclude an overall agreement on the Doha Round by the end of 2006 and set a series of interim deadlines to meet that goal. For example, April 30, 2006, was the new date for establishing "modalities"—broad guidance on the extent of each country's reductions in tariffs, subsidies, and other trade barriers—for agricultural and nonagricultural goods. Members' schedules, reflecting how they propose to apply these modalities in their national commitments, are due July 31, 2006, and will be the basis for the final phase of negotiations.

WTO members and observers recognize that achieving an agreement within the time remaining in 2006 will be challenging, given the limited progress to date and the scope and difficulty of the work outstanding. Members continue to profess high ambitions, however, and most view expiration of TPA on July 1, 2007, as a hard deadline that drives the need to conclude negotiations in 2006. Since Hong Kong, some steps toward achieving their agreed-upon goals have been taken, such as gaining agreement among key members to use simulations of the impact of proposed cuts in subsidies and tariffs as a basis for discussions. Nevertheless, factors such as the failure to meet most prior deadlines, the ongoing impasse on core areas such as agriculture, and the difficult political decisions needed to resolve them, cause experts to be skeptical. In particular, the trade-offs required to finalize the agreement will need to be made when political events such as elections are taking place, which will constrain key countries. Moreover, even if a breakthrough is achieved, many difficult and time-consuming steps must be completed before entering an agreement. Thus, the ability to meet the 2006 deadlines with an ambitious outcome—one that would result in a strengthened and measurably freer global trade environment—is in doubt. While holding out some hope for a satisfactory outcome, several experts in fact warn that outright collapse, substantial delay, or a minimal outcome are possible.

We solicited comments on a draft of this report from the Office of the U.S. Trade Representative (USTR), and the Departments of Agriculture, Commerce, and State; these agencies generally agreed with our substantive findings and offered a few minor technical corrections, which we incorporated.

BACKGROUND

The WTO was established as a result of the Uruguay "Round" on January 1, 1995, as the successor to the General Agreement on Tariffs and Trade (GATT). Based in Geneva, Switzerland, the WTO administers agreed-upon rules for international trade, provides a mechanism for settling disputes, and serves as a forum for conducting trade negotiations. WTO membership has increased since 1995, and there are currently 149 WTO member nations and customs territories that are diverse in terms of economic development; these members negotiate individually or as a member of a group of countries (see table 1 for some of the major country groupings). While the WTO has no formal definition of a "developing country," the World Bank classifies 105 current WTO members—or approximately 72 percent—as developing countries; 32 of these members are officially designated as "least-developed countries" (LDCs).[4] USTR negotiates on behalf of the United States in WTO negotiations.

The WTO ministerial conference held in Hong Kong, China, from December 13–18, 2005, was the sixth since the establishment of the WTO in 1995. These ministerial conferences, convened at least every 2 years, bring together trade ministers from all WTO members. The outcome of a ministerial conference is reflected in a fully agreed-upon ministerial declaration. The substance of these declarations guides future work by outlining an agenda and deadlines for the WTO until the next ministerial conference. Decisions in the WTO are made by consensus—or absence of dissent—among all members, rather than by a simple majority. Periodic "mini-ministerials," or informal meetings among small groups of selected WTO members, are often used to advance dialogue on issues.

At the Hong Kong conference, ministers sought to make progress in the ongoing multilateral trade negotiations, officially known as the Doha Development Agenda. Formally launched at the fourth WTO ministerial conference in Doha, Qatar, in November 2001, the negotiations are the latest in a series of global trade talks (negotiating rounds) dating back nearly six decades.[5] They are intended to reduce trade barriers and facilitate the free flow of commerce throughout the world. A major objective of the Doha negotiations is development—that is, to help developing countries realize the economic benefits of trade and enable them to take advantage of trading opportunities.

Table 1. Major Negotiating Groups in the World Trade Organization

Country group	Countries	Interest
Groups of 4, 5, and 6 (G-4, G-5, G-6)	United States, EU, Brazil, and India (plus Australia in G-5; Japan in G-6)	The G-5 helped negotiate the July 2004 framework agreement on agriculture and variants of this group are now a key negotiating group for the Doha Round
European Union (EU)(currently has 25 members)	Austria, Belgium, Cyprus, Czech Republic, Denmark, Estonia, Finland, France, Germany, Greece, Hungary, Ireland, Italy, Latvia, Lithuania, Luxembourg, Malta, Netherlands, Portugal, Poland, Slovak Republic, Slovenia, Spain, Sweden, and United Kingdom	Political union that negotiates as a group in the Doha Round
Group of 20 (G-20) (currently has 21 members)	Argentina, Bolivia, Brazil, Chile, China, Cuba, Egypt, Guatemala, India, Indonesia, Mexico, Nigeria, Pakistan, Paraguay, Philippines, South Africa, Tanzania, Thailand, Uruguay, Venezuela, Zimbabwe	Developing countries united on agriculture negotiations
Group of 10 (G-10)	Bulgaria, Iceland, Israel, Japan, Liechtenstein, Mauritius, Norway, South Korea, Switzerland, and Chinese Taipei	Net food importers and subsidizers
Group of 90 (G-90)	Members of the African Union; the LDCs; and the African, Caribbean, and Pacific (ACP) Group[a]	Coalition of the poorest and least-developed countries in the WTO
Cotton Four (C-4)	Benin, Burkina Faso, Chad, and Mali	West African cotton-producing countries advocating a WTO initiative to assist their cotton farmers

Source: GAO analysis of WTO documents.

[a] The African, Caribbean, and Pacific Group of States (ACP) is an organization created in 1975. It is composed of African, Caribbean, and Pacific states that are signatories to the partnership agreement between the ACP and the EU, now officially called the "Cotonou Agreement."

The Doha ministerial declaration established a work program with a number of negotiating areas and set the goal for concluding the negotiations by January 1, 2005.[6] Of the 16 current negotiating areas, market access in agriculture, services, and nonagricultural (industrial) products (NAMA) are the three U.S. priorities. WTO members set specific goals for each area and set up various negotiating groups to achieve them. In agriculture, the Doha work program commits countries to lower barriers in world agricultural markets and sets forth three pillars for agricultural trade reform: export competition (subsidies), domestic support (subsidies and other assistance to farmers), and market access (tariffs). Agriculture remains the top issue for many participants and has been described as the lynchpin of the Doha negotiations. Lack of progress in liberalizing agriculture is partly due to the fact that it was first added to the trading system in the last (Uruguay) round, which left high subsidies and tariff barriers in place. Doha negotiations in services aim to ensure increased transparency and predictability of rules and regulations governing services and to promote liberalization of service markets. The goal of the NAMA negotiations is to reduce or eliminate tariffs and non-tariff barriers. The agriculture and NAMA negotiations involve first reaching agreement on "modalities"—the formulas, thresholds, dates, and other numerical benchmarks that members will commit to meet when they revise their WTO schedules of subsidy and tariff commitments. This guidance then is translated into national tariff schedules specifying what tariff will be charged on each product. Members are then "bound" not to exceed these.

Concluding the round will require simultaneous agreement on all issues, because WTO members have agreed it will be a package deal (or "single undertaking" in WTO parlance). As a result, trade-offs are expected to occur among issues to accomplish an overall balance satisfactory to all members. When it is final, the trade agreement will impose legally binding international obligations on WTO members governing the trade barriers they are allowed to maintain (such as tariffs) and the trade rules by which they must abide. Failure to comply is subject to binding dispute settlement and possible trade retaliation.

To date, the negotiations have progressed fitfully. Our January 2004 report explained the factors that caused the September 2003 Cancún ministerial to collapse in acrimony and confusion, including sharp North-South (developed-developing country) divisions on key issues. For example, developing countries rejected the proposed U.S. and EU reductions in agricultural subsidies as inadequate, but the United States and the EU felt developing countries were not contributing to reform by agreeing to open their markets. Moreover, many developing countries remained dissatisfied with proposed responses to their demands for special treatment and for relief from difficulties they were still experiencing in implementing existing WTO obligations. In 2004, the Doha Round negotiations started again on an uncertain note; however, political leadership, intensified dialogue, and a series of conciliatory gestures resulted in WTO members adopting an agreement on key issues in the negotiations known as the "July framework agreement," which is credited with achieving sufficient progress on agriculture to put the global trade talks back on track and reopen discussion of other issues. The main features of the framework agreement were to establish key principles for each aspect of global agricultural trade reform; identify the key elements of negotiations to improve nonagricultural market access; stress the importance of liberalizing access to services markets and addressing outstanding development concerns; and launch negotiations to clarify and improve WTO rules on customsprocedures (trade facilitation).[7] WTO members also agreed to hold their next ministerial in Hong Kong in December 2005. However, our last report[8] noted that, despite the improved negotiating atmosphere, the negotiations were effectively 2 years behind schedule and considerable work remained on the numerous issues that would constitute a final agreement. Pursuant to the Trade Act of 2002, in March 2005, the president requested a 2-year extension of TPA, and the extension went into effect.

LIMITED PROGRESS SINCE MID-2004 CAUSES WTO MEMBERS TO RECALIBRATE GOALS FOR HONG KONG

Despite the impetus provided by the framework agreement, the Doha negotiations moved slowly throughout 2005. As we reported last year, WTO negotiators began 2005 with a resolve to complete the round in 2006 and set the stage by agreeing to make progress in 6 of the 16 Doha negotiating areas by the end of 2005—agriculture, NAMA, services, trade facilitation, development issues, and WTO rules. However, limited progress was made before the Hong Kong ministerial, as the talks stalled in fall 2005 amid stalemate over fundamental issues on agriculture and NAMA. To avoid another failed meeting, such as at the last ministerial in Cancún, Mexico, expectations for the Hong Kong ministerial were lowered. The agenda for the meeting shifted from making key decisions on the six core areas to focusing on narrower initiatives, particularly in agriculture and development, that could help the talks move forward, if only marginally (see fig. 1).

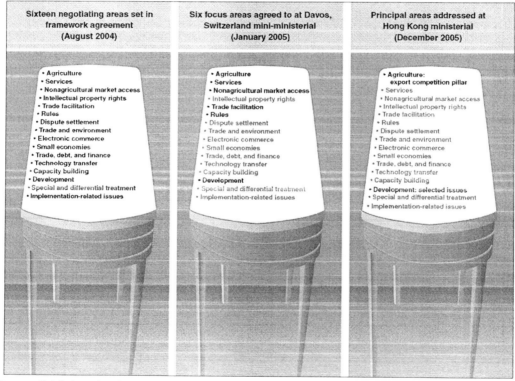

Source: GAO, based on WTO information.

Figure 1. Agenda for Hong Kong Focused on Only 2 of the 16 Doha Negotiating Areas.

Some Technical Progress Achieved but Key Milestones Missed

In early 2005, at a mini-ministerial meeting in Davos, Switzerland, and subsequently at a February meeting among all WTO members, WTO members agreed that the goal of the Hong Kong ministerial was to set the stage for the final phase of the Doha negotiations, which would enable the round to conclude in 2006. To that end, they agreed to seek to finalize modalities for both the agriculture and NAMA negotiations at Hong Kong, and to make significant progress in four other core areas—services, trade facilitation, development issues, and WTO rules (which covers subjects such as subsidies, antidumping measures, and regional trade agreements). Deliverables in these six areas are critical in determining how ambitious the Doha Round will be in terms of cuts in tariffs, subsidies, and other barriers to trade, as well as the ultimate balance across member interests and issues.

Despite these ambitious goals, the overall pace of the negotiations was slow throughout most of 2005, and even progress on technical issues was difficult to achieve. For example, in the agriculture and NAMA talks, negotiators were able to agree on a preliminary basis to methodologies for converting specific tariffs into *ad valorem* equivalents (tariffs based on a percentage of value), a necessary step before potential tariff reductions could be calculated and considered.[9] However, reaching this agreement for agriculture proved to be contentious and occupied the negotiators' time through early May, delaying the discussion of more central issues such as how to make tariff and subsidy cuts. On many issues, negotiators made incremental progress by narrowing the number of options under consideration or fleshing out principles or methods without coming to full agreement. On NAMA, for example, a list of products to be covered by the negotiations was compiled, but there was disagreement about including some items, and no agreement on whether the list should be considered definitive or just a guideline.

In 2005, WTO members missed the key milestones they had set to keep the talks on schedule for completion at the end of 2006 (see fig. 2). In the services negotiations, many WTO members failed to submit offers for opening their markets to foreign services-providers by a May 2005 deadline. Just before the ministerial, the services negotiating group chair reported having 69 initial and 30 revised offers, but 23 members had not yet submitted any offer.[10] In addition, the chair described many of the offers as disappointing, because they did not provide new market access or bind access at existing levels. In development, the negotiating group made little progress toward a July 2005 deadline to prepare recommendations to improve special and differential treatment.[11] WTO members also missed an informal but important milestone to reach agreement in July 2005 on a "first approximation" of the modalities for agriculture, NAMA, and other issues, which negotiators had hoped to finalize at the Hong Kong ministerial. As deadlines were missed during the spring and summer of 2005, WTO's then-Director-General warned negotiators that the talks were not moving fast enough to reach this goal. In early July, the Director-General stated flatly that "these negotiations are in trouble," adding that WTO members faced "a crisis of immobility" that threatened their ability to deliver decisions at the Hong Kong ministerial.

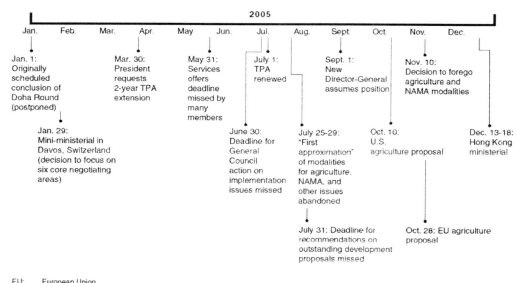

Figure 2. Key Milestones and Deadlines Missed in the WTO Negotiations in 2005.

We noted in our last report that U.S. and EU leadership has been essential to making progress in the WTO trade negotiations and that relations between their newly appointed trade principals could influence success at Hong Kong. However, a number of events made the leadership transition and U.S.–EU relations more difficult in 2005. A gap of several months occurred between the time when then-current U.S. Trade Representative Robert Zoellick was nominated Deputy Secretary of State in early January 2005 and when his replacement, Rob Portman, was confirmed in late April by the Senate as the new Trade Representative. At that time, a U.S.–EU aircraft dispute was flaring, and influential U.S. congressmen took umbrage at comments by the new EU Trade Commissioner, Peter Mandelson, directed at U.S. policies on cotton subsidies. In addition, some U.S. negotiators were also occupied with finalizing the Dominican Republic–Central America–United States Free Trade Agreement and ensuring its approval by Congress, which was finally secured on July 28, 2005.

Countries Still Divided Over Toughest Issues in Fall 2005

Fundamental divisions among WTO members became very clear in the fall of 2005 when members found themselves deadlocked over conflicting market access goals. In October, key members and country coalitions put forth detailed agriculture proposals that were intended to re-energize the negotiations and resolve key issues before the Hong Kong ministerial. The United States; the EU; the Group of 20 (G-20) coalition of developing countries; and the Group of 10 (G-10)—a coalition of primarily developed countries that import most of their food—laid out their positions on cutting agricultural subsidies and tariffs and what they expected in return from trading partners.[12] The differences among these parties' positions were particularly evident in their approaches to market access (see table 2). The U.S. proposal centered on an offer to cut U.S. domestic farm subsidies substantially, along with aggressive tariff cuts ranging from 55 to 90 percent for all developed countries. However, the offer was contingent on higher subsidy cuts and "ambitious" market access improvements by other countries, particularly the EU and the G-20. Many WTO members received the proposal as a significant effort to unblock the negotiation, but some countries were doubtful that the proposed subsidy cuts were as substantial as billed. The EU proposed smaller agricultural tariff cuts, with more exemptions for protecting "sensitive" products from competition from imports. This offer was contingent on certain concessions from other members, notably substantial market opening in NAMA and services from the more advanced developing countries of the G-20, especially Brazil and India. The G-20 proposal on agricultural market access, submitted earlier in the year, was presented as a middle ground, as the suggested tariff cuts for developed countries fell between the U.S. and EU proposals.[13]

Table 2. Agriculture Market Access Proposals Revealed Wide Differences among Key Players in Expectations for Developed Countries

	U.S.	G-20	EU[a]	G-10[b]
Tariff rate reduction goals	55–90%	45–75%	20–60%	27–45%
Maximum tariff rate (cap)	75%	100%	100% (no cap on sensitive products)	None
Sensitive products, as a percentage of all agricultural products	1%	1%	Up to 8%	15%

Sources: U.S., G-20, EU, and G-10 proposals.
[a] These terms are from the EU's second proposal of Oct. 28, 2005; the 20% tariff reduction minimum takes into account the "pivot" concept.
[b] The G-10 proposal included two approaches to tariff reductions—"linear" and "flexible." This table presents the G-10's linear approach to facilitate comparison with the other members' proposals that are also based on the linear approach.

The EU's market access offer became the focus of criticism before the ministerial, as neither the United States nor the G-20 considered it acceptable. They demanded that the EU cut its tariffs further and reduce the number of sensitive products that would be exempted from the standard tariff cuts. USTR noted that the EU's proposal would allow for tariff cuts of as little as 20 percent on about four-fifths of EU tariff lines.[14] Also, according to USTR, the EU could effectively limit competition from imports, due to the large number of sensitive products it had proposed to shield from liberalization (about 142 tariff lines). Although the EU revised its offer at the end of October 2005, it was again quickly rejected as insufficient.

The EU held the stance in the Doha Round that its chief gains were to be found in the industrial and services sectors underpinning its economy. Specifically, the EU wanted countries such as India and Brazil to offer realimprovements in access to their industrial and services markets.[15] EU members had already agreed to reform the EU's domestic support programs and to eliminate export subsidies as part of the framework agreement and believed they had gotten little in return. In internal consultations in late October, France warned the EU negotiating team that it should not overstep its mandate, which in its view was strictly tied to existing agricultural subsidy spending and the 2003 reform of the EU's Common

Agricultural Policy, by making concessions in the negotiations that would not be acceptable to EU member states.

The stand-off continued, as Brazil and India refused to make improved NAMA or services offers until the EU made a better agricultural market access offer. As leaders of the G-20, Brazil and India complained that the EU wanted developing countries to accept much lower tariffs in NAMA than it was willing to offer in agriculture—an export area where many developing countries have a competitive advantage. They insisted that developed countries' market access offers in agriculture be proportional to the market access demanded of developing countries in NAMA and services. However, the EU said its offer was not only final, but conditional, and would be withdrawn if demanders persisted in seeking "something for nothing"—or in the EU Trade Commissioner's words, "real cuts by Europe, paper cuts by others."

Despite the intense focus on agriculture, negotiations continued on industrial goods and services trade, but the knotty conflicts we reported last year continued to impede their progress. On NAMA, negotiators circled around the problem of what tariff reduction formula to use, with signs of potential agreement on a "Swiss" formula that would even out tariff levelsby cutting higher tariffs more than lower ones.[16] However, negotiators could not agree on the type of Swiss formula to use and the selection of coefficients that would determine the reductions for developed and developing countries. In addition, the treatment of unbound tariffs[17] was not settled, and the degree to which developing countries would have the flexibility to deviate or exempt products from the formula was controversial. On services, negotiators were stalled over proposals to alter the bilateral negotiating format, speed the pace of the negotiations, and encourage greater participation and better market access offers by more countries. Suggestions included the use of numerical targets, with members covering a certain percentage of service sectors in their offers, and a plurilateral negotiating approach whereby groups of countries collectively present "requests" to other groups of countries for market access improvements and then the recipient countries reply with market access "offers" to the demanding countries. However, developing countries criticized these suggestions as overly prescriptive, and a constraint on their freedom to opt out of services liberalization or selectively liberalize sectors.

The trade facilitation negotiations made good progress throughout the year, as did the negotiations on rules, but remained at the stage of exploring proposals versus bridging gaps in positions.[18] Trade facilitation negotiators put forward a large number of proposals for expediting the movement of traded goods, and developing countries participated actively. Negotiations on various trade "rules" intensified, with the debate focusing on the divide between the traditional and new users of trade remedy laws (measures used to counter unfairly priced and subsidized imports)—including the United States—and non-users that have called for significant change in users' antidumping and countervailing duty regimes. Rules negotiators conducted in-depth discussions of such proposed changes and narrowed the list of issues somewhat, according to U.S. officials. While proposals aimed at U.S. practice remain a concern, U.S. officials report that proponents had difficulty justifying or gaining consensus for their more radical proposals. Rules negotiators also considered U.S. proposals to improve transparency and due process in trade remedy proceedings and made progress on developing new disciplines on subsidies (including fish subsidies) and transparency for regional trade agreements.[19]

Goals Lowered for December 2005 Hong Kong Ministerial

The flurry of activity in October gave way to the realization in November that the gaps between key negotiating positions were still too wide for negotiators to reach any major decisions by December, and the agenda for Hong Kong was scaled back. New WTO Director-General Pascal Lamy, whom members had installed that fall with hopes that his energetic style might bring negotiators to decisions more quickly, had begun his term by declaring that his goal for Hong Kong was to take the Doha negotiations "two thirds of the way" to conclusion. By early November 2005, Lamy concluded that members had not bridged their differences enough to draft texts with specifics on modalities in the core negotiating areas and urged members to "recalibrate" their expectations for the ministerial. He suggested that members focus on what could reasonably be achieved, rather than risk a failure reminiscent of previous ministerials in Cancún and Seattle. The text for a Hong Kong ministerial declaration should thus try to capture progress or any decisions made since the framework agreement and provide a range of numbers (or "outer parameters") to indicate how other decisions had been clarified, if not narrowed down. Members recognized that no one would be served by presenting the ministers with an overly full and unresolved agenda. They agreed to focus on what was achievable, while stressing they remained committed to an ambitious outcome for the round.

The agenda for Hong Kong quickly changed to reflect these scaled-back expectations and focus on several development issues. Lamy called for the ministerial to deliver on several narrow measures to benefit the 32 LDCs that are WTO members. In addition, the EU and certain developing countries voiced the view that an "early harvest" on development issues was important symbolically. Immediately before the ministerial, the Group of 90 (G-90)—a coalition of the African Union; the LDCs; and the African, Caribbean, and Pacific Group— issued a statement reminding WTO members that the Doha ministerial declaration had placed the needs and interests of developing countries at the heart of the Doha Round and that they expected concrete benefits from Hong Kong. India and other developing-country coalitions made similar statements. The EU Trade Commissioner emphasized the importance of making a "down payment" on the trade agreement to the poorest countries at Hong Kong. He stated that the Doha negotiations were a development round and "not an agricultural exporters' round," leading the U.S. Trade Representative and key members of Congress to question whether the EU's efforts to shift the focus to development were somewhat self-serving.

The draft declaration text, as transmitted in early December for consideration at the ministerial, contained few provisions for new agreements to be made at Hong Kong. The provisions included calling on ministers to adopt decisions on five LDC proposals and to set new deadlines for completing modalities and other aspects of the negotiations. Annexes to the draft text on the six core negotiating areas represented full agreement by WTO members in only one area—trade facilitation. The annexes on the five other core areas simply summarized the members' positions at that point in time, and postponed key decisions that would be necessary before member-to-member bargaining over each nation's schedules of commitments could begin.

HONG KONG RESULTED IN SEVERAL LIMITED NEW COMMITMENTS, BUT POSTPONED KEY DECISIONS ON CUTTING TARIFFS AND OTHER BARRIERS

WTO members arrived in Hong Kong intent on avoiding a stalemate and ensuring continued progress in the negotiations. The ministerial declaration that was adopted reflects commitment to complete the Doha negotiations in 2006 and agreement on a narrow set of issues. Agriculture, of critical concern for many members, continued to occupy much of the negotiators' attention at the ministerial. Economic development issues also were featured prominently at Hong Kong, with nearly round-the-clock negotiations finally yielding several concrete steps to alleviate some concerns of the WTO's poorest members. Other U.S. priorities, however— notably services and NAMA—made little progress at the ministerial.

Members Formally Commit to Conclude Negotiations by 2006

Negotiators at Hong Kong succeeded in avoiding deadlock and meeting—or even exceeding—the lowered expectations for the ministerial. Having failed to meet many of the important milestones they had set for themselves in 2005, and aware of the difficult ground still to be bridged, in Hong Kong members reaffirmed their commitment to a successful and timely completion of the round. In doing so, they agreed to a new deadline for completing the round by the end of 2006 and interim deadlines under a compressed schedule by which to reach agreement on the difficult issues that had eluded them thus far. For example, they set April 30, 2006, as the deadline for WTO members to agree on modalities for cutting tariffs and subsidies for agricultural and nonagricultural goods. The next key deadline is July 31, 2006, when countries will be expected to submit national schedules of commitments embodying the modalities for agriculture and NAMA, and to present revised offers for liberalizing trade in services.

Ministers Focused on Export Competition Issues and Cotton, but Made Little Progress on other Aspects of Agricultural Negotiations

In Hong Kong, negotiators focused primarily on three agricultural issues: elimination of export subsidies, in-kind food aid, and the demands of a group of African countries on cotton. However, they did not address the underlying differences on agricultural market access and made little progress on other areas in the agriculture negotiations.

First and most significantly, members agreed to eliminate all forms of agricultural export subsidies on a parallel basis by 2013. Reaching consensus on this deadline proved to be difficult, however. The EU, the largest user of agricultural export subsidies, insisted on progress in developing parallel disciplines on export credit programs, state trading enterprises, and other aspects of export competition before agreeing on a deadline to end export subsidies. On the other hand, the G-20 and other major agricultural exporters, including the United States, wanted a 2010 deadline for abolishing agricultural export subsidies before turning to other export competition issues. Heated debate on an export subsidies deadline continued throughout the ministerial, with Brazil reportedly threatening to pull out of the talks at one point. The compromise adopted involved a commitment to eliminate a substantial part of the export subsidies in phases by the end of 2010 if an agreement enters into force in January 2008.

Second, negotiators devoted considerable time to discussing whether in-kind food aid distorts international commodities markets, but they failed to reach consensus on this issue. The EU maintains that in-kind food aid is trade-distorting and represents a form of export subsidy. At Hong Kong, EU negotiators sought a commitment from other members to phase out in-kind food aid and to move toward an international system of cash-only assistance that would allow countries in need to purchase food from the most convenient and commercially viable sources. The United States, however, as the main provider of in-kind food aid, resisted this move, arguing that in-kind food is often critical in emergencies such as famines and natural disasters. The ministerial declaration deferred setting disciplines on food aid until April 30, 2006, in conjunction with the adoption of overall modalities for agriculture. The ministers did agree to certain principles, including a guarantee that such disciplines would include a mechanism, called a "safe box," to ensure the availability of food for needy populations in emergency situations.

Third, negotiators in Hong Kong also addressed the demands raised by a group of four African countries,[20] known collectively as the Cotton Four (C-4). Since the Cancún ministerial, the C-4 countries have sought to bring attention to the plight of African farmers, who face falling international prices for cotton and diminishing opportunities in overseas markets. At Hong Kong, the C-4 countries, supported by others, obtained a commitment by developed countries to eliminate all forms of export subsidies for cotton in 2006. This provision, aimed primarily at the United States, coincides with existing U.S. plans to eliminate cotton export subsidies by that time.[21] The C-4 also obtained a commitment from developed countries to provide duty-free, quota-free access for cotton exports from least-developed countries when the agreements resulting from the Doha negotiations are implemented. Moreover, the C-4 secured a new commitment that the overall Doha agreement on agriculture would entail deeper and faster cuts in domestic cotton subsidies relative to cuts in domestic support for agricultural commodities in general.

The Hong Kong ministerial declaration reflects more limited progress on several other agricultural issues. On the domestic support pillar, the declaration contained a new commitment to ensure that the total of all trade-distorting domestic support to farmers must be reduced, possibly involving cuts beyond those agreed to for specific categories of farm payments—known as "boxes" in WTO parlance. The declaration also adopted a framework with three levels or "bands" for reducing domestic farm subsidies, which were based on the amount of financial support provided by members. The United States would fall in the middle of these bands, along with Japan, while the EU would be in the top band, and other countries that provided domestic support to farmers would be in the lowest band. Members in the higher bands would be expected to make deeper cuts. Similarly, in the market access pillar, the declaration reflects convergence on an arrangement calling for four bands for tariff reductions, with higher cuts for higher tariffs. Finally, the Hong Kong declaration noted that developing countries will be granted additional flexibility to protect their domestic agricultural production by self-designating special products and having access to a volume- and price-based special safeguard mechanism to protect against import surges.

Several Proposals on Development Issues Were Also Adopted at Hong Kong

The Hong Kong ministerial conference also devoted substantial attention to certain development issues. The prominence of these issues may have contributed to a public show of unity among some 110 developing countries at Hong Kong. Nevertheless, a number of developing-country officials expressed concerns about their different needs and priorities at the ministerial, and in private meetings in the weeks just before the conference.[22]

Formal adoption of five proposals made by LDCs was among the most significant agreements related to development at the ministerial. Among these proposals was a controversial initiative to secure duty-free, quota-free access to developed countries' markets. LDCs, supported by the EU, had sought complete duty-free, quota-free access for all of their products. However, the United States opposed this initiative for various reasons, including the fact that, as proposed, the initiative exceeded the current U.S. statutory authority, which sets conditions on preferential market access to protect U.S. commercial interests and to advance certain U.S. policy goals. U.S. Trade Representative Portman also indicated that numerous developing countries that do not qualify for LDC status had raised concerns about being disadvantaged in the U.S. market. In the end, the compromise called for duty-free and quota-free access for at least 97 percent of tariff lines of developed countries' imports from LDCs, and for steps to be taken to achieve complete coverage thereafter.[23] The declaration also urged developing countries to take on the same commitment to LDCs if they were able.

Moreover, following up on 2005 work,[24] the declaration invited the creation of a WTO task force to recommend how "aid for trade" can contribute to Doha development goals by helping developing countries take advantage of new trade opportunities. The declaration also called for members to increase their financial commitments for technical assistance and capacity building to help developing countries participate in trade negotiations and implement the WTO agreements. At Hong Kong, the United States and others made new commitments outside the WTO declaration. Notably, the United States pledged it would double its "aid for trade" to developing countries to $2.7 billion a year by 2010; the EU announced it would raise its commitment to 2 billion euros per year by 2010; Japan offered to provide $10 billion from 2006 through 2008.

Little Progress Made in other Important Areas

Little progress was made in two other areas of the Doha negotiations critical to U.S. interests—NAMA and services.

In NAMA, negotiators decided to:

- postpone reaching agreement on modalities until April 30, 2006;
- call for comparable levels of ambition[25] in market access for agriculture and NAMA; and
- reaffirm the goal of reducing or eliminating tariffs in various ways, notably by adopting a Swiss formula approach that cuts high tariffs more than lower tariffs to achieve these reductions.

However, negotiators did not agree on specific numbers (coefficients) for the Swiss formula, which would determine the depth of cuts and final tariff ceilings for members. The range of cuts proposed by members prior to Hong Kong is wide. Moreover, they left unresolved the controversy over how much flexibility developing countries will retain to deviate or exempt products completely from the formula.

In services, members agreed to:

- accelerate negotiations by adopting a plurilateral approach, whereby groups of countries jointly present offers to other groups; and
- clarify that participation in plurilateral negotiations would be voluntary, as members would be able to decide whether or not to respond to the requests presented to them.

The Hong Kong declaration addressed numerous other issues, ranging from trade facilitation to rules, but they received minimal attention at the conference. On trade facilitation, for example, the declaration categorized previous proposals and endorsed drafting a text of new commitments. On rules, WTO members reaffirmed their commitment to substantial results, set several new goals, and authorized the chair of the Committee on Rules to produce a draft text embodying proposed changes to existing WTO agreements on antidumping and subsidies to serve as the basis for final negotiations.

Several Factors Make Meeting 2006 Deadlines Challenging, and Have Raised Doubts about the Likelihood of an Ambitious Outcome within the TPA Time Frame

WTO members and observers recognize that achieving a balanced and ambitious outcome for global trade talks within the TPA time frame will be challenging, and the window of opportunity is quickly closing. Efforts to make progress are under way. However, a mix of motivating and constraining factors creates tension between the feasibility of meeting the 2006 deadlines and members' ambition for a far-reaching agreement. Motivating factors include a desire to reap the economic benefits that some experts forecast would result from further trade liberalization and the fact that the outlines of a "grand bargain"—or key trade-offs involved in any deal—are becoming clearer. On the other hand, factors constraining progress include the difficulty of breaking the ongoing impasse over agriculture, political constraints in key WTO member states, and the significant amount of work to be done in the time remaining. Some officials maintain that success remains possible, but emphasize that members need a greater sense of urgency and the political will to cut trade barriers from current levels. Other officials and many experts are skeptical that success is possible within the TPA timeframe. In the event that an ambitious agreement cannot be reached within the TPA timeframe, members may be forced to consider extending the talks or concluding them with more modest results.

Expiration of TPA Is Seen as a Hard Deadline

Generally seen by the United States and other WTO members as a hard deadline, the expiration of TPA on July 1, 2007, is a motivating factor to concluding the negotiations. Failure to meet that deadline would risk expiration of TPA and make U.S. approval of an agreement more difficult. The Doha Round agreement would be eligible for approval under TPA, provided it was signed by the president before July 1, 2007, when the authority lapses.[26] Continuing negotiations without TPA is possible but would jeopardize the president's ability to present a final Doha agreement to Congress for an "up or down" vote within a fixed period of time. Congress would then be in a position to avoid acting on the legislation or to demand that certain parts of the agreement be renegotiated. According to USTR, the WTO agreement would need to reach Congress by the spring of 2007 to meet the TPA deadline. As discussed later, renewing TPA is not presently contemplated. (When TPA was renewed in 2002, after an 8-year lapse, the legislation passed the House of Representatives by only three votes.)

Most Members Continue to Profess High Ambition and Work Has Resumed in Earnest

Most WTO members maintain that they are committed to the goal of achieving an ambitious Doha agreement. The concept of ambition refers to the scope and level of trade liberalization to which WTO members are willing to commit. A high level of ambition, for example, would result in a comprehensive agreement in which members commit to significant reductions in tariffs, subsidies, and other trade barriers across most, if not all, core issues under negotiation. Such a robust agreement should result in a strengthened and measurably freer global trade environment and added impetus for economic growth and development. An outcome with a low level of ambition, on the other hand, would result in little actual trade liberalization and create few new opportunities for growth.

WTO members and the Director-General continue to work on ways to facilitate the successful conclusion of the negotiations. Since the talks resumed in late January 2006, negotiators have been engaged in a flurry of activities designed to speed up the process and find practical ways to narrow their differences. These include holding a series of mini-ministerials among small groups of WTO members and intensified bilateral consultations, setting more interim deadlines, developing questionnaires and reference papers to advance dialogue, and conducting simulations on the effects of tariff cuts under various scenarios. In February, Director-General Lamy indicated that these activities represented a needed shift from general principles to discussion of concrete numbers and text, and were resulting in a heightened awareness of the need for movement by all players, in concert, toward a middle ground. At that time, he stated that he had no indication that agreeing on modalities would not be possible by April 30, 2006. Shortly thereafter, U.S. Trade Representative Portman reported that the United States and the EU were making progress in narrowing some differences on agriculture. In addition, the first deadline since the Hong Kong ministerial was successfully met, as members submitted plurilateral requests in the services negotiations by the agreed-to deadline of February 28, 2006. Over 14 requests for market access in sectors such as financial and express delivery services were submitted, with the United States participating in 10; more are expected.

Members Further Motivated by Risks of Forfeiting Potential Economic Benefits

Also motivating the negotiations is the risk of foregoing the expected benefits from a successful Doha agreement. The economic benefits from trade liberalization occurring as a result of the Doha Round could be significant. The Organization for Economic Cooperation and Development and trade experts in general agree that only a comprehensive multilateral process of negotiation, in which political and economic trade-offs are maximized, can realize all the benefits of market opening and rules strengthening. Agricultural reform in particular has largely been kept out of regional agreements and would need to involve the present WTO protagonists to be meaningful. Some estimates, as reported in a Congressional Research Service report,[27] indicate that economic gains could be as high as $574 billion globally and $144 billion in the United States.[28] Other estimates are more modest. For example, a 2005 World Bank study projects global gains ranging from $84 billion to $287 billion annually by the year 2015,[29] while a Carnegie Endowment study predicts income gains of $40 to $60 billion from what it deems plausible outcomes of the Doha Round.[30] Although this represents a small share of global and U.S. income, some economists and development advocates argue that global trade liberalization—particularly of agricultural products and other products of interest to developing countries—could still play a role in promoting economic opportunity and alleviating poverty. For example, the additional income would equal or surpass aid flows to developing countries, and leading developing country exporters such as Brazil, India, China, Thailand, and Argentina would stand to capture sizeable gains.

Nevertheless, such projected overall gains can mask important differences, and several authoritative studies suggest that some groups and nations face potential losses and near-term adjustment costs that merit particular consideration in the negotiations.

Clearer Outlines of a Grand Bargain Enable Concerted Effort

Another factor that could facilitate reaching agreement in the negotiations relates to the outlines of a "grand bargain" (the necessary trade-offs, or benefits and concessions, among the players) that, according to some observers, are becoming more apparent. According to WTO Director-General Lamy, each country or group now knows what it needs to do. The United States, for example, is expected to make further reductions to its domestic agricultural subsidies and clarify how it will handle countercyclical payments to compensate farmers for low commodity prices,[31] and the EU is expected to reduce its domestic agricultural subsidies and cut agricultural tariffs. In return, large developing countries such as Brazil, India, and China are expected to lower barriers to agriculture, industrial goods, and services sufficiently to create new market opportunities. In general, other developing countries would be asked to liberalize as their capacity allows and would benefit from special treatment and trade capacity building assistance. The clarity of the trade-offs necessary for a deal—although requiring difficult reforms—could result in a concerted effort among key nations to bridge their differences and address areas of importance to their trading partners.

Impasse on Agriculture Continues to Constrain Progress

Despite indications of an outline for a "grand bargain," the negotiations to date have centered on agriculture and remain deadlocked on this issue. In mid-February, and again in late March, U.S. Trade Representative Portman remarked that the negotiations have largely lost the momentum generated by the United States' October 2005 proposal on agriculture. According to WTO Director-General Lamy, the United States, the G-20, and the Cairns Group regard the EU's market access offer as inadequate. Since Hong Kong, the EU has held firmly to its position that its October 2005 offer is serious and that others must first make concrete and commercially meaningful proposals in areas of interest to the EU before it would even contemplate improvements in its offer. According to the EU, these would restore needed "balance" among the key players' market access interests. However, it remains unclear whether the European Commission has the flexibility to improve its October offer.[32] In fact, a March 2006 memo to the European Commission signed by 13 of its 25 member nations stated that the EU's October 2005 offer "exhausted and may have exceeded" all the room for maneuver they had on domestic support and market access, and that even improved offers on NAMA and services would not justify an improvement. The United States also faces pressure from many WTO members to improve and clarify its agricultural offer, particularly on domestic support. Brazil and India, negotiating on behalf of the G-20, maintain that until there is more movement on agriculture, they will not negotiate reciprocal concessions on the other core issues—namely NAMA and services. They also insist that any cuts in NAMA and services must be proportional to those by developed countries on agriculture and that, in general, developed countries should cut their tariffs more than developing countries. As a result, they argue, developed-country demands for across-the-board cuts that harmonize tariff levels across countries and bring developing-country tariffs below presently applied rates are excessive. A group of 11 developing countries that includes Brazil and India recently stressed that they need flexibility to shield products from liberalization so that they can pursue industrial policies and manage structural adjustment. A March mini-ministerial among six key players—the EU, the United States, Japan, Australia, Brazil, and India—failed to yield breakthroughs. Rather than moving in concert, as they had pledged in January, players signaled little or no flexibility, according to reports. Since the meeting, U.S. Trade Representative Portman and Secretary of Agriculture Mike Johanns have said publicly they are increasingly doubtful that sufficient "political will" exists to conclude a deal in 2006.

"Political Will" to Break Deadlock Still Absent and Timing for Making Hard Political Choices Is Not Propitious

Breaking the impasse over agriculture remains key to reaching agreement on the whole of the Doha agenda. However, the political will to liberalize and make the quality of offers and concessions necessary to break the impasse is not yet evident. In addition, the political timing of elections scheduled for 2006 in several countries, including the United States, the EU, and Brazil, could make concessions at this time even more difficult.

In the United States, 2006 is a congressional election year, and Congress already seems to be divided on support for further trade liberalization. Faced with increasing trade deficits, heightened competition from China, and workers' displacement as jobs move overseas, the approval of free trade agreements has become a difficult proposition. Congressional deliberations on the Dominican Republic–Central America Free Trade Agreement in 2005 were extremely contentious, and it passed Congress by only two votes. U.S. Trade Representative Portman has attempted to rebuild bipartisan consensus on U.S. trade policy. However, some leaders in Congress have publicly stated that unless the United States gains significant market access on agriculture, NAMA, and services—particularly in the large developed and developing nations that U.S. business groups have identified as liberalization priorities—they will not agree to a deal.

Timing is sensitive for other reasons as well. For example, most provisions of the present U.S. farm bill expire in September 2007, and Congress will begin work on the legislation to reauthorize U.S. farm programs in 2006. Congressional leaders want to take into account the framework likely to emerge from the WTO negotiations when drafting a bill, in part to avoid exposing farmers to the uncertainty associated with WTO challenges to U.S. programs. However, some are skeptical that a WTO agreement will be completed in time and urge the drafting of legislation independent of WTO negotiations. Other congressional members and some farm organizations advocate the extension of the current farm bill until the outcome of the Doha negotiations is clear. In the meantime, certain members of Congress have urged the administration not to "tie their hands" in drafting a new farm bill and have asked executive branch agencies to coordinate closely with congressional committees to ensure that they can work with any result being negotiated at the WTO.

Other key players also face political constraints. The EU's current political problems range from member states' rejection of the EU constitution to violent protests by disaffected immigrants and youths. One expert recently noted that EU budget negotiations in December did not deliver an agreement to cut back on the EU's agricultural support spending, as some EU members such as the United Kingdom had hoped.[33] Instead, only agreement to review spending in 2008-2009 was achieved. France, in particular, has been adamant in its opposition to any further EU concessions on agriculture in the WTO negotiations, but it is not alone. EU Commissioner Mandelson has recently affirmed that the EU member states are united in insisting that all main parties to the talks should be prepared to offer more to get more in the talks, while stressing that others need to offer more in areas of interest to the EU. Brazil will hold presidential elections in the fall of 2006; however, its negotiating strategy is not expected to change. In its powerful role as leader of the G-20 and as one of the nations with the most to gain from the negotiations, Brazil is likely to hold fast to its position that any movement on NAMA and services will be proportional to (and dependent on) what it achieves in agriculture. India's new government has kept its markets open to certain imports, but remains reticent about commitments to liberalize its agriculture and industrial markets further; the government's stance is attributed to the perceived benefits of retaining "policy space" for development, and concerns that its many small domestic producers would be unable to withstand heightened competition from China and other foreign nations. Several officials stated that they believe China's rise as a manufacturing and export power has made many nations wary of committing to cut tariffs at the WTO. China, in turn, has not played a visible role in pressing for liberalization in the Doha negotiations.

These political constraints have led some observers and stakeholders to propose high-level political intervention to break the impasse. Notably, some trade experts and at least two heads of state have suggested a "trade summit" at which national leaders from key countries such as the EU, the United States, Brazil, and India could meet to make the commitments necessary in the core negotiating areas and break the impasse. In early March, British Prime Minister Tony Blair and Brazilian President Luiz Inacio Lula da Silva issued a public call for such a WTO summit. On the one hand, they recognize that this action would require commitment to strengthening the world's economy and global trading system at a time when protectionist tendencies may be on the rise. Yet, they argue that the risks of letting the Doha talks fail or languish in uncertainty would be contrary to members' and the institution's best interests. U.S. officials offer mixed reactions to the idea of a "trade summit": some think a leaders' meeting may be desirable if the ministers' efforts fail, and others question its usefulness. U.S. Trade Representative Portman, for example, recently stated that summits between the leaders of Britain and France within the EU, rather than broader international summits, may be more productive.

Against Looming Deadlines, Many Difficult and Time-Consuming Steps Remain

Shortly after the Hong Kong ministerial, the Director-General estimated that 40 percent of the work necessary for completing the negotiations remained; he noted that the most recent 5 percent of the work had taken nearly 17 months to complete. However, just over a year remains before the president would have to enter into a final WTO agreement to qualify for TPA consideration by Congress. Keeping to the deadlines is critical if the major issues are to be dealt with and necessary steps completed, according to U.S. and WTO officials. However, the track record for meeting deadlines in these negotiations is not promising. We noted in our last report that the talks were unlikely to conclude before December 2006, which would be 2 years after the originally established deadline of January 2005. Indeed, most interim deadlines in the negotiations have been repeatedly deferred.

Even if a political breakthrough on agriculture were to be achieved, U.S. and WTO officials agree that finalizing each country's schedule of WTO commitments on agriculture, NAMA, and services would be time-consuming, with little margin for missed deadlines (see fig. 3 for a timeline of negotiation deadlines in 2006). First, members must make up for lost time after missing the critical deadline of April 30, 2006, for agreeing to modalities in agriculture and NAMA. This means they must agree on the formulas, thresholds, dates, and other numerical benchmarks that members will be committed to meet when they revise their current WTO commitments. However, to finalize these commitments, a host of technical issues fraught with political and practical implications must be addressed. In February 2006, for example, the chairman of the negotiating group on agriculture presented a list of 70 questions that he believed would need to be addressed to complete modalities.[34] In mid-March, a U.S. official told us that WTO members had been focusing on about 15 modalities issues but had not come close to compromise on any. In NAMA, meanwhile, the negotiating chair identified 14 issues in his March 27 report that still need work to finalize modalities—

particularly the tariff reduction formula, treatment of unbound tariffs, and flexibilities for developing countries. The list did not include how to interpret the linkage between ambition in agriculture and NAMA established at Hong Kong, which has since been the topic of heated debate.

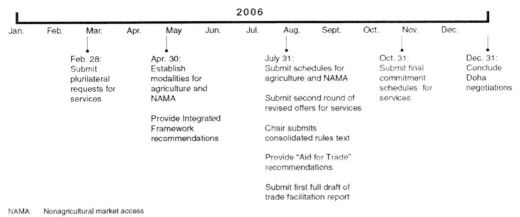

Figure 3. Key Selected Deadlines in 2006 for the Doha Negotiations.

Second, once modalities are agreed to, the United States and other members must take a series of important and time-consuming steps to reach a final agreement. For example, members must draft revisions of their national tariff schedules to indicate how they intend to meet their modalities commitments for each product or tariff line. The draft commitment schedules in agriculture and NAMA are to be completed by July 31, 2006. A U.S. official told us that only when the draft schedules are submitted will other members see which products will be liberalized. Then, a process of verifying schedules, finalizing sectoral agreements, and bargaining among individual members (known as "request–offer") begins. According to U.S. officials, verification is critical because the modalities text will allow different interpretations of commitments, and only countries' national schedules are legally binding. They said that most experienced observers agree that this process is vital to achieving intended results and may require 6 to 8 months to complete. Even if the current schedule for submitting schedules is met, little time would remain in 2006 to do this work.

Third, as indicated in table 3, before and after an agreement is finally entered into, the United States must take certain steps to comply with TPA. The president must notify and solicit input from Congress and ask the International Trade Commission (ITC) for an assessment of the agreement's likely impact on the U.S. economy and specific industries before signing an agreement. The agreement itself must be entered into before July 1, 2007. Once an agreement is entered into, the U.S. administration would have to draw up an implementing package that would include implementing legislation and a plan, known as a statement of administrative action, to carry out the agreement under existing law; this is likely to be a laborious effort, according to U.S. officials. The implementation package for the Uruguay Round, for example, filled hundreds of pages. U.S. officials said the plan must specify how existing U.S. programs, regulations, and legislation will be adjusted to comply with WTO commitments. The implementing package, one official noted, must also contain a series of reports (e.g., an analysis of how the agreement serves U.S. commercial interests) and a description of how the agreement meets TPA-mandated negotiating objectives.

Table 3. Principal U.S. Government Activities to Conclude Doha Round Agreements

U.S. Government activities	Time frames
TPA requires USTR to consult closely with congressional revenue committees (i.e., the House Ways and Means and Senate Finance Committees), the Congressional Oversight Group, and other congressional committees with jurisdiction over areas affected by the WTO Doha agreement.	Time frames
Negotiate agriculture and NAMA modalities.	January–April 2006
Develop national tariff schedules and other binding commitments based on modalities for agriculture and NAMA. Prepare and submit revised services offers	May–July 20
Verify schedules, finalize sectoral and non-tariff barrier agreements, and engage in "request-offer" negotiations with individual WTO members or groups.	August–December 2006
TPA requires that at least 180 days before entering into a trade agreement, the president must report to congressional revenue committees on the range of proposals being negotiated that could require amendments to U.S. trade remedy laws, and how the proposals relate to the principal U.S. negotiating objectives concerning those laws.	December 31, 2006
TPA requires that at least 90 days before entering into an agreement, the president must notify Congress of his intent to enter into the agreement.	April 1, 2007
TPA requires that at least 90 days before entering into agreement, the president must provide the ITC with details of the agreement "as it exists at that time" and request ITC to prepare and present to the president and Congress an assessment of the agreement's likely impact on the U.S. economy and specific industry sectors. Between the time of the president's request and the ITC's submission of the assessment, the president must "keep ITC current with respect to details of the agreement."	April 1, 2007
TPA requires that no later than 30 days after the president notifies Congress of intent to enter into an agreement, private sector advisory committees must submit reports on the agreement to Congress, the president, and USTR.	May 1, 2007
The president must enter into an agreement before this date for the agreement to qualify for approval under TPA's expedited procedures.	July 1, 2007
TPA requires that within 60 days after entering into an agreement, the president must submit to Congress a description of the changes to existing law he believes would be required to bring the United States into compliance with the agreement.	August 31, 2007
TPA requires that no later than 90 days after the president enters into the agreement, the ITC must submit its impact report to the president and Congress	September 30, 2007
The president is required by TPA to submit to Congress the final text of the agreement, together with a draft of the implementing bill, a statement of administrative action, and supporting information.	No date specified, but both houses of Congress must be in session

Source: GAO analysis of WTO milestones and TPA requirements.

Fourth, a series of other complex and difficult issues that are crucial to some members may need to be resolved before a final WTO agreement is possible; however, WTO members have largely postponed dealing with them until after the core issues are resolved. This sequential approach—putting off some issues until other issues are decided—puts further stress on the time available to conclude an agreement. For example, a variety of developing-country concerns and calls for changes to WTO rules in areas such as antidumping, trade facilitation (customs reform), and services are on the agenda; several of these issues may prove intractable. The crosscutting issue of erosion of preferences illustrates the complexities. A number of WTO members are small developing countries with economies dependent on one or two commodity exports. Currently, some of them rely heavily on the preferential tariff treatment they receive for their exports in the EU, the United States, and other developed countries. As a result, they regard reducing worldwide tariffs as a clear threat to their economic wellbeing. Yet foregoing or delaying the benefits of multilateral liberalization so these countries can retain their preferred access is not acceptable to many other WTO nations. A seminar to explore options for dealing with this issue was held in April 2006.

Difficulty Foreseen in Meeting Deadline with an Ambitious Outcome Leads Experts to Float other Options

WTO member states still say that they remain committed to the goal of concluding the Doha Round with robust results by the end of 2006. The fact that all members continue to be engaged in efforts to accomplish this task is a positive sign; if the political will can be found to accommodate each others' ambitions and produce an acceptable "grand bargain," then it would be difficult but not impossible to conclude the Doha Round successfully within the TPA timeframe. However, the limited progress to date and the significant amount of work remaining has raised questions about the feasibility of an ambitious outcome by the 2006 deadline, particularly without more active leadership from the highest levels. A January poll of negotiators, policy makers, and experts located in Geneva and key country capitals revealed that none of the Geneva respondents believe WTO members will meet their goal for completing the negotiations in 2006 and only 2 percent of all respondents believed they would meet the April 30 modalities deadline.[35] Moreover, the officials and experts we consulted believe that by July 2006, it will be clear whether the goal of completing an agreement within the TPA timeframe can be met. Backloading modalities on agriculture and NAMA to July would, however, "guarantee failure," according to WTO Director-General Lamy. These concerns have led numerous experts and observers to suggest that there may be different outcomes, including (1) no results in the round, (2) negotiations continuing beyond mid-2007 with uncertain results, or (3) conclusion of the round with modest results within the TPA timeframe.[36] Each involves trade-offs.

1. No Results in the Round

At Davos in late January, the EU Trade Commissioner was quoted as stating that so little was being offered by other countries that the EU would stand to lose next to nothing if the Doha negotiations failed. (His official remarks since then, however, emphasize the EU's commitment to Doha's success, while stressing the need for reciprocity.) In February, WTO Director-General Lamy indicated that without sufficiently ambitious results, there will be no Doha outcome. U.S. Trade Representative Portman has said the United States is committed to doing everything it can to bring an agreement together. Yet he added that if the Doha negotiations are not concluded by the end of 2006, "there is a real danger the Doha Round could drift into a long, unpredictable period of stagnation." Some analysts and business groups also warn the round has gone off course for lack of political will, and accepting various premises for avoiding liberalization; they say that a pause or collapse would be better than reaching a "bad deal." Yet a complete collapse of the Doha Round is generally seen as the least desirable outcome by observers, who believe that members will try to avoid total failure because so much is at stake. In addition to forfeiting the economic and welfare gains expected from Doha's successful conclusion, WTO Director-General Lamy and numerous observers warn that failure to achieve agreement may pose risks to the credibility of the WTO as an effective or even relevant institution. Although the WTO itself—with its extensive set of binding commitments and vast coverage in terms of country membership and world trade volume—would no doubt continue, experts caution that Doha's failure could strain the global trading system. For example, Director-General Lamy has expressed the view that developing countries, particularly the smallest and weakest, would be among the biggest losers. Others say one potential outcome of a failed round could be the proliferation of regional and bilateral trade agreements, further weakening the "most favored nation" principle—the concept of equal treatment for all members that is a pillar of the multilateral trading system. The United States has already announced its intention to move vigorously in 2006 to negotiate new bilateral and regional agreements. In fact, some in Congress have encouraged the United States to pursue bilateral free trade agreements with countries such as Korea, in part to encourage countries that are resisting liberalization at the WTO to take notice. Other WTO functions, such as the legitimacy of the dispute settlement system, also could be weakened.

2. Negotiations Continue beyond Mid-2007 with Uncertain Results

Another possible outcome would be to continue the talks in the hope of a more robust outcome at a later date. Experts note that past rounds have taken longer than originally planned, and the last round—which involved fewer countries—took 7.5 years to complete. However, because of the importance of TPA for U.S. ratification, it is unclear whether countries would choose to continue negotiations without TPA or let the negotiations pause until TPA is extended or renewed. One scenario would be to continue the negotiations without TPA, with the hope that TPA is eventually renewed, although congressional observers believe that extension or renewal of TPA is an uncertain and difficult proposition in the near term. A second scenario would be to put the negotiations on hold for an indefinite time until TPA is extended or renewed. Some experts think that renewal or extension of TPA would probably have a better chance if it were linked to an extension of the U.S. farm bill or if the Doha negotiations showed potential of concluding with an ambitious result. Because of these uncertainties, the difference between outright failure of the round and continuing or suspending the negotiations may only be clear after some years have passed.

3. Concluding the Round with Modest Results within TPA's Timeframe

This scenario would avoid the risks of outright failure and the uncertainty inherent in continuing the talks beyond mid-2007. However, a modest outcome may not be acceptable to many WTO members as it may not include sufficient gains to offset the costs; or—in trade negotiators' language—the agreement would not result in a "balanced package." EU Trade Commissioner Mandelson stated publicly early in 2006 that the EU would "reluctantly settle" for a minimalist outcome, but WTO Director-General Lamy said a "cheap round is not an option," and U.S. Trade Representative Portman quickly rejected "Doha-lite" as falling short of success and being difficult to promote domestically. In addition, a more modest package would leave countries with more ambitious goals little alternative but to pursue other avenues for liberalization, such as bilateral agreements.

CONCLUDING OBSERVATIONS

WTO members undertook an ambitious set of goals when they launched the Doha Development Agenda more than 4 years ago. Our May 2005 report ended by noting that some of the experts we had consulted were confident that an ambitious, balanced outcome of the round could be attained—if 2005 resulted in sufficient progress. Other experts warned that hard decisions were necessary and time was short if an outcome living up to Doha's promises were to be achieved. Progress in 2005 through the Hong Kong ministerial, however, was considerably less than WTO members hoped. With nearly all tough decisions put off until 2006, the tension between members' original high ambitions and the TPA time frame has become acute. This is evident in the increasing divide between the official statements of WTO members and the expectations of experts on whether the round can be completed before TPA's expiration on July 1, 2007. U.S. officials often call the Doha Round a "once in a generation opportunity" because the last global trade round took a decade to launch and complete and another decade to implement. WTO Director-General Lamy recently stressed that WTO members will soon face the "moment of truth" for the Doha Round. In part for this reason, some observers expressed dismay at the timing of the president's announcement that he was nominating U.S. Trade Representative Portman to be Director of the Office of Management and Budget. At press time, WTO Director-General Lamy had just announced the April 30 modalities deadline would be missed, necessitating a shift to continuous text-based negotiations in the coming weeks. He urged members to deal coolly and constructively with the situation, avoiding recrimination and showing fresh determination to accelerate progress. With just over a year left to produce an agreement that qualifies for TPA, it remains unclear whether the WTO can create an environment where members perceive it is in their interest to make the significant changes in their current positions, and other decisions, that cumulatively would fulfill the vision of the Doha Development Agenda.

APPENDIX I. OBJECTIVES, SCOPE, AND METHODOLOGY

In this report, we (1) provide the status of the Doha negotiations on the eve of the Hong Kong ministerial, (2) review the outcome of the Hong Kong ministerial, and (3) discuss the prospects for concluding the Doha Round before U.S. Trade Promotion Authority (TPA) expires in July 2007.

We followed the same overall methodology to complete all three of our objectives. We obtained, reviewed, and analyzed documents from a variety of sources. From the World Trade Organization (WTO), we analyzed the 2001 Doha ministerial declaration; the Doha work program decision adopted by the General Council on August 1, 2004, known as the "July framework agreement"; the final and earlier versions of the December Hong Kong ministerial conference declaration; reports by the Director-General and negotiating chairs; and negotiating proposals and other documents from WTO member countries. From U.S.

government agencies and foreign country officials, we obtained background information regarding negotiating proposals and positions. We also obtained information on day-to-day developments from trade publications.

To assess the status of the Doha negotiations before Hong Kong, we met with a variety of U.S. government agencies, including the Office of the U.S. Trade Representative (USTR) and the Departments of Agriculture, Commerce, and State, to obtain information on progress on the negotiations and on the issue areas and factors affecting the negotiations. We also met with representatives from Brazil in Washington, D.C. Further, we met with officials from the Mauritius Sugar Syndicate, the Food Trade Alliance, the National Farmers Union, and the National Cotton Council. In addition, we attended conferences and seminars, such as those sponsored by the American Bar Association in partnership with the Washington International Trade Association, and the Global Business Dialogue.

With the assistance of USTR and the State Department, in October 2005 we traveled to WTO headquarters in Geneva and European Union (EU) headquarters in Brussels. We met with WTO member country officials at each location, including those from the EU, Japan, Mauritius, Australia, Benin, Burkina Faso, Chad, Mali, and members of the African, Caribbean, and Pacific group. We also met with WTO officials, including the industrial (nonagricultural) market access, services, and trade facilitation negotiating group chairs. Upon returning from our trip, in November 2005, we briefed your staff on the status of the Doha negotiations prior to the Hong Kong ministerial conference.

To assess the outcome of the Hong Kong ministerial conference, we attended the Hong Kong conference in December 2005. In Hong Kong, we attended USTR congressional briefings and went to press conferences and meetings open to country delegates. We also collected the views of experts, relying primarily on (1) published articles in reputable sources such as *Foreign Affairs* and *Foreign Policy*; (2) publications put out by a range of organizations following the ministerial and Doha talks, such as the Institute for International Economics, the International Food and Agricultural Trade Policy Council, the Center for Economic Policy Research, the International Centre for Trade and Sustainable Development, the Center for Global Development, Bryan Cave, the American Society of International Law, Oxfam, and the South Centre, as well as officials at the World Bank, the Organization for Economic Cooperation and Development, the EU, and the Congressional Research Service; and (3) seminars and conferences sponsored by the Department of Agriculture and groups such as the Georgetown Law School and the American Bar Association, the Cordell Hull Institute, the American Enterprise Institute, Women in International Trade, the Washington International Trade Association, the Woodrow Wilson Center for International Scholars, the Center for Strategic and International Studies, and the Carnegie Endowment for International Peace. Though many of these seminars and conferences we attended occurred in Washington, D.C., collectively they represent a range of perspectives from "think tanks," government, academia, business, nongovernmental organizations, and former trade officials in the United States and elsewhere. Also, we reviewed news media reports, news releases on the developments at the ministerial conference, and statements about the outcome of the ministerial conference from the WTO, U.S. and foreign governments, and other international organizations.

To assess prospects for success, we relied on the perspectives of participants and experts, as well as our own analysis. We defined success with an "ambitious outcome" as meeting

WTO members' originally agreed goals and U.S. objectives as set forth in TPA legislation and associated requirements.

We performed our work from May 2005 through March 2006 in accordance with generally accepted government auditing standards.

REFERENCES

[1] The negotiations are formally called the Doha Development Agenda but are commonly referred to as the "Doha Round."

[2] Title XXI of the Trade Promotion Authority (TPA) Act of 2002 (P.L. 107-210) gives the president the authority to conclude trade deals around the world and to submit legislation approving and implementing the agreement subject to an up or down vote by Congress using expedited procedures within a set time period. To qualify, any agreement resulting from the Doha negotiations must be entered into by the president before July 1, 2007. Expedited consideration is also contingent on the president's compliance with requirements for consultations with and notices and reports to Congress before, during, and after negotiation of the agreement. In negotiating the Doha Round on behalf of the United States, the Office of the United States Trade Representative is guided by the goals outlined by TPA, including overall and principal objectives and promotion of certain priorities.

[3] GAO, *World Trade Organization: Global Trade Talks Back on Track, but Considerable Work Needed to Fulfill Ambitious Objectives*, GAO-05-538 (Washington, D.C.: May 31, 2005); GAO, *World Trade Organization: Cancún Ministerial Fails to Move Global Trade Negotiations Forward; Next Steps Uncertain*, GAO-04-250 (Washington, D.C.: Jan. 15, 2004); GAO, *World Trade Organization: Early Decisions Are Vital to Progress in Ongoing Negotiations*, GAO-02-879 (Washington, D.C.: Sept. 4, 2002).

[4] The WTO recognizes as least-developed countries those countries that have been designated as such by the United Nations. Since 1971, the United Nations has denominated LDCs "a category of States that are deemed highly disadvantaged in their development process... facing more than other countries the risk of failing to come out of poverty." In its 2003 review of LDCs, the United Nations identified LDCs as countries with a 3-year average estimate of gross national income per capita under $900, among other criteria.

[5] The Doha Round is the ninth round of trade liberalizing negotiations under the auspices of the GATT/WTO since 1947. For additional information on the fourth ministerial conference and the Doha Development Agenda, see GAO-02-879.

[6] There are currently 16 negotiating areas in the Doha work program. These 16 areas are implementation-related issues and concerns; agriculture; services; market access for nonagricultural products; trade-related aspects of intellectual property rights; trade facilitation; WTO rules; dispute settlement understanding; trade and environment; electronic commerce; small economies; trade, debt, and finance; trade and transfer of technology; technical cooperation and capacity building; least-developed countries; and special and differential treatment. Originally, the Doha declaration set forth three other negotiating areas: transparency of government procurement, interaction between trade

and competition policy, and relationship between trade and investment. Members agreed to drop these three areas in the July 2004 framework agreement.

[7] The full framework (WTO, "Doha Work Program: Decision Adopted by the General Council on 1 August 2004," WT/L/579, Aug. 2, 2004) is available at http://www.wto.org/english/tratop_e/dda_e/draft_text_gc_dg_31july04_e.htm (downloaded April 19, 2006).

[8] GAO-05-538.

[9] The Department of Agriculture reports that agreement on *ad valorem* equivalents has not yet been fully completed. Isolated products remain to be confirmed, some WTO members have only recently responded to questions in discussions on this point, and members are not fully agreed on the process for verification.

[10] This number excludes least-developed countries, which were not required to prepare services offers.

[11] "Special and differential treatment" refers to specific provisions that provide more time or leniency, greater market access, or other more favorable terms to developing and least-developed countries in implementing WTO agreements.

[12] For a detailed comparison of the agriculture proposals by the United States, the Group of 20, the EU, and the Group of 10, see Charles Hanrahan and Randy Schnepf, *WTO Doha Round: The Agricultural Negotiations*, Congressional Research Service, RL33144 (Washington, D.C.: Jan. 12, 2006).

[13] Although this debate centered on the extent of market access in the EU and other developed countries, the proposals also offered schemes for reducing developing countries' agriculture tariffs, though to a lesser extent than in developed countries.

[14] A tariff line is a single item or product in a country's schedule or list of tariffs, associated with a particular tariff rate.

[15] The EU has stated that real improvements on market access would require reductions in their applied, as opposed to bound, tariff rates. An applied tariff is the actual tariff rate levied for a product, while a bound tariff is the maximum allowed tariff rate for a product, which a country has agreed at the WTO not to go above. Many developing countries' bound tariff rates are considerably higher than the tariffs they currently apply. For example, Brazil had an average bound tariff of 31 percent and a 12 percent average applied rate in 2004, according to WTO country statistics.

[16] The Swiss formula is a nonlinear mathematical formula that (1) produces a narrow range of final tariff rates from a wider set of initial tariffs and (2) specifies a maximum final rate, no matter how high the original tariff. A key feature is a number (the coefficient) that is negotiated and plugged into the formula to determine the maximum final tariff rate. This formula was first proposed by Switzerland in the 1970s in the Tokyo Round of trade negotiations.

[17] An unbound tariff is one that a country can raise to any level because it has made no commitment to keep the tariff rate below a maximum allowed (bound) level.

[18] The WTO rules negotiations address provisions concerning antidumping measures, subsidies and countervailing measures (including fishery subsidies), and regional trade agreements.

[19] On antidumping, the negotiating group's chair reported in November 2005 that in-depth debate over proposals had progressed to the point that work was being carried out almost exclusively on the basis of specific legal texts. The chair also indicated he

sensed a broad agreement on three principles: (1) avoiding unwarranted use of antidumping measures, while preserving the basic concepts, principles, and effectiveness of the instrument and its objectives where such measures are warranted; (2) limiting the costs and complexity of proceedings for interested parties and the investigating authorities; and (3) strengthening the transparency and predictability of proceedings.

[20] The four countries are Benin, Burkina Faso, Chad, and Mali.

[21] The United States planned to eliminate its export subsidies for cotton producers during 2006 to come into conformity with an adverse ruling from the WTO on a cotton case filed by Brazil.

[22] For example, representatives of several African, Caribbean, and Pacific nations have raised questions about whether large developing countries such as Brazil and India could effectively represent the interests of small, less developed countries. At the ministerial, differences among developing countries were also evident in the opposing positions taken by Latin American and Caribbean negotiators on the EU banana import regime.

[23] The exemption of up to 3 percent of tariff lines, insisted upon by developed countries, would allow these countries to shield certain sensitive products such as sugar and textiles. This provision is to take effect by 2008, or by the start of implementation of Doha agreements.

[24] Recently, the World Bank, the International Monetary Fund, WTO, and other researchers have issued papers exploring the benefits and costs of trade liberalization for developing countries and how international institutions could help them adjust. See, for example, Joint Note by the Staffs of the IMF and the World Bank, "Aid for Trade: Competitiveness and Adjustment" (Washington, D.C.: Apr. 11, 2005); WTO Committee on Trade and Development, "Developmental Aspects of the Doha Round of Negotiations" (Geneva, Switzerland: revised Nov. 22, 2005).

[25] "Comparable ambition" was not defined in the ministerial declaration. Members are debating how it should be defined.

[26] The president, however, must fulfill a number of procedural requirements and meet certain time frames established by TPA. As a result, we concluded in our last report that the Doha negotiations need to conclude by the end of 2006 to meet TPA's statutory requirements.

[27] Congressional Research Service, *The World Trade Organization: The Hong Kong Ministerial*, RL32060, (Washington, D.C.: Jan. 20, 2006).

[28] Drusilla Brown, Alan Deardorff, and Robert Stern, "Computational Analysis of Multilateral Trade Liberalization in the Uruguay Round and Doha Development Round," University of Michigan Discussion Paper 490, Dec. 12, 2002. Available at http:/www.spp.umich.edu/rsie/workingpapers/wp.html (downloaded April 19, 2006).

[29] Thomas W. Hertel and Roman Keeney, "What is at Stake: The Relative Importance of Import Barriers, Export Subsidies and Domestic Support," in Anderson and Martin, eds., *Agricultural Trade Reform and the Doha Development Agenda* (Washington, D.C.: World Bank, 2005); and Kym Anderson, Will Martin, and Dominique van der Mensbrugghe, "Doha Merchandise Trade Reform: What's at Stake for Developing Countries," July 2005, available at http://www.worldbank.org/trade/wto (downloaded April 19, 2006). Results vary depending on the type of model (static vs. dynamic), key

assumptions in the model, and the ambition of the liberalization scenario. The World Bank studies, for example, do not attempt to quantify services liberalization.

[30] Sandra Polanski, *Winners and Losers: Impact of the Doha Round on Developing Countries* (Washington, D.C.: Carnegie Endowment for International Peace, 2006).

[31] U.S. countercyclical payments compensate farmers for low commodity prices. Specifically, U.S. producers of wheat, feed grains, rice, upland cotton, oilseeds, and peanuts are eligible to receive countercyclical payments whenever the effective (market) price for these commodities falls below the target price set by federal legislation.

[32] For example, on March 21, 2006, EU Trade Commissioner Mandelson stated that "certain WTO members continue to expect more from us on agricultural market access…we are ready to play a constructive role, including on agriculture… but we need to see real cuts in industrial tariffs." On March 22, Mandelson said "the members of the WTO realize that a new offer on agriculture is not on the agenda," and Commissioner for Agriculture Mariann Fischer Boel "confirmed that the EU had no intention of making new proposals."

[33] Simon Evenett, "The WTO Ministerial Conference in Hong Kong: What Next?" (University of St. Gallen and the Centre for Economic Policy Research, Jan. 18, 2006).

[34] These questions from the agriculture chair include, among others, (1) the range of cuts for domestic support expected in each of the three bands set in the Hong Kong ministerial declaration, (2) the number of tariff lines that developing countries will be able to designate as special products, and (3) the definition of an "emergency situation" that would qualify for in-kind food aid.

[35] Institute for International Business, Economics and Law, *Global Trade Opinion Poll, Survey No. 12*, Jan. 2006 (Adelaide, Australia: The University of Adelaide).

[36] See, for example, Gary Clyde Hufbauer and Jeffrey J. Schott, "The Doha Round After Hong Kong," *Policy Briefs in International Economics* (Washington, D.C.; Institute for International Economics, Feb. 2006).

In: The World Trade Organization: Another Round
Editor: Harold B. Whitiker, pp. 33-85
ISBN: 978-1-60021-816-3
© 2007 Nova Science Publishers, Inc.

Chapter 2

POTENTIAL CHALLENGES TO U.S. FARM SUBSIDIES IN THE WTO[*]

Randy Schnepf and Jasper Womach

ABSTRACT

Prior to its expiration on January 1, 2004, the World Trade Organization's (WTO's) Peace Clause (Article 13 of the Agreement on Agriculture) provided protection from trade remedy consideration and WTO dispute settlement for domestic farm subsidies provided they met certain compliance conditions. Absent the Peace Clause, challenges to U.S. farm subsidies now appear to confront a lower threshold for success, that of establishing "serious prejudice" under Articles 5(c) and 6.3 of the Agreement on Subsidies and Countervailing Measures (SCM). In particular, the criteria for establishing serious prejudice claims include demonstrating (1) the magnitude of a commodity's subsidies either as a share of returns or as an important determinant in covering production costs; (2) the relevance of the subsidized commodity to world markets as a share of either world production or world trade; and (3) a causal relationship between the subsidy and the adverse effect in the relevant market. Evidence of these criteria favors a successful challenge ruling by a WTO panel, as demonstrated by Brazil's successful WTO challenge of the U.S. cotton program.

A review of current U.S. farm programs measured against these criteria suggests that all major U.S. program crops are potentially vulnerable to WTO challenges. In addition, a review of recent economic analyses suggests that a partial policy reform of the nature suggested by the U.S. Doha-Round Proposal would do little to diminish the causal relationship between U.S. crop subsidies and adverse effects in international markets. Instead, the most clear method for decreasing exposure to WTO legal challenges is through extensive decoupling of U.S. programs — i.e., removing the linkage between payments and producer or consumer behavior. Such decoupling would sever the causality linkage necessary to consummate a successful WTO challenge.

The potential success of WTO challenges against U.S. farm programs is of concern to the U.S. Congress. If such challenges occur and are successful, the WTO remedy likely would imply either the elimination, alteration, or amendment by Congress of the programs in question to remove their adverse effects. Since most governing provisions

---

[*] Excerpted from Crs Report RL33697, dated April 26, 2007.

over U.S. farm programs are statutory, new legislation could be required to implement even minor changes to achieve compliance. Alternately, in light of an adverse ruling the United States could choose to make compensatory payments (under agreement with the challenging country) to offset the alleged injury.

This article provides background regarding the vulnerability of U.S. agricultural support programs to potential WTO dispute settlement challenges. It does not predict which WTO members might challenge U.S. commodity subsidies, nor the likelihood that such challenges will be brought. Instead, this article reviews the general criteria for successfully challenging a farm subsidy program, and then uses available data and published economic analyses to weigh U.S. farm programs against these criteria.

GLOSSARY OF ACRONYMS

AA	Agreement on Agriculture (WTO)
ABARE	Australian Bureau of Agricultural and Resource Economics
AD	Anti-Dumping
AMS	Aggregate Measure of Support
CCC	Commodity Credit Corporation
CCP	Counter-Cyclical Payment
CEG	Certificate of Exchange
CVD	Countervailing Duty
DEIP	Dairy Export Incentive Program
DP	Direct Payments (under the 2002 farm bill)
DSB	Dispute Settlement Body (WTO)
DSU	Understanding on Rules and Procedures Governing the Settlement of Disputes (WTO)
EEP	Export Enhancement Program
EU	European Union
FAPRI	Food and Agricultural Policy Research Institute
FSA	Farm Service Agency (USDA)
GATT	General Agreement on Tariffs and Trade
LDP	Loan Deficiency Payment
MILC	Milk Income Loss Contract
MLA	Market Loss Assistance
MLG	Marketing Loan Gain
OECD	Organization for Economic Cooperation and Development
PFC	Production Flexibility Contract payments (under the 1996 farm bill)
RMA	Risk Management Agency (USDA)
SCM	Agreement on Subsidies and Countervailing Measures
TRQ	Tariff-Rate Quota
USDA	U.S. Department of Agriculture
WTO	World Trade Organization

INTRODUCTION

The combination of three relatively recent events — the expiration of the World Trade Organization's (WTO's) Peace Clause[1] on January 1, 2004; Brazil's successful challenge of certain provisions of the U.S. cotton program in a WTO dispute settlement proceeding (upheld on appeal in March 2005); and the indefinite suspension of the Doha Round of WTO trade negotiations in July 2006 — have raised concerns among U.S. policymakers that U.S. farm programs could be subject to a new wave of WTO dispute settlement challenges.

Prior to its expiry, the Peace Clause had provided a degree of protection from WTO challenges — under both domestic countervailing duty proceedings and the WTO dispute settlement process — to most domestic agricultural support measures provided they met certain compliance conditions. The success of Brazil in challenging U.S. cotton program provisions within the WTO's dispute settlement process demonstrated the vulnerability of U.S. commodity programs to WTO challenges in the absence of the Peace Clause.[2] Furthermore, those countries most likely to bring new WTO challenges against U.S. commodity programs may feel more inclined to do so in light of the diminished likelihood of further negotiated reductions in U.S. domestic support following the indefinite suspension of the Doha Round of trade talks.

Nevertheless, some trade specialists argue that, despite the indefinite suspension of Doha Round talks and the substantial market distortions linked to several of the major U.S. domestic support programs, a large number of additional WTO challenges of U.S. farm support is unlikely. They contend that the fact-intensive nature of WTO challenges, their extensive costs, and the potential negative consequences in broader geopolitical terms may far outweigh any potential trade gains achieved through WTO litigation or dispute settlement proceedings.[3] In addition, others have argued that there is a large inherent risk involved in bringing a challenge against another country's subsidy program — if the challenge fails, it could legitimize those very programs that it had sought to discipline. Furthermore, some argue that Brazil's successful cotton case is indicative of the substantial investment Brazil has made over the past decade in human and institutional capacity to monitor trade issues and to use the WTO's dispute settlement process in protecting its interests. Few, if any, other developing countries have developed a similar capacity.

The potential success of WTO challenges against U.S. farm programs is of concern to the U.S. Congress. The current 2002 farm bill is set to expire in 2007, at which time Congress is expected to either extend, amend, or rewrite the current farm bill. USDA Secretary Johanns has stated that one of his primary objectives for the next farm bill is to make U.S. farm programs "beyond challenge."[4] If such challenges occur and are successful, the WTO remedy likely would imply either the elimination, alteration, or amendment by Congress of the programs in question to remove their adverse effects. Since most governing provisions over U.S. farm programs are statutory, new legislation could be required to implement even minor changes to achieve compliance. Alternately, in light of an adverse ruling the United States could choose to make compensatory payments (under agreement with the challenging country) to offset the alleged injury.

REPORT OVERVIEW AND DISCLAIMER

This article provides background concerning the potential vulnerability of U.S. domestic agricultural programs to new challenges under current WTO agreements. In addition, it provides a brief summary of the current status of the major ongoing WTO challenges against U.S. agricultural products. However, it is not an official CRS legal analysis of U.S. program vulnerability to WTO challenge, and it does not attempt to predict which WTO members might challenge U.S. commodity subsidies, the likelihood that such challenges will be brought, or the potential outcome of such challenges. Instead, this article reviews the general criteria for successfully challenging a farm subsidy program, then uses available data and published economic analyses to weigh U.S. farm programs against these criteria. As such, it acts as a primer on the issue of the vulnerability of domestic farm programs to WTO challenges, and provides numerous references for those seeking greater detail and more background information.

The chapter is divided into four sections. The first section briefly summarizes the recent developments concerning ongoing WTO dispute settlement (DS) challenges against U.S. farm programs. The second section reviews some provisions of WTO agreements that would be implicated in potential WTO challenges. A review of both the policy commitments and compliance rules established during the Uruguay Round is important in understanding which particular commodities would be most vulnerable to potential challenges and how a challenge might be framed. This section also includes a discussion of Brazil's successful WTO challenge of certain provisions of the U.S. cotton program, since it is also suggestive of how future cases against U.S. farm programs may be fashioned, as well as being indicative of the policy consequence of such challenges.

The third section of the chapter provides a review of U.S. domestic support, by program and by commodity, with a discussion of how each program fits into the scheme of WTO liberalization commitments. This section includes a review of various crop-specific measures that might suggest farm program vulnerability to a WTO challenge and discusses how U.S. programs could be altered to minimize the threat of challenge.

The final section briefly reviews several broader issues related to WTO challenges of commodity subsidy programs, including likely remedies under successful challenges, defining subsidy criteria under the serious prejudice claim, and potential redesign of farm programs to reduce their vulnerability to WTO DS challenges.

RECENT DEVELOPMENTS:
WTO CHALLENGES OF U.S. FARM PROGRAMS

Two significant WTO DS cases against U.S. farm programs remain active —the Brazil case (DS267) against certain features of the U.S. cotton program and the Canada case (DS357) against certain features of U.S. farm programs, in general, and more specifically against the U.S. corn program.

Concerning the cotton case, a WTO Appellate Body (AB) issued a final ruling in March 2005 recommending that the United States remove both the prohibited subsidies and the adverse effects defined by the case.[5] In response, the United States eliminated the Step 2 program (August 1, 2006) and indicated that the market loss payments cited in the case have also ended. However, Brazil claims that additional permanent modifications to U.S. farm programs are still needed to fully comply with the WTO ruling. On August 21, 2006, Brazil submitted a request for a WTO compliance panel to review whether the United States has fully complied with panel and AB rulings. A compliance panel was established on October 25, 2006. On January 9, 2007, the compliance panel's chairman announced that work would be finished in July 2007. If the compliance panel finds that the United States has not fully complied with the AB rulings, Brazil could ask a WTO arbitration panel to resume its work that was temporarily suspended in mid-2005. Brazil has claimed the right to retaliate against $3 billion in U.S. exports to Brazil based on the prohibited subsidies, and proposed $1 billion in retaliation based on the actionable subsidies.

On January 8, 2007, Canada requested consultations with the United States under the auspices of the WTO DS process to discuss three explicit charges against U.S. farm programs (all three charges derive directly from the legal precedent of the Brazil cotton case).[6] First, Canada contends that U.S. corn subsidies have caused serious prejudice to Canadian corn producers in the form of market price suppression in Canadian corn markets during the 1996 to 2006 period. Second, Canada argues that the U.S. export credit guarantee program operates as a WTO-illegal export subsidy. Third, Canada claims that U.S. fixed direct payments are not green box compliant and should therefore be included with U.S. amber box payments, in which case the United States would be in violation of its $19.1 billion amber box spending limit for 1999, 2000, 2001, 2004, and 2005. If successfully litigated, this case could affect broader U.S. agricultural policy, since the charges against the U.S. export credit guarantee and direct payment programs extend beyond corn to all major program crops.

Consultations are still ongoing and Canada has not yet requested the formation of a WTO panel. If a WTO panel is requested and ultimately agreed to by the WTO Dispute Settlement Body, it would set in motion the full rules and timetables of the WTO DS process in examining Canada's case. Should any eventual changes in U.S. farm policy be needed to comply with a WTO ruling in Canada's favor, such changes would likely involve action by Congress to produce new legislation. Congress will be revisiting U.S. farm legislation this year and could potentially address some of the issues raised by Canada's WTO challenge.

WTO COMMITMENTS, RULES, AND CHALLENGES

Overview

The linkage between agricultural subsidies and market distortions has long provided a basis for trade remedy claims.[7] Article VI of the General Agreement on Tariffs and Trade (GATT) of 1947 helped to standardize international trade remedies where claims of dumping and subsidization were alleged. Article XVI of the GATT also addressed subsidies. However, agricultural support policies and their linkage to commodity markets and trade were first addressed in the Uruguay Round (UR) of multilateral trade negotiations in 1994 under the Agreement on Agriculture (AA). This agreement attempted to specify and discipline agricultural support policies, and to develop a process for settling disputes between member countries concerning the use of agricultural subsidies.[8] Both anti-dumping (AD) and countervailing duty (CVD) trade remedies have remained available to member countries of the WTO since its establishment in 1994. However, Article 13 of the AA (the so-called Peace Clause) called for due restraint among WTO members in seeking CVD or WTO dispute settlement claims, particularly if the subsidies in question remained within certain limits as spelled out in the AA and in each member country's schedule of concessions. Article 13 was limited by a sunset provision that fixed its duration to the nine-year implementation period running from January 1, 1995, through December 31, 2003.

As part of WTO membership, countries agreed to disciplines in agricultural support including rules and definitions governing the nature of agricultural support (e.g., market distorting or non-distorting), as well as formal, clearly defined commitments to reduce or limit agricultural support.[9] In addition, WTO members have agreed to formal procedures for resolving disputes concerning compliance with WTO disciplines. This chapter assumes a general knowledge of WTO rules and procedures; however, those aspects deemed most relevant for understanding potential challenges to U.S. agricultural programs are briefly described below.

Wto Agreements

Within the WTO's multitude of legal texts and supporting documents, the following are most relevant to issues related to agricultural subsidies and challenges to the WTO legality of those subsidies:[10]

- General Agreement on Tariffs and Trade of 1994 (GATT 1994).
- GATT 1994 subsumes the original GATT 1947 under the WTO and includes a series of "understandings" that provide additional precision to the interpretation of earlier GATT 1947 legal texts and rules.
- Agreement on Agriculture (AA). The AA provides the legal framework for administering the agricultural policy reforms agreed to in 1994 by members.
- Country Schedules to the AA.[11] Each individual member has a unique schedule of concessions and commitments that includes such details as the implementation period for subsidy and tariff reductions or quota expansions, subsidy caps, and other country-specific terms.
- Agreement on Subsidies and Countervailing Measures (SCM).
- The SCM establishes formal definitions and rules for subsidies, including whether they are "prohibited"or "actionable," as well as providing special and additional rules for consultations and dispute settlement.
- Understanding on Rules and Procedures Governing the Settlement of Disputes (DSU). The DSU establishes a binding dispute settlement system to enforce WTO rules.[12] It is only within the framework of the DSU that a member country may bring a formal challenge against another member country for alleged violation of rules or provisions of the AA or SCM.

Article 13 and Annex 2 from the AA, along with Articles 1, 5, and 6 from the SCM, are included as attachments at the end of this chapter.

Agricultural Policy Reform Commitments

To limit and reduce the amount of distortive subsidies directed to their agricultural sectors, WTO members have agreed to disciplines in agricultural support in three broad areas — domestic support programs, export subsidies, and market access. Since much of the potential for new challenges of U.S. farm programs involves compliance with these policy reform commitments, each of these broad policy reform areas is briefly discussed below.

Domestic Support

In Article 6 of the AA, domestic support programs were categorized based on their potential to distort commodity markets.[13] Domestic support that is deemed to have a "direct effect" on agricultural markets is measured by an index referred to as the Aggregate Measure of Support (AMS).[14] The AMS combines the monetary value of all non-exempt agricultural support into one overall measure. The AMS includes budgetary outlays in the form of actual or calculated amounts of direct payments to producers under various commodity programs such as marketing loan provisions, input subsidies, and interest subsidies on commodity loan programs, as well as revenue transfers from consumers to producers as a result of policies that distort market prices. Once measured, the AMS is then subject to reductions and a cap. However, to accommodate legitimate domestic policy goals, the AA defined four major categories of domestic support, three of which are eligible for exemption from reduction commitments:[15]

- Green Box. This category covers domestic programs deemed to be minimally or non-market distorting, such as agricultural research and extension programs.[16]
- Blue Box. This category includes support that is production-limited for either crop or livestock production.[17]
- Product- and Non-Product-Specific De Minimis Exemptions.
- U.S. commodity-specific support that is below 5% of a commodity's value of production is deemed sufficiently benign that it does not have to be included in the AMS calculation.[18] Such commodity-specific support can be evaluated for each individual commodity. Similarly, non-product specific support that is below 5% of the total value of production for all commodities may be exempted from AMS limits. Since the value of U.S. agricultural production averages in excess of $200 billion annually, this latter exemption can cover as much as $10 billion in non-product specific support.
- Amber Box. After excluding all of the exempted categories, the remaining AMS support is placed in the Amber Box. U.S. Amber Box AMS has been capped at $19.1 billion since 2000.

Each WTO Member has certain obligations to notify the WTO of spending under each of these domestic support categories (amber box, blue box, de minimis, and green box).[19] The AA is fairly specific on the criteria for designating domestic support programs into the various AMS categories. However, each country makes its own designations and there is not always a clean fit between a domestic program and a WTO AMS category. As a result, disagreement may arise between WTO members over a particular program designation (e.g., exemption status with respect to the AMS) or whether the support under a particular program has been fully counted. Such disagreements may manifest themselves as formal DSU challenges. For example, as part of its WTO cotton case, Brazil successfully challenged the U.S. designation of Production Flexibility Contract (PFC) payments as fully "decoupled" and, therefore, green box compliant.[20] However, increasing tardiness in notifying domestic crop subsidies to the WTO, particularly on the part of those countries with the largest domestic subsidies — the United States, the EU, and Japan — has diminished the ability of third countries to use notifications as a basis for challenge.

Export Subsidies

The AA imposes limits on direct agricultural export subsidies, but not on indirect export subsidies. Indirect methods of export subsidization include government subsidized financing for exports (e.g., export credit guarantees), export promotion and information activities, tax benefits, or other forms of assistance that may lead to lower than normal costs for exported products.[21] WTO members agreed to both volume and value reductions in the use of direct export subsidies from a 1986-90 base period. Each country's schedule specifies both how much can be exported with subsidy as well as the permitted subsidy expenditure for each listed commodity. A WTO member may not initiate new export subsidies for commodities that are not in its country schedule.[22] Because indirect export subsidies are less transparent, but may still provide substantial market support, their use represents a potential source for dispute between nations and may lead to new challenges. For example, as part of the WTO cotton case, the panel found that U.S. export credit guarantees operated as prohibited export subsidies and were permissible only to the extent that they complied with the export subsidy commitments listed in the U.S. country schedule.

Market Access

Market access refers to the extent to which a country permits imports. Within the WTO, market access refers more specifically to the conditions governing tariff and non-tariff measures agreed to by members for the entry of specific goods into their markets.[23] WTO members agreed to bind the maximum tariff rates that may be applied to imported products at base period (1986-88) levels. Member countries are free to apply tariff rates that are below the bound rate, but may never apply a tariff rate in excess of the bound rate without first consulting the other members most likely to be affected by such a change and agreeing on some level of compensation.[24] In addition to the binding of maximum tariff rates, member countries have agreed to reductions in the bound rates as specified in their country schedules. In some countries, a tariff-rate quota (TRQ) was established for "sensitive" products that included a minimum low-tariff, access quota component and a more protected above-quota component. The specific quota and tariff rates for all TRQs are listed in the country schedules. Violations of tariffs and TRQ provisions are challengeable, as are indirect import restrictions in the form of variable import levies, discretionary import licensing, non-tariff measures maintained through state trading enterprises, voluntary export restraints, and most border measures other than ordinary customs duties. However, the Peace Clause did not apply to market access commitments. As a result, the status of WTO legal challenges of market access commitments has not changed with the expiration of the Peace Clause.

WTO Subsidy Challenges under the Peace Clause

Subsidies under the SCM Agreement

As mentioned earlier, the Agreement on Subsidies and Countervailing Measures (SCM) establishes formal definitions and rules for subsidies, including whether they are "prohibited" or "actionable," as well as providing for consultations and dispute settlement.

Prohibited Subsidies

The SCM is explicit in its prohibition of subsidies that directly affect trade.[25] Two types of subsidies are prohibited: subsidies contingent upon export performance and subsidies contingent upon the use of domestic over imported goods. These prohibitions apply except as provided in the AA.[26] For example, in the WTO cotton case, U.S. Step 2 cotton payments to exporters were identified as unscheduled export subsidies, while Step 2 cotton payments to domestic users were identified as illegal import substitution subsidies.[27] Thus, both Step 2 payments were subject to the SCM agreement prohibition. In the WTO's dispute settlement process, prohibited subsidies are treated with greater urgency than are actionable subsidies. If a policy measure is found to constitute a prohibited subsidy under DSU challenge, then the DSU panel "shall recommend that the subsidizing Member withdraw the subsidy without delay."[28]

Actionable Subsidies

Actionable subsidies (i.e., those subsidies that are not expressly prohibited but against which legal action may be taken) are broadly defined in SCM Article 5 as those subsidies (defined in SCM Article 1) which cause:
... adverse effects to the interests of other Members, i.e.:

a) injury to the domestic industry of another Member ;
b) nullification or impairment of benefits accruing directly or indirectly to other Members under GATT 1994 in particular the benefits of concessions bound under Article II of GATT 1994;
c) serious prejudice to the interests of another Member.[29]

Trade analysts have argued that the adverse effects criteria represent a lower threshold for achieving successful challenges to agricultural support programs than the injury requirement under a countervailing duty claim. This is because under SCM Article 5, "serious prejudice," but not injury, must be established (discussed below).[30] Prior to its expiration, the Peace Clause had provided protection from trade remedy consideration for actionable subsidies provided that they met certain compliance conditions (discussed in the following section).

The Peace Clause

During the nine-year period from January 1, 1995, through December 31, 2003, Article 13 of the AA, known as the "Due Restraint" or so-called Peace Clause, exempted most domestic commodity support measures from domestic countervailing duty (CVD) and DSU challenge, so long as the support provided for any specific commodity (a) was in compliance with the provisions of Annex 2 of the AA, or (b) was in compliance with the criteria for AMS, green box, blue box, and de minimis from Article 6 of the AA and did not exceed the level of support received during the benchmark 1992 marketing year.[31] In other words, for those agricultural support programs in full compliance with the terms of the AA, the Peace Clause provided relief from domestic CVD and DSU challenge provided the value of the support did not exceed the 1992 spending benchmark.

The intention of the Peace Clause was to allow WTO members sufficient time to comply fully with their policy reform commitments, recognizing that some policies would likely take several years to bring into full compliance due to the dynamics of each country's internal political process. With the expiry of the Peace Clause, the full substantive and procedural legal apparatus of the WTO may be used to challenge any type of agricultural subsidy — including export subsidies, Amber Box, Blue Box, Green Box, and De Minimis measures — even if a subsidy remains within spending limits defined under the country schedule.

The Peace Clause did not provide protection from DSU challenges to all agricultural policy support measures. Prior to the Peace Clause's expiration, DSU challenges with respect to agricultural commodities could encompass issues arising from noncompliance with WTO commitments, particularly from prohibited subsidies. In addition, DSU challenges could encompass issues arising from violation of other WTO rules, such as those covering dumping or sanitary and phytosanitary measures including emerging issues such as biotech trade disputes. CVD actions also were available for injury resulting from subsidized trade, although, as noted earlier, members were requested to use "due restraint" in seeking countervailing duties. At the time of the Peace Clause expiration, over 128 DSU cases involving agricultural products (including fisheries and forestry) were in some stage of determination.[32]

U.S. trade negotiators have sought to include a new Peace Clause in the negotiating text of the Doha Round in order to protect domestic support programs while a new round of domestic support disciplines is being adopted. However, the proposal for a new Peace Clause has met stiff resistance from nearly all negotiating partners.

Brazil's WTO Case Against the U.S. Cotton Program

On March 21, 2005, the WTO Dispute Settlement Body (DSB) adopted the reports from both the WTO Appellate Body and the original WTO panel hearing Brazil's claims against the U.S. cotton program.[33] Several of the rulings from the cotton case have important implications for future DSU challenges against U.S. farm programs and are briefly summarized below.[34]

First Ruling: Peace Clause Violation

The existence of the Peace Clause did not prevent Brazil from bringing its case against the U.S. cotton program, in part because Brazil thought it could prove that the United States was in violation of the Peace Clause's 1992 spending limit. After reviewing the evidence presented, the panel found that U.S. cotton support levels for each of the marketing years 1999 through 2002 exceeded the Peace Clause's 1992 benchmark spending threshold. As a result, according to the panel the Peace Clause exclusion could not be used to protect the U.S. policy measures. Had Brazil failed to show a violation of the Peace Clause's 1992 support threshold, it is unlikely the panel would have pursued the case further, thus demonstrating the important protection provided to domestic support measures by the now-expired Peace Clause.

A key element of the panel's determination regarding the Peace Clause was that U.S. Production Flexibility Contract (PFC) payments made under the 1996 farm bill and Direct Payments (DP) made under the 2002 farm bill failed to fully meet the Green Box conditions for decoupled income support. Disqualification arises because of planting restrictions on fruits, vegetables, and wild rice. As a result, the panel ruled that they should count against the U.S. 1992 spending benchmark. In its notifications for 1996 through 2001, the United States notified PFC payments as fully decoupled green box support, thereby not counting against the U.S. AMS limit of $19.1 billion.

Although the panel did not declare that PFC and DP payments should be notified as amber box payments, the panel implied as much. This particular finding was not a part of the "serious prejudice" finding that required remedy; however, it establishes a precedent for interpreting the notification status of U.S. direct payments. As such, the ruling represents an obvious vulnerability should another country choose to specifically challenge the notification status of PFC and DP payments. Such a DSU challenge, if successful, would have important implications for the United States' ability to meet its domestic support commitments. What would happen if PFC and DP payments are included as amber box rather than green box? Two economic analyses conclude that the United States would have violated its AMS limit of $19.1 billion during the years 1998, 1999, 2000, 2001, and 2006.[35] New legislation would be necessary to make these direct payments green box compliant.

Second Finding: Prohibited Subsidies

On Sept 8, 2004, the panel found that both the Step 2 cotton program and the export credit guarantee program acted as prohibited subsidies and should be withdrawn (i.e., terminated) within six months of adoption of the panel report by the WTO (or by July 1, 2005, whichever was earlier).[36] Furthermore, the panel found that this applied, not just to cotton, but to all commodities that benefit from U.S. commodity support programs and receive export credit guarantees. As a result, U.S. export credit guarantees for any recipient commodity are subject to previously scheduled export subsidy commitments for that commodity (as listed in the Country Schedule). For the United States, this refers to export subsidies listed under the Export Enhancement Program (EEP) and the Dairy Export Incentive Program (DEIP).[37] Among those commodities eligible for EEP or DEIP, the panel found that U.S. rice exports received export credit guarantee benefits in excess of its EEP volume commitments. The panel found that all "unscheduled" program commodities, such as cotton, receiving export credit guarantee benefits were also in violation of WTO commitments.

The panel ruling on export credits hinged on a determination that the financial benefits returned to the government failed to cover long-run program expenses, thus implying that they functioned effectively as export subsidies.[38] An amendment to the statute is needed to eliminate the alleged subsidy component of export credit guarantees — i.e., below market user fees due to a 1% cap on user fees for GSM-102 (the primary export credit program). This statutory cap prevents charging higher risk-based fees as recommended by the panel. Other U.S. trade assistance programs, such as the various market development programs, appear to operate within WTO rules; however, if brought under more intensive scrutiny, they could be vulnerable to interpretation charging that they effectively function as export subsidies, which would potentially subject them to scheduled export subsidy commitments.[39]

Third Finding: Serious Prejudice

The panel ruled that the United States should remove the prejudicial effects of price-contingent support measures including marketing loan provisions, Step 2 payments, market loss payments, and counter-cyclical payments. The extent of program change needed for compliance is not clear, particularly since the Step 2 program ended on August 1, 2006, and no market loss payments have been made since 2002. However, Brazil claims the right to impose retaliatory tariffs valued at $1 billion. On August 21, 2006, Brazil requested the establishment of a compliance panel to determine whether current U.S. actions are sufficient to comply with the original WTO rulings and recommendations.[40] Although the United States successfully blocked Brazil's first attempt to form a compliance panel, Brazil's second request on September 28, 2006, resulted in the establishment of a compliance panel.[41]

Post-Peace-Clause DSU Challenges

Following the expiry of the Peace Clause, both export and domestic subsidies on agricultural products that are otherwise in compliance with WTO commitments may be subject to DSU challenge under various legal provisions of the GATT 1994 and the SCM Agreement.[42] One legal analysis of the potential for post-Peace-Clause DSU challenges, undertaken by Steinberg and Josling, suggests that the most likely avenue for future DSU challenges against the alleged "adverse effects" of U.S. farm programs under SCM Article 5 would be claims of "serious prejudice" as defined in SCM Article 5(c), primarily because this provision contains the lowest threshold that a challenge must meet.[43] SCM Article 6 defines the nature of "serious prejudice" and the cases in which it may be said to exist. In particular, Article 6.3 provides that:

> Serious prejudice in the sense of paragraph (c) of Article 5 may arise in any case where one or several of the following apply: (a) the effect of the subsidy is to *displace or impede the imports of a like product* of another Member into the market of the subsidizing Member; (b) the effect of the subsidy is to *displace or impede the exports of a like product* of another Member from a third country market; (c) the effect of the subsidy is *a significant price undercutting* by the subsidized product as compared with the price of a like product of another Member in the same market or significant price suppression, price depression or lost sales in the same market; (d) the effect of the subsidy is *an increase in the world market share of the subsidizing Member* in a particular subsidized primary product or commodity as compared to the average share it had during the previous period of three years and this increase follows a consistent trend over a period when subsidies have been granted.[44]

SCM Article 6.4 adds further precision to the nature of market displacement identified in Article 6.3(b) by indicating that displacement may be demonstrated by showing that a change in relative market shares has occurred to the disadvantage of a non-subsidized "like" product.

Steinberg and Josling conclude that the biggest challenge to making a trade remedy claim under SCM Article 6.3 would be to credibly and reliably establish that agricultural subsidies are causing serious prejudice as defined by the above provisions.[45] Steinberg and Josling provide a roadmap for developing a case under these legal provisions including the incorporation of economic and statistical modeling for showing causal linkages between agricultural support policies (i.e., subsidization) and prejudicial market effects as measured by market share, quantity displacement, and/or price suppression. Steinberg and Josling argue that a strong *prima facie* case under the legal standards of SCM Article 6.3 and 6.4 could be made if:

- regression analysis, partial equilibrium modeling, or general equilibrium modeling confirmed each of the relationships being tested, and
- those analyses were complemented by a confirmatory narrative about the relationships in particular markets.

Brazil's successful challenge of the U.S. cotton program followed this general course, but used a serious prejudice argument based on "significant price suppression" in world markets. Econometric model results were included to support the argument of strong adverse policy-to-price linkages.[46] Specifically, the WTO panel cited four main grounds that supported a causal link between the implicated U.S. cotton subsidies and significant price suppression:[47]

- the United States exerts a substantial influence in the world cotton market due to the relative magnitude of U.S. cotton production and exports;
- the relevant U.S. subsidies are price contingent, i.e., linked directly to world prices for upland cotton, thereby insulating U.S. producers from low prices;
- there is a discernible temporal coincidence of suppressed world market prices and the price-contingent U.S. subsidies; and
- there is a divergence between U.S. cotton producers' total costs of production and their revenue from cotton sales, suggesting that it is the U.S. subsidies that permit cotton sales at prices that fail to cover costs.

These same criteria are relevant for evaluating the potential vulnerability to future WTO legal challenges for U.S. commodities. Appendix A provides a brief review of several published economic analyses of the market effects of U.S. agricultural policies. As a general rule, these studies support the idea that U.S. (and other developed country) agricultural support programs negatively influence international market prices and tend to disadvantage third-country trade of non-subsidized "like" products.

The following section reviews actual U.S. program outlays by commodity, as well as various market statistics (e.g., share of world production and trade) for major U.S. program crops that correspond with the causal linkage criteria listed above.

U.S. FARM PROGRAM SUBSIDIES

Overview

As mentioned earlier, each WTO member country is expected to routinely submit notification reports on the implementation of its specific policy reform commitments, including domestic farm support outlays, to the WTO.[48] The country notifications, along with any other publicly available information on domestic support outlays, provide the basis for evaluating and challenging compliance with WTO commitments. As of this writing, the United States has notified domestic support outlays for only calendar years 1995 through 2001. However, USDA routinely publishes estimates of U.S. farm program support for historical, current, and projected crop years.[49] In building its case against the U.S. cotton program, Brazil made ample use of USDA public data sources. Furthermore, a critical issue for U.S. commodity subsidies with respect to their inclusion in a WTO legal challenge is, not how they were notified to the WTO, but the extent to which they can be linked to a specific commodity.

This section reviews both U.S. domestic support notifications and publicly available USDA data since 1996 to evaluate the potential vulnerability of U.S. farm commodities to new WTO legal challenges. This section begins with a review of U.S. farm support programs, including a discussion of differences between actual USDA outlays and the AMS support levels notified to the WTO. This is followed by an evaluation of domestic support for each of the major U.S. program crops against the criteria for measuring potential linkages between policy and market effects as developed in the first section of this chapter.

U.S. Domestic Support Outlays and Notifications

The United States operates a wide range and large number of federal programs that both directly and indirectly support U.S. agricultural production. For example, in FY2006, USDA and related agencies (the Food and Drug Administration and the Commodity Futures Trading Commission) received budget authority of an estimated $99.9 billion that included domestic food assistance programs, agricultural research and extension, rural development, conservation, foreign aid, and commodity programs.[50] However, most of these programs and activities are considered minimally production and trade distorting under the terms of the WTO Agreement on Agriculture (AA).

A WTO challenge under SCM Articles 5 or 6.3 appears likely to focus on those programs that are categorized under the WTO criteria as production and trade distorting (i.e., amber box) or that are have been exempted from the amber box under the blue box, de minimis, or green box criteria but can be shown to cause adverse effects in certain markets. Table 1 presents a list of U.S. agricultural support programs by WTO category based on the domestic support notifications submitted by the United States during 1995-2001.

During the 1995-2001 period, the United States notified an annual average of $15.3 billion in domestic spending under the AMS amber box and de minimis categories (Table 2). The United States has used the blue box only once (in 1995) since qualifying target-price deficiency payments were eliminated by the 1996 farm bill. During that same 1995-2001 period, the United States notified an annual average of $50 billion in green box support outlays.

The 2002 farm bill (Farm Security and Rural Investment Act of 2002, P.L. 107-171), made some changes to commodity support programs including the creation of two new programs — the Counter-Cyclical Payments (CCP) program and the Milk Income Loss Contract (MILC) program. Neither of these programs has yet been notified as belonging to a particular WTO category. U.S. commodity programs are briefly described below.

Farm Support Programs

Domestic commodity support provisions in the 2002 farm bill include three major payment programs: Direct Payments, Counter-Cyclical Payments (CCP), and benefits under marketing loan provisions — i.e., loan deficiency payments (LDPs), marketing loan gains (MLGs), and certificate exchange gains (CEGs).[51] Over 62% ($110 billion) of USDA CCC outlays were made under these three programs during 1996-2006 (table 3).

CCP payments and marketing loan benefits (LDP, MLG, and CEG) vary with market prices and make outlays when market prices fall below target prices (CCP) or loan rates (marketing loan benefits). Marketing loan benefits have been notified as product-specific AMS support (see table 2, heading 2, "Non-Exempt Direct Payments"). Like marketing loan benefits, CCP payment are specific to a commodity. Unlike marketing loan benefits which depend on actual production, CCP outlays are based on historical base acres and national average prices. As a result, CCP payments are decoupled from producer planting decisions, but do retain a link to market prices. Because CCP payments were not made until calendar 2003, they have yet to be notified to the WTO. However, the commodity-decoupled, but price-linked nature of CCP payments suggests that they would likely be notified as non-product specific AMS support under current WTO criteria. As a result, CCP would likely qualify for exemption from the AMS limit under the non-product-specific de minimis exemption.

Direct payments (DP) are paid annually and are based on historical base acres and yields. As a result, they do not vary annually based on current production or market conditions. DP under the 2002 farm bill are an extension of the Planting Flexibility Contract (PFC) payments of the 1996 farm bill (P.L. 104-127). The principal difference between DP and PFC payments is that farmers were allowed to adjust their declared base acres and crops at sign-up time for the 2002 farm bill. As a result, the share of DP payments across program crops shifted slightly between the 1996 and 2002 farm bills. The United States has always notified both DP and PFC to the WTO as decoupled green-box support. However, the WTO panel and Appellate Body hearing the cotton case (DS267) found that DP payments are not fully decoupled because of a prohibition on planting fruits, vegetables, and wild rice on payment acres. As a result, the panel ruled that DP payments did not qualify for inclusion in the green box and therefore were counted against the 1992 "Peace Clause" spending limit discussed earlier. This raises the question of whether or not the U.S. will continue to classify direct payments as green box or report them in the future as amber box.

Table 1. Categorized List of U.S. Support Programs, 1995-2001

Green Box Programs — non or minimally production and trade distorting programs exempt from disciplines.	
•	USDA research, cooperative extension, and economics programs;
•	Animal and Plant Health Inspection Service (APHIS) pest and disease programs;
•	Food Safety and Inspection Service (FSIS) meat and poultry inspection;
•	Agricultural Marketing Service (AMS), Grain Inspection, Packers and Stockyards Administration (GIPSA), and other marketing services, including grading, quality inspection, and market news;
•	Domestic food assistance programs, including food stamps, school food, the special supplemental food program for women, infants, and children (WIC), and Section 32 food purchases for domestic assistance;
•	Food security commodity reserve;
•	Disaster payments for livestock and crop losses due to natural disasters;
•	Conservation programs like conservation operations and the Environmental Quality Incentives Program (EQIP);
•	Farm credit including Farm Service Agency (FSA) farm ownership and operating loans; and state mediation programs;
•	The Conservation Reserve Program (CRP); and
•	CCC production flexibility contract payments made under the Agricultural Market Transition Act (AMTA) of 1996.
Blue Box Programs — production limiting programs exempt from disciplines.	
•	Target price deficiency payments (which ended with 1996 farm law).
Amber Box Programs — potentially production and trade distorting programs that are subject to disciplines. They are defined as either product- or non-product specific.	
Product-specific support:	
•	Dairy price support;
•	Sugar price support;
•	Peanut price support;
•	Benefits under marketing loan provisions; and
•	Storage payments.
Non-product specific support:	
•	Irrigation subsidies on Bureau of Reclamation Projects in 17 Western States;
•	Subsidies for grazing livestock on federal land;
•	Federal crop and revenue insurance subsidies; and
•	Farm storage facility loan subsidies.

Source: U.S. notifications to the WTO; G/AG/N/USA/# for #'s 10, 17, 27, 36, 43, and 51.

Nearly all of the payments made under these three programs — DP, CCP, and marketing loan provisions — are directed to a relatively small number of commodities (see following section). However, several other federal programs provide substantial annual direct support to a broader list of crops. Such programs include livestock grazing subsidies, crop and revenue insurance subsidies, irrigation subsidies, storage payments, and commodity loan interest subsidies. In addition, over $37 billion in emergency assistance payments were made to agricultural producers during FY1996-FY2006. Although most disaster assistance qualifies for the WTO green box exclusion, U.S. emergency payments included $16 billion in *ad hoc* market loss assistance (MLA) payments that were made to grain, oilseed, cotton, tobacco, and dairy producers in response to low farm commodity prices during the 1998-2002 period.[52]

Based on specific AMS criteria, the United States notified support under many of these smaller programs (including MLA payments) as non-commodity-specific domestic support such that they qualified for the de minimis exemption (see table 2, heading 5, "Non-product specific support"). However, in many instances payments from these programs can be linked directly to specific crops using publicly available information sources. For example, MLA payments were based on specific crop yield conditions. Similarly, the United States has notified its crop insurance subsidies as non-commodity-specific support since all crop production is universally eligible for such insurance. However, most crop insurance subsidies (with the exception of adjusted gross revenue insurance) can be linked directly to a specific insured crop.[53]

Government support of crop insurance has expanded greatly in the past decade and is currently available to all crops grown in the United States. As a result, federal crop insurance subsidies have greatly expanded the pool of subsidized commodities in the United States. Crop insurance support is administered by USDA's Risk Management Agency (RMA) and funded through the Federal Crop Insurance Fund rather than from the CCC, therefore crop insurance subsidies are not included in CCC budget tables. Since FY2002, government net outlays (including premium subsidies and government loss-sharing) have averaged over $3 billion annually. However, the recent growth in federal crop insurance subsidies, coupled with projections for continued growth (FAPRI projects federal crop insurance net outlays to exceed $4 billion by 2008 and to reach $4.6 billion by 2015[54]) could potentially bring the crop insurance program under greater scrutiny from WTO competitors.

Program Commodities

Most direct program subsidies are available only for about 25 agricultural commodities. The 2002 farm bill defines two classes of commodities: "covered commodities" and "loan commodities." The classes determine which types of payments are available. For example, DP and CCP payments are available only to the covered commodities, while marketing loan benefits are available to the larger group of loan commodities. *Covered commodities* include wheat, feed grains (corn, grain sorghum, barley, and oats), upland cotton, rice, soybeans, and other oilseeds (sunflower seed, rapeseed, canola, safflower, flaxseed, mustard seed, crambe, and sesame seed). *Loan commodities* include the covered commodities, plus extra long staple cotton, wool, mohair, honey, dry peas, lentils, and small chickpeas. Peanuts are classified separately, but receive payments like the covered commodities.

U.S. dairy and sugar sectors also receive substantial support, but their support is of a less direct nature than cash payments or certificate exchanges. Dairy prices are supported (at a producer liquid milk-equivalent price of $9.90 per hundredweight) through federal purchases of surplus nonfat dry milk, butter, and cheese. In addition, dairy producers also receive a counter-cyclical "milk-income loss contract" (MILC) payment when prices fall below a target price. Although they have yet to be notified, MILC payments are linked to production and market prices (much like loan deficiency payments for crops) and can be expected to qualify as amber box payments. Demand for dairy products is supported by the Dairy Export Incentive Program (DEIP), which subsidizes export of U.S. dairy products. Finally, domestic prices are provided border protection by a system of TRQs for most dairy products.

Table 2. WTO Notifications of U.S. Domestic Support: Amber Box Categories and De Minimis Exemptions, 1995-2001

AMS Policy category[a]	Base 1986-88	1995	1996	1997	1998	1999	2000	2001	Average 1995-01
					($ million)				
1. Market Price Support[b]	6,956	6,213	5,919	5,816	5,776	5,921	5,840	5,826	5,902
Dairy	5,409	4,693	4,674	4,455	4,332	4,437	4,377	4,483	4,493
Sugar	1,041	1,108	937	1,045	1,093	1,180	1,133	1,032	1,076
Peanuts	347	412	308	315	350	303	330	311	333
Beef[c]	158	0	0	0	0	0	0	0	0
2. Non-Exempt Direct Pmts[d]	12,393	88	7	578	4,437	10,403	10,567	8,435	4,931
Loan Def. Payment	56	0	0	3	2,780	6,210	6,273	5,593	2,980
Marketing-Loan Gain	387	0	0	161	1,039	1,685	733	610	604
Certificate-Exch. Gains	0	0	0	0	6	175	619	1,975	396
Cotton Step 2 payments	0	35	6	416	280	446	237	182	229
Other non-exempt pymnts	2,244	88	7	414	613	2,332	2,943	256	951
3. Total Other Support[e]	1,995	10	12	80	338	567	457	367	262
Storage payments	573	4	0	24	78	144	43	62	51
Interest subsidies	1,599	115	78	141	344	443	466	367	279
NE dairy compact benefits	0	0	0	0	28	55	20	0	15
Fees paid by producers	(177)	(109)	(67)	(84)	(112)	(74)	(72)	(62)	(83)
4. Product-Specific Totals (= 1 + 2 + 3)	21,343	6,311	5,937	6,475	10,550	16,891	16,865	14,628	11,094
5. Non-prod-specific support	901	1,543	1,113	568	4,584	7,406	7,278	6,828	4,189
Crop market loss payments	0	0	0	0	2,811	5,468	5,463	4,640	2626
Crop insurance costs	289	906	633	120	747	1,514	1,396	1,770	1,012
Irrg. subsidies-W. States	543	543	381	348	348	316	316	300	365
Other	69	94	99	100	677	108	103	118	186
For Non-Specific "De Minimis" (DM) Calculations									
5% of value of prod.[f]	7,146	9,505	10,285	10,194	9,544	9,237	9,476	9,925	9,738
6. Total Before Exemptions (= 4 + 5)	22,245	7,855	7,051	7,042	15,134	24,297	24,143	21,456	15,283

Table 2. (Continued).

AMS Policy category[a]	Base 1986-88	1995	1996	1997	1998	1999	2000	2001	Average 1995-01
					($ million)				
7. Exemptions	1,634	(1,642)(1,174)		(812)	(4,750)	(7,435)	(7,341)	(7,045)	(4,314)
Non-prod-specific DM[f]	(901)	(1,543)(1,113)		(568)	(4,584)	(7,406)	(7,278)	(6,828)	(4,189)
Prod-specific DM[f]	(692)	(99)	(61)	(244)	(166)	(29)	(63)	(217)	(126)
Credit in base period[g]	3,228	0	0	0	0	0	0	0	0
8. Total Non-Exempt AMS Outlays (= 6 + 7)	23,879	6,212	5,876	6,231	10,384	16,862	16,802	14,411	10,968
9. AMS Ceiling[h]	23,879	23,083	22,287	21,491	20,695	19,899	19,103	19,103	20,809
10. Unused AMS Ceiling	—	16,869	16,390	15,253	10,303	3,037	2,301	4,690	9,835

Source: USDA/ERS, WTO database at [http://www.ers.usda.gov/briefing/farmpolicy/usnotify.htm] and recent U.S. notifications to the WTO. Reproduced from CRS Report RL30612, *Agriculture in the WTO: Member Spending on Domestic Support*.

Notes: a. Categories correspond to those in official domestic support notifications to the WTO, as shown in Supporting Tables DS: 4, 5, 6, 7, and 9. Domestic support is measured by WTO index called the aggregate measurement of support (AMS).
b. Market price support is total eligible production times the difference between the current administered price and the fixed, 1986-88 world reference price.
c. The United States also notified the value of beef purchases made to offset the effect of the dairy herd buy-out program. No fixed world reference price was used.
d. See Appendix Table 11 of CRS Report RL30612, *Agriculture in the WTO: Member Spending on Domestic Support*, for details on non-exempt direct payments. Support in the 1986-88 base period was defined to include payments related to production reduction programs. Such payments were exempt (excluded) from the AMS reduction commitments after the base period and were notified in Supporting Table DS:3 (blue box). U.S. deficiency payments included in the blue box were re-calculated using a fixed, 1986-88 reference price. The 1995 value in the blue box was $7,030 million. This payment was eliminated after 1995 by the 1996 Farm Act.
e. Product-specific support only.
f. Under the de minimis provision, if the calculated individual product support level or the non-product-specific total is not larger than 5% of its respective total value of production, the support does not have to be included in the current total AMS.
g. For the 1986-88 base period only, countries could increase their AMS by using the higher of the 1986 value or the 1986-88 value. The U.S. increased its AMS by $3,227 million. This was done to give credit for reductions in support already accomplished during the first three years of the Uruguay Round.
h. Under the Uruguay Round Agreement, the AMS commitment ceiling was derived as the 1986-88 base value minus 3.3% per year during 1995 through 2000 (20% divided by six years = 3.33333%).

No direct payments are made to U.S. sugar growers and processors; however, U.S. sugar production is supported indirectly through import quotas, domestic marketing allotments, and non-recourse loans to processors of domestically grown sugar. The non-recourse loan rate varies for refined sugar from sugar cane (18¢ per lb.) and from sugar beets (22.9¢ per lb.). As a result of these indirect support programs, U.S. farm prices for sugar cane and sugar beets are maintained at levels that are substantially above international market prices.

Because of the absence of direct payments, price support under the sugar and dairy programs is defined by the WTO as the difference between the higher protected domestic price and the unprotected international market price times annual production. The relevant parameters for calculating price support were measured at the farm gate and fixed by agreement during the Uruguay Round. As a result, these reference prices do not change, even as world market conditions fluctuate. For dairy, the U.S. administered domestic price of $9.90 per cwt. is compared with the international reference price of $7.25 per cwt. to obtain the difference of $2.65 of subsidy per cwt of domestic milk production. For sugar, the U.S. administered price of 17¢ per lb. is compared with the international reference price of 10.5¢ per lb. to obtain the difference of 6.5¢ of subsidy per lb. of domestic sugar production. WTO-measured support for dairy and sugar varies annually with the volume of domestic production. Because of the indirect nature of government support, USDA direct outlays for dairy and sugar are significantly less than the level of annual AMS support notified to the WTO. Prior to the 2002 farm bill, U.S. peanut support was calculated in a similar manner based on a U.S. administered price of 30.5¢ per lb. and an international price of 18.75¢ per lb. However, the U.S. peanut program was revised as part of the 2002 farm bill such that peanuts are now essentially a "covered commodity" and qualify for both market loan benefits and CCP payments.

The list of commodities that normally do not receive direct support includes meats, poultry, fruits, vegetables, nuts, hay, and nursery products. Producers of these commodities, however, may be affected by the support programs because intervention in one farm sector can influence production and prices in another. For example, program commodities such as corn are feed inputs for livestock. Congress and the Administration often provide periodic assistance to some non-program commodities. For example, the 2002 farm bill provided $94 million to apple growers for 2000 market losses, and $200 million annually to purchase fruits, vegetables, and specialty crops for food assistance under USDA's Section 32 program.[55] Also, many of these programs benefit from other USDA programs including subsidized crop insurance, ad hoc disaster payments, and low-interest loans.

Which U.S. Program Crops Might Be Vulnerable to WTO Challenge?

If subsidies are challenged as being in violation of U.S. WTO commitments under SCM Articles 5 and 6.3, the challenges must be specific to commodities. This section uses the criteria discussed in this report's first section — i.e., magnitude of commodity support and linkage to adverse effects in the marketplace — to identify those subsidized U.S. commodities that are potentially vulnerable to WTO legal challenges under current WTO rules.

Table 3. USDA Net Outlays by Major Programs, 1996 to 2006

	1996	1997	1998	1999	2000	2001	2002	2003	2004	2005[a]	2006[a]	Ave.
	$ billions											
Direct Payments[b]	6.0	6.1	6.0	5.0	5.0	4.0	3.9	6.4	5.2	5.2	5.3	5.3
Market Loan Benefits[c]	0.0	0.0	2.0	6.8	7.6	6.2	2.8	1.3	3.5	7.0	2.9	3.6
CCP[d]	0.0	0.0	0.0	0.0	0.0	0.0	0.2	2.3	1.1	4.1	4.2	1.1
Ad Hoc Emergency[e]	0.0	0.0	2.8	7.9	8.6	8.5	1.7	3.1	0.6	3.2	1.3	3.4
Conservation	2.1	2.0	1.6	1.6	1.7	1.9	2.0	2.2	2.3	2.8	2.9	2.1
Other[f]	0.0	0.0	0.0	0.1	0.0	0.1	1.9	1.2	0.2	2.1	1.7	0.7
Total CCC Outlays[g]	8.1	8.1	12.4	21.5	22.9	20.7	12.4	16.5	13.0	24.3	18.2	16.2
Crop Insurance Net Govt Outlays[h]	1.8	1.0	1.3	1.7	2.3	2.5	3.0	3.3	3.3	2.9	2.9	2.4

Source: CCC outlays are on a calendar year basis from USDA, ERS, Farm Income and Costs Briefing Room, Farm Sector Income Forecasts; available at [http://www.ers.usda.gov/Briefing/FarmIncome/Data/GP_T6.htm]; crop insurance net government outlays are on a fiscal year basis from USDA, RMA, Summary of Business Online database, available at [http://www3.rma.usda.gov/apps/sob/].

a. Years 2005 and 2006 are forecasts.
b. Includes Direct Payments from the 2002 farm bill and Production Flexibility Contract Payments from the 1996 farm bill.
c. Marketing loan benefits include loan deficiency payments, marketing loan gains, and certificate exchange gains
d. Counter-cyclical payments were not available under the 1996 farm bill, but were started by a provision in the 2002 farm bill.
e. Includes market loss payments and disaster assistance.
f. Includes Milk Income Loss Contract (MILC) payments, peanut quota buyout payments, tobacco transition payments, and other miscellaneous outlays.
g. CCC outlays are on a calendar year basis.
h. Crop insurance subsidies are on a fiscal year basis and include both premium subsidies and loss cost-sharing by the federal government.

First, USDA data are used to identify both those crops that depend heavily on government subsidies, and the specific subsidies on which they depend (to the extent that this varies across commodities). Three questions are addressed:

- How important are farm subsidies relative to the commodity's market returns?
- How important are farm subsidies relative to the commodity's costs of production?
- Which programs provide most of the farm subsidies for the commodity?

Second, those commodities identified as depending heavily on government subsidies are evaluated in terms of the potential for their farm subsidies to be linked to adverse effects in international commodity markets.

- How important is U.S. production and trade for an identified commodity relative to world markets?

How Important Are Farm Subsidies Relative to the Commodity's Market Returns?

The commodities receiving mandatory federal support are listed in Table 4 and ranked by the level of subsidy as a share of cash receipts (over the past 10 years beginning with 1996). With the exception of some minor oilseeds, all of the "covered commodities" receive subsidy payments amounting to more than 10% of cash receipts. At the top of the list is rice at 72%, followed by upland cotton at 58%. The other top-ranking crops are sorghum (45%), wheat (34%), barley (30%), corn (25%), sunflower seed (21%), and canola (20%). While these shares are high, they actually understate the situation because they are 10-year averages. Challenges in the WTO likely would identify the years when the subsidies were at their highest levels relative to market revenues. In FY2000, for example, rice and cotton subsidy payments amounted to 174% of cash receipts, and sorghum, wheat and corn payments were respectively 110%, 101%, and 66% of cash receipts.[56] Figures 2-8 display agricultural subsidies by program for the major covered commodities during fiscal years 1996 through 2005.

How Important Are Farm Subsidies Relative to the Commodity's Costs of Production?

Data in **Table 5** show that, on average for the seven major commodities examined, per unit market revenue has covered operating costs but not total costs of production during recent three- to nine-year periods. In declining rank order, per unit market revenue as a share of per unit total costs are: soybeans, 91%; corn, 85%; rice, 70%; peanuts, 76%; cotton, 63%; wheat, 61%; and sorghum, 47%. It is only with the subsidies that these commodities cover their total cost, and even this was not accomplished for sorghum and wheat (see figure **1**). In the most extreme case, market revenue for rice amounted to 70% of total costs, but with the addition of subsidies the total revenue amounted to 146% of total cost.

These comparisons suggest that it is only with the aid of subsidies that a substantial portion of U.S. production is made economically sustainable. Unanswered is the question of whether production would decline without the subsidies. Some, and possibly a substantial portion of the lost production from high cost farms that would leave the sector in the absence of subsidies would be offset by increased production from low cost farms that would likely expand their operations. However, the substantial contribution of subsidies toward covering otherwise unmet production costs implies a high chance for adverse rulings for any of the major covered commodities.

Table 4. Commodity-Specific Program Support and Insurance Subsidy Payments, Yearly Average, FY1996-2005

Commodity	Av. Subsidy Payments			Subsidy Payment		Cash Receipts	
	CCC[a]	Crop Ins.[b]	Total	Period Min	Period Max	Total Value	Subsidy Share of Total Value
($ millions)							Percent
Rice	981	9	990	450	1,786	1,379	72%
Upland Cotton	2,221	247	2,468	736	6,522	4,229	58%
Sorghum	376	63	439	188	991	984	45%
Wheat	2,024	288	2,312	1,374	5,418	6,798	34%
Barley	171	18	190	86	414	636	30%
Corn	4,390	88	4,478	1,120	10,149	18,024	25%
Oats	19	4	23	9	64	93	25%
Sunflower Seed	47	29	76	0	178	368	21%
Canola	18	10	27	0	60	137	20%
Flaxseed	5	1	6	0	21	49	13%
Dry Peas	5	1	6	0	36	49	12%
Peanuts	73	31	104	0	332	909	11%
Soybeans	1,362	120	1,481	0	3,520	14,772	10%
Rapeseed	0	na	0	0	0	1	5%
Mustard Seed	0	0	0	0	0	8	5%
Safflower Seed	1	1	1	0	4	45	3%
Wool	1	na	1	0	5	26	3%
Honey	4	na	4	0	28	170	2%
Dairy	302	0	302	0	1,769	23,132	1%
Lentils	1	na	0	0	3	0	1%
Mohair	0	0	0	0	0	8	0%
Crambe	0	na	0	0	1	na	na
Chickpeas	0	na	0	0	0	na	na
Sesame	0	na	0	0	0	na	na
Other	17	267	284	57	551	na	na
All Commodities	12,019	1,388	13,407	3,788	25,914	207,092	6%

NA = not available.
Source: CCC outlays are from USDA, Farm Service Agency, Budget Division, "Table 35, CCC Net Outlays by Commodity and Function"; crop insurance net government outlays are from USDA, RMA, Summary of Business Online database, available at [http://www3.rma.usda.gov/apps/sob/]. Cash receipt data are from USDA, Economic Research Service and are tabulated on a calendar year basis. For lack of correspondence between data sets, FY2000 subsidy payments are compared with calendar year 2001 cash receipts.
a. Government support for the sugar and dairy sectors derive primarily from import restrictions rather than direct payments.
b. Crop insurance subsidies are the excess of indemnity payments over farmer-paid premiums. Hence, it also includes the portion of the total premium that is paid by the government on the farmer's behalf.

Table 5. Commodity Revenue and Cost Per Unit of Production, National Averages for Major Program Crops for Selected Periods

Commodity, Data Time Frame, (Unit of Measure)		Revenue Per Unit			Subsidy as Share of Total Revenue	Per Unit of Production			Share of Total Cost	
		Market[a]	Federal Subsidy[b]	Total[c]		Operating Costs[d]	Total Costs[e]		Market Revenue	Total Revenue
		$/unit	$/unit	$/unit	%	$/unit	$/unit		%	%
Corn	1996-04 (bu)	$2.15	$0.43	$2.58	17%	$1.12	$2.54		85%	102%
Soybeans	1997-04 (bu)	$5.45	$0.62	$6.07	10%	$1.90	$6.00		91%	101%
Wheat	1998-04 (bu)	$2.98	$1.28	$4.26	30%	$1.68	$4.90		61%	87%
Cotton	1997-04 (lb)	$0.51	$0.30	$0.81	37%	$0.43	$0.80		63%	101%
Rice	2000-04 (cwt)	$5.95	$6.53	$12.48	52%	$4.25	$8.56		70%	146%
Sorghum	1996-04 (bu)	$2.01	$0.86	$2.87	30%	$1.71	$4.24		47%	68%
Peanuts	2002-04 (lb)	$0.19	$0.06	$0.25	24%	$0.12	$0.25		76%	100%

Source: Calculations are by the authors based on primary data from the USDA. The time period varies across commodities based on the consistency of program operations and the availability of data. Season average crop price and cost of production data are from USDA, Economic Research Service; CCC commodity subsidy data are from USDA, Farm Service Agency. Crop insurance data are from USDA, Risk Management Agency.

a. Season average farm price.
b. Sum of total fiscal year CCC crop subsidy payments, and crop insurance indemnities not offset by farmer-paid premiums, per unit of total production.
c. Sum of market revenue and federal subsidy payments.
d. Per acre costs divided by yield.
e. Operating costs plus fixed and economic costs divided by yield.

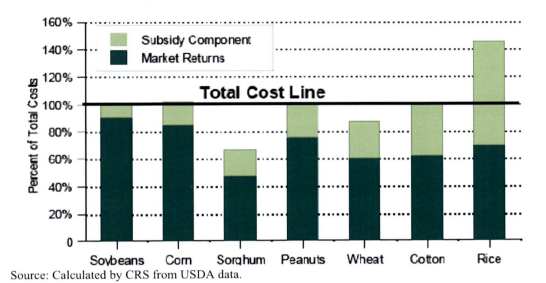

Source: Calculated by CRS from USDA data.

Figure 1. U.S. Revenue Components as Share of Total Costs, Selected Program Commodities.

Which Programs Provide Most of the Farm Subsidies for the Commodity?

Under the 2002 farm bill, the largest and most stable commodity subsidy payments, on average, are direct payments. Counter-cyclical payments and marketing loan program payments, as well as milk income loss contract payments are the least stable and are large when prices are low. The cotton user marketing program, commonly called the Step 2 program, has been terminated by a change in U.S. law subsequent to the WTO ruling and expenditures drop to zero in FY2007. There are purchase programs for milk and sugar to remove supplies when prices fall below mandated support levels, but costs are comparatively low because price support largely is achieved through import restrictions. Table 6 shows yearly subsidy expenditures by program.

The variation in commodity subsidy payments by crop, by program, and by year are large, as illustrated in Figures 2-8 and the minimum and maximum ranges of Table 4. From FY1996 through FY2005, corn subsidies averaged $4.5 billion per year, but ranged from $1.1 billion in FY1996 to $10.1 billion in FY2000. The abnormally large corn payments in FY2000 were from market loss assistance. Upland cotton subsidies averaged $2.5 billion, but ranged from $0.7 billion to $6.5 billion. Especially large cotton commodity certificate payments were made in FY2003 and FY2005 under the marketing loan program. Wheat, rice, soybeans, and dairy payments also showed considerable variation over the 10-year period.

While crop insurance is available for nearly all crops in most production locations, 68% of the subsidy over the FY2002-FY2006 period went to five crops —corn (20%), wheat (18%), soybeans (16%), cotton (9%), and sorghum (6%) — and 75% of the total crop insurance coverage went to the price- and income-supported crops, while the remaining 25% went to the non-supported crops. When total premiums (including federal contributions) are compared to indemnity payments, the loss ratio was 1.09, giving the overall appearance of approaching actuarial soundness. However, if the federal premium subsidy is excluded, the loss ratio is 2.70 (indemnities were 2.7 times as high as farmer premium payments).

Table 6. Commodity Subsidy Outlays, by Program, FY2002-FY2007 (forecast)

Program	FY02	FY03	FY04	FY05	FY06F	FY07F
	($ million)					
Direct Payments Program[a]	3,968	3,857	5,278	5,235	4,949	4,170
Counter-Cyclical Payments Program	—[b]	1,743	809	2,772	3,975	3,147
Marketing Loan Program	5,987	4,752	1,047	5,608	5,693	402
Loan Deficiency Payments	5,345	693	461	3,856	4,576	351
Commodity Certificate Gains	0	3,869	268	1,520	1,106	32
Marketing Loan Gains	642	190	318	232	11	19
Milk Income Loss Contract	0	1,796	221	9	515	600
Cotton User Marketing Program	182	455	363	582	312	0
Total CCC Commodity Payments	16,124	17,355	8,765	19,814	21,137	8,721
Dairy Price Support Program	622	698	74	(30)	88	145
Sugar Price Support Program	(130)	(84)	61	(86)	0	0
Total Commodity Purchase Operations	492	614	135	(116)	88	145
Crop Insurance Indemnities in Excess of Farmer-Paid Premiums	1,772	2,892	1,871	1,500	750	na
Total Commodity-Specific Support	18,388	20,861	10,771	21,198	21,975	8,866

Source: Data are from USDA, FSA, CCC Net Outlays by Commodity and Function, July 11, 2006. Numbers for FY2006 and FY2007 are budget forecasts.
[a.] Direct payments outlays for FY2002 includes funding for the predecessor contract payments program.
[b.] The CCP program was created by the 2002 farm bill.

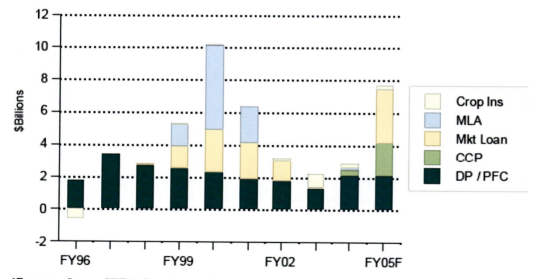

*Forecast. Source: USDA, Farm Service Agency.

Figure 2. U.S. Corn Subsidies, FY1996 to FY2005F*.

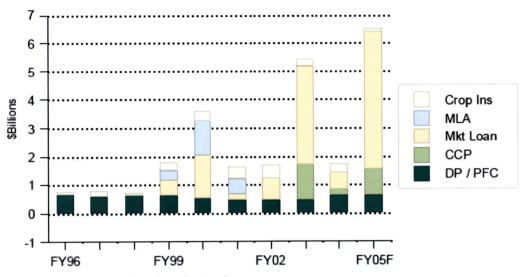

*Forecast. Source: USDA, Farm Service Agency.

Figure 3. U.S. Upland Cotton Subsidies, FY1996 to FY2005F*.

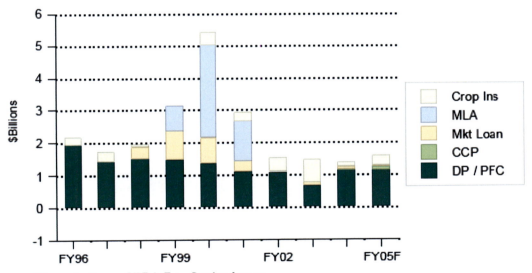

*Forecast. Source: USDA, Farm Service Agency.

Figure 4. U.S. Wheat Subsidies, FY1996 to FY2005F*.

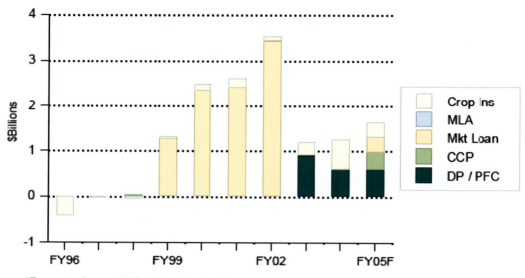

Figure 5. U.S. Soybean Subsidies, FY1996 to FY2005F*.

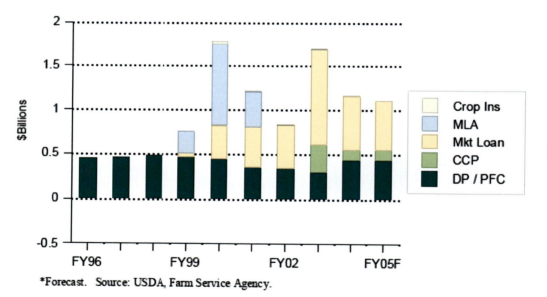

Figure 6. U.S. Rice Subsidies, FY1996 to FY2005F*.

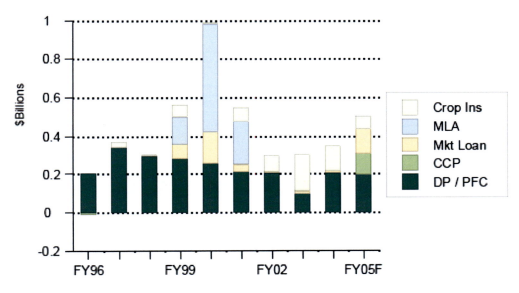

*Forecast. Source: USDA, Farm Service Agency.

Figure 7. U.S. Grain Sorghum Subsidies, FY1996 to FY2005F*.

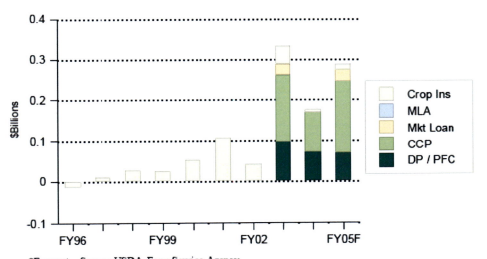

*Forecast. Source: USDA, Farm Service Agency.

Figure 8. U.S. Peanut Subsidies, FY1996 to FY2005F*.

How Important Is U.S. Production and Trade for an Identified Commodity Relative to World Markets?

The most heavily subsidized commodities (with the exception of milk) also are this nation's largest agricultural exports. Not only do exports provide a market for a large proportion of U.S. production, these exports are a large proportion of the entire world's exports.

During the 2002 to 2005 period, cotton exports accounted for 70% of U.S. production and 40% of world trade (Table 7). Similarly, U.S. rice exports accounted for 52% of U.S.

production and 13% of world trade; wheat exports were 50% of U.S. production and 25% of world trade; sorghum exports averaged 47% of U.S. production and 83% of world trade; and soybeans exports averaged 35% of U.S. production and 44% of world trade. Figure 9 illustrates the large share of world exports held by the United States and begs the question of how this is accomplished when market prices do not cover total costs.

Table 7. U.S. Share of World Production and Trade for Selected Commodities, Yearly Average, 2002-2005

Commodity	Farm Cash Receipts	Farm Value of Exports	U.S. Exports: Share of U.S. Production	U.S. Share of: World Production	World Exports
	($ million)		(percent)	(percent)	
Corn	19,587	3,468	18%	40%	61%
Soybeans	16,631	5,791	35%	38%	44%
Wheat	6,807	3,398	50%	9%	25%
Cotton	5,204	3,644	70%	20%	40%
Rice	1,216	638	52%	2%	13%
Sorghum	869	412	47%	18%	83%
Peanuts	761	92	12%	6%	11%
Source: Calculations are by CRS based on USDA, FSA marketing-year data.					

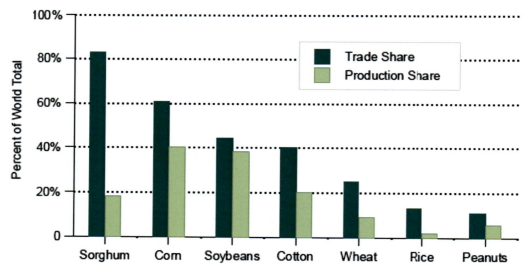

Source: Calculated by CRS from USDA, Farm Service Agency data.

Figure 9. U.S. Share of World Production and Trade, Selected Program Commodities.

Marketing Loan Benefits a Export Subsidies

Another important issue surrounds the nature of marketing loan provisions and the contention by other WTO members that their benefits should be classified as prohibited export subsidies. Under U.S. marketing loan provisions, a commodity's loan rate functions as a guaranteed price. If market prices fall below the loan rate, producers of "loan" crops are eligible for additional subsidies as either loan deficiency payments (LDPs), marketing loan gains (MLGs), or certificate exchange gains (CEGs). All of a farmer's production of a "loan crop" is eligible for marketing loan benefits based on current market conditions making the subsidy payments potentially market distorting. When market prices are low, the subsidies arguably encourage greater production in spite of market signals to do just the opposite, in part because the subsidies (on average) help to cover costs that low market returns are unable to cover. Thus, marketing loan benefits, on average, offset what would otherwise be revenue losses and encourage greater production than the market wants.

Other WTO members such as the EU have argued that, if the surplus U.S. production generated by the marketing loan benefits is then exported at a market price that is below the loan rate (and in many cases below the commodities' cost of production), the marketing loan subsidy is "effectively behaving like an export subsidy." Similarly, they contend that the subsidized production displaces imports from other non-subsidizing countries. As a result, critics argue that, because the subsidy provides a benefit to a U.S. commodity that is not available to a competitor's exports of "like-products" in either the U.S. or third-country market, it bears all of the hallmarks of a prohibited export subsidy.

However, under SCM Article 3 an export subsidy must be based specifically on export performance or upon use of domestic over imported goods. "The mere fact that a subsidy is granted to enterprises that export shall not for that reason alone be considered to be an export subsidy."[57] In addition, the United States maintains that all of its farm programs (including the marketing loan provisions) operate within the framework of U.S. commitments to the WTO and are therefore in compliance. Furthermore, since the WTO's establishment in 1995 no WTO member has challenged the benefits obtained by U.S. producers under the marketing loan provisions as prohibited subsidies.

REDUCING VULNERABILITY TO WTO CHALLENGE

WTO Remedies

In the event of a successful WTO dispute settlement challenge of a subsidy program, the remedy depends on the nature of the subsidy — prohibited versus actionable — and on the recommendation of the panel hearing the case. Prohibited subsidies are to be withdrawn without delay (SCM Article 4.7). In other words, prohibited subsidies are inconsistent with the WTO obligations of the United States and would have to be eliminated within a time period specified by the panel in its recommendation. If the recommendation is not followed within the specified time frame, then the Dispute Settlement Body (DSB) "shall grant authorization to the complaining Member" to take appropriate retaliatory countermeasures, unless the DSB decides by consensus to reject the request (SCM Article 4.10). The complaining member may also ask for a compliance panel under the DSU, as Brazil has done in the WTO cotton case. On the other hand, the defending member can ask for arbitration of the retaliation request if it thinks it to be excessive (DSU Article 22.6), then the arbitrator will decide whether the countermeasures are appropriate (SCM Article 4.11).

With respect to actionable subsidies, the remedy under a successful challenge of a subsidy causing adverse effects (SCM Article 7.8) is to remove the adverse effects or withdraw the subsidy. Furthermore, SCM Article 7.9 states that if the recommendation is not followed within six months of the adoption of Panel report (or the Appellate Body report on appeal), then in the absence of a compensation agreement, the DSB "shall grant authorization to the complaining Member" to take appropriate retaliatory countermeasures commensurate with the degree and nature of the adverse effects determined to exist. An arbitrator may be asked to determine whether proposed countermeasures are commensurate with the adverse effects.

In lay terms, actionable subsidies causing adverse effects are to be altered so as to remove the adverse effects. The subsidizing party is given some leeway in deciding how to remove the adverse effect. Options would include eliminating the subsidy program, reducing the subsidy amounts, reducing the linkage between the subsidy and the adverse effects (e.g., decoupling), or suffering the consequences of trade retaliation. Alternately, the subsidizing member could make some sort of mutually acceptable compensatory payment to offset the adverse effects.

What Constitutes an Acceptable Subsidy?

Pedro Camargo Neto — former Secretary of Trade and Production of the Ministry of Agriculture of Brazil during 2000-2002 — suggests that "a country should not be permitted to export production that received trade-distorting support covering production costs."[58] Furthermore, Neto argues that the Doha Round (assuming resumption of negotiations) should produce a negotiated understanding of "serious prejudice" in relation to the effects of domestic trade-distorting support for agriculture in order to avoid further litigation. Neto offers language for clarifying serious prejudice as used in SCM Articles 5(c) and 6.3, "[s]erious prejudice occurs when an agricultural product receives any kind of trade-distorting support of over 10% of the cost of production and reaches the international market with at least a 2% market share."[59]

Mr. Neto's suggested serious prejudice criteria might be viewed as extremely narrow and, as such, would appear to encompass all major U.S. program crops. Serious prejudice criteria, if established within the Doha Round, would be the product of a negotiated understanding and could involve percentage levels substantially larger than suggested by Neto. However, the evidence provided in Tables 5 and 7 suggests that most major U.S. program crops would still remain vulnerable to potential challenge under subsidy percentage levels of 15% to 20% of the cost of production and an international trade share of 10%.

Decoupled Program Support

Several options for decoupling existing farm programs have been considered or discussed as part of the on-going 2007 farm bill debate.[60] These include fully decoupled direct payments, whole-farm revenue-insurance-type programs, and conservation or green payments. A major attraction for such programs is their potential for exclusion from WTO AMS spending limits by qualifying under WTO green box criteria.[61]

Fully Decoupled Direct Payments

Annual payments to a qualifying producer based strictly on historical criteria with no linkage either to current market conditions or to producer behavior would potentially be eligible for inclusion in the green box.[62] As previously noted, the WTO cotton ruling contradicted the U.S. claim that the direct payments made under the 1996 and 2002 farm bills are minimally production and trade distorting. The ruling found that direct payments are not decoupled from production because fruits, vegetables, and wild rice production are prohibited on payment acres. Unless a legislative change for this problem is adopted, other countries might challenge any categorization other than non-product specific AMS or amber box for the direct payments. Counter-cyclical payments are tied to the same payment acres as direct payments and likely would be categorized the same as direct payments.

Whole Farm Revenue Insurance Type Programs

Current federally subsidized revenue insurance products, offered to producers as part of the federal crop insurance program, indemnify for diminished crop-specific revenue, whether from reduced yield or from low market prices. A possible option for the next farm bill is to expand current programs so that a producer can insure the revenue of the entire farm (possibly including livestock), rather than individual crops. Analysis at Iowa State University indicates that modifications can be made to current revenue insurance products that make them ideally suited to hit congressionally determined revenue targets. In addition, rationalizing commodity, disaster, and crop insurance programs by replacing them with a single-payment program would increase program transparency, eliminate program duplication, reduce administrative costs, and largely eliminate over- and under-compensation of farmers, according to Iowa State University researchers.[63]

Current crop and revenue insurance products are classified as non-product specific amber box under WTO rules because of their linkage to current prices and current planted acres. As a result, they are exempted from AMS limits under the de minimus exclusion. Whether modifications could make them comply with current or new international subsidy rules is uncertain.[64] For example, provision 7(b) of the AA's Annex 2 specifically limits compensation under an income safety-net program to less than 70% of producer's income loss. Presently, a U.S. producer can purchase revenue insurance coverage for up to 90% of losses depending on the particular policy selected.[65]

Green Payments

The term "green payments" refers to providing financial rewards to producers based on the scope or intensity of their conservation activities.[66] A shift from commodity subsidies to green payments is seen by some as attractive because it could provide a new mechanism to support farm income, forge a stronger link between conservation and farm income objectives, and still comply with WTO obligations if the program is not considered to be production and trade distorting.

The Conservation Security Program (CSP), enacted in the last farm bill, is one model for translating the concept of green payments into a program. This program was enacted as the first true entitlement program for conservation, meaning all producers who meet eligibility qualifications would receive payments. However, there is some concern over whether CSP fully qualifies for the green box in accordance with AA, Annex 2, provision 12(b) which states that environmental payments "shall be limited to the extra costs or loss of income" due to requirements of a government program, "including conditions related to production methods or inputs."[67] Thus, any sort of incentive payment associated with green payments may be sufficient to bring the qualification criteria into question.

New Farm Bill

During the past year, Agriculture Secretary Mike Johanns has been advocating that a new farm act should be designed to place U.S. farm policy "beyond challenge." On January 31, 2007, the Administration released a proposal for U.S. farm policy reform that, if incorporated into a new farm act, potentially could alleviate many of Canada's concerns while minimizing the likelihood of future WTO challenges.[68] The proposal includes removal of the planting restriction on base acres receiving direct payments. It also includes adjustments to the export credit guarantee program to make them more compatible with WTO rules. Finally, the proposal includes adjustments to price-contingent commodity programs (i.e., the marketing loan program and the CCP) that would likely make them more WTO compliant and potentially lower the vulnerability to challenges under the "serious prejudice" charge.[69]

Program Buyout

An alternative to program decoupling that has received some attention as part of the 2007 farm bill debate is the idea of program buyout.[70] Under a buyout program, Title I commodity programs would be eliminated entirely, and replaced with either a lump sum payment or a stream of annuity-like payments reflecting a portion of the present discounted value of projected future commodity support under existing law. The proposed buyout payments would be completely decoupled from production and, therefore, notified as WTO green box compliant. Furthermore, by eliminating all price-contingent amber box program payments, the buyout plan would insulate the United States from any future challenges by other WTO members.

Precedents cited for buyout programs include the 2004 buyout of the U.S. tobacco program, and the 2002 buyout of U.S. peanut production quotas. In addition, the recent EU sugar reform includes some buyout dimensions.[71]

REFERENCES

ABARE, U.S. Agriculture Without Farm Support by McDonald, Daniel; Roneel Nair, Troy Podbury, Belinda Sheldrick, Don Gunasekera, and Brian S. Fisher, ABARE Research Report 06.10, September 2006.

Babcock, Bruce A., and Chad E. Hart. "Crop Insurance: A Good Deal for Taxpayers?" Iowa Ag Review, Vol. 12, No. 3, Summer 2006.

CRS Report RL30612, Agriculture in the WTO: Member Spending on Domestic Support, by Randy Schnepf.

CRS Report RL32916, Agriculture in the WTO: Policy Commitments Made Under the Agreement on Agriculture, by Randy Schnepf.

FAPRI, Potential Impacts on U.S. Agriculture of the U.S. October 2005 WTO Proposal, FAPRI-UMC Report #16-05, December 15, 2005.

Hart, Chad E. "The WTO Picture After the Cotton Ruling," Iowa Ag Review, Vol. 11, No. 2, Spring 2005, pp. 10-11; available at [http://www.card.iastate.edu/ iowa_ag_review/ spring_05/].

Neto, Pedro Camargo, "An End to Dumping through Domestic Agricultural Support," Bridges, No. 8, August 2005, pp. 3-4.

OECD, Agricultural Policies in OECD Countries: Monitoring and Evaluation 2005.

Oxfam International, Truth or Consequences: Why the EU and the USA must reform their subsidies, or pay the price, Oxfam Briefing Paper No. 81, November 30, 2005; available at [http://www.oxfam.org/en/policy/pa2005/].

Steinberg, Richard H., and Timothy Josling. "When the Peace Ends: the Vulnerability of EC and US Agricultural Subsidies to WTO Legal Challenge," Journal of International Economic Law, Vol. 6, No. 2, pp. 369-417, July 2003.

Stewart, Terence P., and Amy S. Dwyer. "Doha's Plan B: the Current Pause and Prospects for the WTO," paper presented to the Global Business Dialogue, Inc., September 13, 2006; the authors are with Stewart and Stewart, Washington, D.C.

Sumner, Daniel A. A Quantitative Simulation Analysis of the Impacts of U.S. Cotton Subsidies on Cotton Prices and Quantities, Paper presented to the WTO Cotton Panel (DS267). October 26, 2003; available at [http://www.fao.org/es/esc/ common/ecg/ 47647_en_sumner.pdf].

Sumner, Daniel A. Boxed In: Conflicts between U.S. Farm Policies and WTO Obligations, CATO Institute Trade Policy Studies, No. 32, December 5, 2005; available at [http://www.freetrade.org/pubs/pas/pas.html].

WTO, The Legal Texts, Agreement on Subsidies and Countervailing Measures, Cambridge University Press; © World Trade Organization 1999. WTO Legal Texts are available at [http://www.wto.org/english/docs_e/legal_e/legal_e.htm].

APPENDIX A. REVIEW OF ECONOMIC STUDIES OF CAUSAL LINKAGE: U.S. FARM POLICY VS. WORLD MARKETS

This appendix reviews several economic studies that have investigated the causality linkage between U.S. agricultural policy support and the adverse world market effects identified in SCM Article 6.3 — i.e., lost market share, quantity displacement, and suppression of market prices. The studies reviewed here are cited in the reference section at the end of this article and include:

- Steinberg and Josling (2003);
- Sumner (2003);
- Sumner (2005);
- FAPRI (2005);
- Oxfam Briefing Paper No. 81 (2005); and

- ABARE (2006).

As a general rule, these studies support the idea that U.S. (and other developed country) agricultural support programs negatively influence international market prices and tend to disadvantage third-country trade of non-subsidized "like" products. While one may disagree with their results, the modeling techniques used in these studies are not out of the mainstream of accepted modeling methodology found in the professional economics literature and as taught in agricultural economics departments at U.S. land-grant universities. They are included here because of both their adequacy as economic analyses and their usefulness in indicating those commodities and programs that are most vulnerable to potential WTO challenge from another WTO member country.

Steinberg and Josling (2003)

Steinberg and Josling developed a series of regression models to evaluate the market effects of seven classes of U.S. subsidies for six major commodities (barley, beef, corn, milk, rice, and wheat) based on data for the 1986-2001 period. Their categories of commodity-specific subsidies were based on definitions developed by the Organization for Economic Cooperation and Development (OECD) and included (1) market price support which incorporated the effects of import barriers and export subsidies; (2) payments based on output; (3) payments based on area planted; (4) payments based on historical entitlements; (5) payments based on input use, (6) payments based on input constraints; and (7) payments based on overall farming income.

Steinberg and Josling performed regression analyses for each commodity market using the market share and export volume criteria of Article 6.3(b) and the relative market share criteria of Article 6.4 for the ten largest exporting non-subsidizing WTO members (i.e., potential complainants) as the dependent variable. Each of the subsidy categories was included as an independent variable along with other relevant control variables. A second regression was included that incorporated the subsidies as a single aggregate category. Steinberg and Josling evaluated these regressions for impacts in both U.S. and third-country markets. With respect to the U.S. market, their analyses found a significant negative relationship between U.S. subsidies and imports of non-subsidized third-country product for barley and milk — i.e., higher U.S. subsidies are associated with lower U.S. imports of non-subsidized "like" products. In third-country markets, their regressions found widespread negative effects of U.S. subsidies on both non-subsidized product market share and volume. Table 8 provides a list of countries affected in third-country markets for each commodity studied. Steinberg and Josling did not evaluate the causal linkage between commodity support and market price changes.

Table 8. Third-Country Markets Impacted by U.S. Subsidies

Subsidized Commodity	Third-Country Markets With Statistically Significant Effects[a]
Barley	Canada[d], Cyprus[b], Japan[b], Mexico[d]
Beef	Colombia[b], Japan[d], Jordan[c], Nicaragua[b], Saudi Arabia[ba]
Corn	Algeria[d], Argentina[b], Canada[d], Costa Rica[d], Ecuador[b], Egypt[b], El Salvador[d], Grenada[c], Guatemala[d], Honduras[d], Indonesia[b], Jamaica[b], Korea[b], Mexico[c], Nicaragua[b], Panama[b], Philippines[d], Senegal[d], Trinidad and Tobago[b], Venezuela[b]
Milk	Algeria[b], Australia[b], Canada[c], Chile[b], China[b], Ecuador[b], Nicaragua[d], Venezuela[c]
Rice	Argentina[b], Australia[b], Brazil[b], Chile[d], China[b], Colombia[d], Costa Rica[d], El Salvador[d], Honduras[c], Indonesia[c], Mexico[d], Nicaragua[d]
Wheat	Algeria[d], Bolivia[c], China[d], Colombia[d], Cyprus[b], Ecuador[b], Egypt[b], Honduras[b], Japan[b], Kenya[b], Korea[b], Morocco[d], Pakistan[d], Tunisia[b], Venezuela[c]

Source: Steinberg and Josling (2003).
a. Statistical significance was tested using a 95% confidence interval.
b. Based on the SCM Article 6.3(b) standard: market share or quantity displacement.
c. Based on the SCM Article 6.4 standard: relative market share.
d. Based on criteria cited in both footnotes (b) and (c).

Sumner (2003)

Brazil's successful WTO challenge of the U.S. cotton program included the submission of an econometric simulation model (referred to hereafter as the Sumner cotton model) in conjunction with its "serious prejudice" arguments to evaluate the international market effects of U.S. cotton program support. Unlike Steinberg's and Josling's regression analyses (which directly evaluate the statistical relationship between a dependent and an independent variable while controlling for the effects of other influential factors), a simulation model is a statistical representation of a market complete with supply, demand, trade, and equilibrium (market clearing) price. A simulation model may be used to test the relationship between subsidies and trade flows or market price by comparing a baseline scenario reflecting the status quo against a hypothetical scenario where the subsidies in question are reduced or omitted.

The Sumner cotton model evaluated the market effect of six U.S. subsidy programs — (1) marketing loan benefits, (2) PFC and DP payments, (3) market loss assistance (MLA) payments and Counter-Cyclical Program (CCP) payments, (4) crop insurance subsidies, (5) Step 2 payments, and (6) export credit guarantee subsidies. A seventh aggregate subsidy category also was evaluated. On the supply side of the simulation model, the subsidies influence U.S. producer behavior primarily through net returns per acre for cotton relative to competing crops. On the demand side, subsidies influence the net price paid by buyers of U.S. cotton. The Sumner cotton model was simulated for the removal of all subsidy programs (as well as for each individual component subsidy) for the five-year period 2003-2007. Because the LDP and CCP program payments vary with market conditions, their influence also varied from year to year as market conditions changed. Over the five-year period, the removal of all U.S. cotton subsidies led to an annual average reduction in U.S. cotton production of over 27%, a reduction in U.S. cotton exports of nearly 43%, and an increase in the world cotton price of almost 12%.

Although the United States argued strongly against inclusion of the Sumner cotton model as relevant evidence of serious prejudice (primarily on technical modeling grounds rather than on the substantive value of econometric modeling per se), the panel noted that:

> we observe that the simulations were prepared by experts, and explained to the Panel by experts. The outcomes of the simulations are consistent with the general proposition that subsidies bestowed by member governments have the potential to distort production and trade and the elimination of subsidies would tend to reduce "artificial" incentives for production in the subsidized Member. This is one of the underlying rationales for the establishment of the subsidy disciplines in the SCM agreement.[72]

As a result, it is not unreasonable to assume that the Sumner cotton model results supported, if not directly contributed to, the Panel's general finding in support of Brazil's challenge.

Sumner (2005)

In follow-up analyses published by the Cato Institute, Sumner used a similar analytical approach to review the vulnerability to WTO legal challenge of U.S. program subsidies for corn, wheat, rice, and soybeans (cotton was also included for comparative purposes).[73] First, looking at the 2004 to 2006 period Sumner evaluated the magnitude of U.S. crop subsidies by comparing total subsidy outlay to the value of production for each crop. The subsidy's share of production ranged in importance from 5% to 7% for soybeans and 15% to 45% for corn, up to 80% for cotton in 2005 and 78% for rice in 2004 (Table 9). In addition, the subsidies were examined in relation to net returns (market revenue minus costs of production). Net returns were evaluated with and without subsidies for 2003 through 2005. For every case, per acre average costs exceeded per acre market returns without subsidies. It is only with the addition of the subsidy that net returns cover costs in 7 out of 12 cases. This preliminary comparison based on a limited number of years would suggest that subsidy payments have had substantial market impact, particularly for rice and corn.

Table 9. Evaluating the Importance of U.S. Crop Subsidies

Crop	Subsidy Share of Production (%)			Net Returns					
				Without Subsidy ($/ac)			With Subsidy ($/ac)		
	2004	2005	2006	2003	2004	2005	2003	2004	2005
Corn	14.7	28.8	44.6	-32.4	-37.0	-70.6	-9.1	0.9	34.7
Wheat	21.8	27.4	50.9	-66.2	-47.6	-54.3	-46.9	-17.9	-17.0
Rice	78.1	32.1	39.6	-164.7	-110.3	-108.9	298.7	171.6	85.4
Soybean	5.4	6.9	6.9	-4.9	-20.8	-16.9	16.3	-8.1	7.8
Cotton	22.7	80.3	65.2	na	na	na	na	na	na
na = not available.									

Source: From Sumner (2005) based on USDA data.

In addition, Sumner used a stylized version of his cotton model to evaluate the causal linkage between U.S. crop subsidies and international market prices. The model assumed that the extent to which subsidies caused market price suppression depended on:

- the subsidy rate relative to the value of production;
- the degree to which the subsidy provided a production incentive (i.e., the extent of coupling);
- the share of the subsidized production in the relevant world market; ! the share of demand in each market; and
- the supply and demand elasticities in the U.S. and world markets.

Sumner found that U.S. subsidies for corn, wheat, and rice were associated with a substantial degree of market price suppression. Removing U.S. subsidies for these crops resulted in world price increases of 9 to 10% for corn, 6 to 8% for wheat, and 4 to 6% for rice. These rates of change compare with a world price impact of over 12% associated with U.S. cotton subsidies in Sumner (2003).

In his Cato Institute paper, Sumner included several additional, highly relevant observations in regards to potential WTO legal challenges of U.S. commodity programs. *In particular, he observed that challenges based on serious prejudice need not be global in scope, but can be restricted to a specific geographic market or product sub-market.*[74] Sumner argues that such geographically restricted claims may in many instance be stronger and more easily defended than claims that embrace one commodity in the global marketplace. For example, Mexico, Japan, and Taiwan are major markets for subsidized U.S. corn and displacement of corn exports from Argentina is likely and could present the opportunity for a geographically-focused challenge. Similarly, U.S. sales of subsidized wheat into major markets like Japan, China, Mexico, and various Middle Eastern and Asian markets are also potentially vulnerable on a geographic basis from competitor wheat-exporting nations such as Australia, Argentina, and Canada.

With respect to product sub-markets, the United States is a large producer and exporter of all major classes of wheat (hard red winter, soft red winter, white wheat, hard red spring, and durum) and rice varieties (indica and japonica). *Sumner observed that, to the extent that many third-country markets are segmented by a preference for a specific wheat class or rice variety, an analysis focused on a specific class or variety might actually implicate the United States as playing a larger market role in terms of production and export share than for the generic commodity.*[75] Also, evidence of displacement of quantities might be more direct in a localized geographic market. As a specific example, Sumner points out that while the United States has a relatively small share of world rice trade for indica (long-grain) rice, the U.S. share of indica rice trade in Central and Latin America and the Caribbean is significantly larger. Uruguay has recently claimed that U.S. exports to those and other markets hinder its ability to market non-subsidized indica rice that competes directly with heavily subsidized U.S. rice.[76]

Sumner also suggests that the U.S. dairy subsidies "probably create more vulnerability to WTO claims than any remaining farm subsidy."[77] Not only are dairy price supports a substantial portion of U.S. AMS notifications — averaging nearly 41% of total U.S. amber box subsidies notified to the WTO during 1995-2001 (Table 2) — but Sumner points out that the price discrimination and pooling schemes under the milk marketing orders stimulate overall milk production and divert milk from beverage products that are generally not traded internationally to manufactured dairy products, e.g., cheese, milk powder, and butter, which are the main traded dairy products. The net result is a lower price of the tradable products and displacement of U.S. imports or stimulation of U.S. exports to the detriment of other dairy export competitors such as Australia or New Zealand.[78]

With respect to the U.S. sugar program, Sumner points out that benefits for U.S. sugar producers derive mainly from the import TRQ scheme and that, although the price support scheme contributes more than $1 billion annually to the U.S. AMS (Table 2), it provides little additional distortion above that caused by the "WTO-scheduled" TRQ. As such, he concludes that the sugar program does not appear to be a likely candidate for WTO legal challenge in its present form.[79]

Sumner expresses concern that *detailed analysis might reveal prohibited subsidies for commodities supported under smaller programs such as market research and development programs, crop insurance, irrigation subsidies, etc.*[80] This might occur, for example, if the program provided a benefit to U.S. commodities that is not available to an imported commodity, or to competitor exports of "like-products" in third-country markets.

As a final observation, Sumner notes that two important domestic support programs — irrigation subsidies and subsidized grazing on government-owned land — have been classified as non-product-specific AMS subsidies. As such they have been excluded from the amber box under the de minimis exclusion throughout the 1995-2001 notification period. Sumner suggests that subsidized grazing fees represent low benefits relative to market revenue for the beef sector (the primary beneficiary) and are therefore, unlikely to contribute to WTO violations. With respect to irrigation subsidies, Sumner notes that, although larger in value than grazing fees, they are also generally small in value relative to the revenue of benefitting crops. Furthermore, irrigation subsidies are both difficult to measure and difficult to attribute to a specific crop. For both of these reasons, Brazil chose not to add irrigation subsidies to the list of U.S. programs supporting cotton in the WTO cotton case.

FAPRI (2005)

In December 2005, the Food and Agricultural Policy Research Institute (FAPRI) released a report summarizing its analysis of the potential market effects of the U.S. policy reform proposal made as part of the Doha Round of trade negotiations.[81] FAPRI employed a large-scale multi-commodity, multi-country economic simulation model to evaluate the various market effects of hypothetical policy scenarios. In its analysis of the U.S. Doha proposal, FAPRI evaluated several policy reform scenarios including a scenario based on unilateral U.S. policy reform (i.e., no policy changes in other countries) with no offsetting green-box direct payment compensation to producers for loss of program benefits. Specifically, the U.S. proposal offered the following reduction in U.S. domestic support:

- a 60% cut in the total amber box ceiling from $19.1 billion to $7.6 billion;
- a cut in the *de minimis* threshold from 5% to 2.5% of total production value;
- product-specific AMS caps based on 1999-2001 levels; and

- a redefined blue box with an expanded definition to permit inclusion of CCP payments, but with a new ceiling on qualifying subsidies of 2.5% of total production value per commodity (blue box subsidies are presently unlimited).

In addition to the domestic subsidy reduction, several market access concessions were incorporated into the study including the elimination of export subsidies by 2010, substantial reductions of tariff upper bounds, and the expansion of TRQs from current levels by 7.5% of average domestic consumption during 1999-2001. It should be noted that an analysis of the U.S. proposed reduction of 60% in amber box support does not compare directly with an analysis of the complete elimination of U.S. farm support as would be needed to investigate their full market effects. However, by studying unilateral U.S. policy reform (i.e., independent of multilateral reform), this partial reform scenario provides, at the least, some indication of the extent to which policy reform can reduce the causal linkage between U.S. farm supports and the adverse market effects of SCM Article 5.

Since there is no unique set of policy adjustments required for the U.S. to meet its proposed support commitments (and the U.S. proposal contained no program-specific recommendations), FAPRI made certain assumptions regarding how support programs would be altered to obtain the proposed 60% reduction in U.S. amber box support. The current regime of U.S. policy parameters offers only a few options with the major policy levers being target prices and loan rates. (Simply reducing absolute spending levels or fully decoupling spending are alternate options not considered by FAPRI.) To remain somewhat neutral regarding the issue of equity across programs and commodities, FAPRI applied uniform percentage cuts to commodity loan rates and target prices so as to achieve the aggregate spending goals.[82] The required cuts included:

- an 11% reduction in commodity loan rates and the milk support price;
- a 16% reduction in sugar loan rates (adopted to avoid public stock accumulation targets under expected import increases);
- a 7% reduction in commodity target prices;
- sugar and butter TRQs were expanded by 7.5% of the 1999-2001 average consumption level; and
- fixed direct payments are assumed to be green-box compliant (in contrast to the non-green-box compliant determination under the WTO cotton case).

Under this scenario of domestic support reductions, USDA Commodity Credit Corporation (CCC) outlays declined by an annual average of $3.5 billion (from $16.5 billion to about $13 billion). Over 80% of the reduction in subsidies was accounted for by three crops — corn (42%), soybeans (19%), and cotton (19%). The majority of the annual average reduction in CCC outlays came from two programs —marketing loan benefits ($1.9 billion) and CCP payments ($1.3 billion). With respect to WTO subsidy categories, U.S. product-specific amber box subsidies declined from an average of $9.4 billion per year in the baseline to $5.0 billion under the scenario, while CCP outlays declined from $3.1 billion to $1.8 billion per year. However, the individual commodity price and trade effects of this limited policy reform scenario were generally very small. Only peanut, rice, and cotton scenario prices exceeded baseline levels by more than 1%. The largest average price change was for peanuts at 2.4%. U.S. annual average export declines under the scenario were greatest for cotton (4.1%) and rice (2.2%).

Part of the relatively small market effects resulting from a 60% cut in the U.S. domestic support ceiling to $7.6 billion results from a significant portion of the reduction being "water" — that is, unused but allowable support under the $19.1 billion ceiling. For example, from 1995 to 2001 U.S. amber box spending averaged $11 billion (see Table 2, Total Non-Exempt AMS Outlays). This would suggest that the effective cut in actual domestic spending under the U.S. proposal is a much smaller 31% from $11 billion to $7.6 billion, than the 60% cut in the AMS ceiling. At any rate, the limited market effects resulting under the U.S. Doha-Round proposal, when compared with the more substantial effects found in Steinberg and Josling (2003), Sumner (2003), and Sumner (2005) suggest that a partial policy reform of the nature suggested by the U.S. Doha-Round Proposal would provide only modest decoupling between U.S. commodity subsidies and their adverse effects. As a result, U.S. subsidy programs would appear to remain vulnerable to WTO challenge under SCM Article 5 and 6.3 following a policy reform like the U.S. Doha Proposal.

Oxfam Briefing Paper No. 81 (2005)

In a paper from a report series written to inform public debate on development and humanitarian issues, the international development organization, Oxfam, published an assemblage of research results that examined the international market effects of both European Union (EU) and U.S. agricultural subsidies. In the wake of the WTO cotton ruling against the U.S. cotton program, Oxfam claims in its report to reveal additional U.S. (and EU) subsidies that are illegal under WTO rules. While several U.S. commodity groups have questioned the objectivity of a report published by a development organization that advocates on behalf of developing countries, the report and its results are indicative of the type of scrutiny under which U.S. farm support programs are likely to be placed in the post-Peace-Clause trade environment.

Based on a review of previously published work, Oxfam suggests that three major U.S. field crops — corn, rice, and sorghum — are particularly vulnerable to future WTO legal challenge (Table 10). According to Oxfam, major exporters of these crops could challenge U.S. domestic subsidy payments under SCM Articles 5(c) and 6.3 (b) and (c) — i.e., serious prejudice due to export displacement and market price suppression; while major importers of those crops from the United States could challenge the U.S. domestic subsidies paid to those crops under SCM Article 5(a) — i.e., injury to the domestic industry of another WTO member. In supporting its arguments, Oxfam cites evidence that, for each crop:

- the United States is a major producer and exporter;
- market returns fail to cover production cost for an average U.S. producer without government subsidies;
- government subsidies provide a substantial portion of annual average returns to each sector; and
- relevant economic analysis exists confirming that U.S. crop subsidies have substantial and significant international market effects, particularly as measured by market price suppression.

Table 10. Potential WTO Cases Against Subsidized U.S. Crops

Crop	Potential plaintiff
Corn	*Major Exporters:* Argentina, Paraguay, and South Africa.
	Major Importers: Columbia, Ecuador, El Salvador, Honduras, Guatemala, Mexico, Peru, and Venezuela
Rice	*Major Exporters:* Guyana, India, Pakistan, Suriname, Thailand, and Uruguay.
	Major Importers: Costa Rica, Ghana, Haiti, Mexico, Peru, Venezuela, and Zambi.
Sorghum	*Major Importers:* Kenya, Mexico, and South Africa.

Source: *Truth or Consequences*, Oxfam Briefing Paper No. 81, November 2005.

ABARE (2006)

In September 2006, the Australian Bureau of Agricultural and Resource Economics (ABARE), released a report summarizing its analysis of the potential market and welfare effects of abolishing both U.S. agricultural domestic support as well as all import tariffs on agricultural products.[83] ABARE used a dynamic simulation model of the world economy to evaluate several scenarios involving the elimination of all U.S. farm support programs. By including the removal of border restrictions, the ABARE analysis was able to capture the hypothetical effects of government support on the sugar sector in addition to the usual field crops. The hypothetical effects for the U.S. dairy sector are not reported by ABARE in sufficient detail.

ABARE's simulation results suggested large shifts in production away from program crops and towards non-program crops. The largest declines in U.S. production are projected to occur for sugar (31%), while cotton and rice production experience projected declines of 13% and 11%, respectively. U.S. wheat and corn production decline by 3% each and soybean production is projected to fall 1%. Although the ABARE study does not report projected price changes, the production effects are substantial and would likely have important international market price consequences. ABARE suggests that reduced U.S. production of the scale projected by its results could potentially have a noticeable upward effect on world prices, particularly for those crops where the U.S. plays a major role in international markets.[84] As a result, the ABARE study would appear to confirm the important causal link between U.S. farm policy and international market prices and trade.

APPENDIX B. AGREEMENT ON AGRICULTURE, ARTICLE 13: DUE RESTRAINT (THE PEACE CLAUSE)[85]

During the implementation period [i.e., the nine-year period January 1, 1995-December 31, 2003], notwithstanding the provisions of GATT 1994 and the Agreement on Subsidies and Countervailing Measures (SCM):

i) *domestic support measures* that conform fully to the provisions of the Green Box [AA, Annex 2] shall be:

- (i) non-actionable subsidies for purposes of countervailing duties;
- (ii) exempt from actions based on Article XVI of GATT 1994 [dealing with the treatment of general subsidies] and Part III of the SCM [dealing with the treatment of actionable subsidies]; and
- (iii) exempt from actions based on non-violation nullification or impairment of the benefits of tariff concessions accruing to another Member;

ii) *domestic support measures* that conform fully with AA domestic support commitments as reflected in each Member's Schedule, including direct payments that conform to the requirements of Blue Box payments, as well as domestic support within de minimis levels, shall be:
- (i) exempt from the imposition of countervailing duties unless a determination of injury or threat thereof is made in accordance with Article VI of GATT 1994 and Part V of the SCM [i.e., Countervailing Measures], and due restraint shall be shown in initiating any countervailing duty investigations; (ii) exempt from actions [as expressed in (a)
- (ii) above], provided that such measures do not grant support to a specific commodity in excess of that decided during the 1992 marketing year; and
- (iii) exempt from actions based on non-violation nullification or impairment of the benefits of tariff concessions accruing to another Member, provided that such measures do not grant support to a specific commodity in excess of that decided during the 1992 marketing year;

iii) *export subsidies* that conform fully to the provisions of AA Part V, as reflected in each Member's Schedule, shall be:
- (i) subject to countervailing duties only upon a determination of injury or threat thereof based on volume, effect on prices, or consequent impact in accordance with Article VI of GATT 1994 and Part V of the SCM, and due restraint shall be shown in initiating any countervailing duty investigations; and
- (ii) exempt from actions [as expressed in (a)(ii) above].

APPENDIX C. AGREEMENT ON SUBSIDIES AND COUNTERVAILING MEASURES; PART I, ARTICLE 1: DEFINITION OF A SUBSIDY

Part I: General Provisions; Article 1: Definition of A Subsidy

1.1. For the purpose of this Agreement, a subsidy shall be deemed to exist if:

(a)(1) there is a financial contribution by a government or any public body within the territory of a Member (referred to in this Agreement as "government"), i.e. where:

- i) a government practice involves a direct transfer of funds (e.g. grants, loans, and equity infusion), potential direct transfers of funds or liabilities (e.g. loan guarantees);
- ii) government revenue that is otherwise due is foregone or not collected (e.g. fiscal incentives such as tax credits) ;

iii) a government provides goods or services other than general infrastructure, or purchases goods;
iv) a government makes payments to a funding mechanism, or entrusts or directs a private body to carry out one or more of the type of functions illustrated in (i) to (iii) above which would normally be vested in the government and the practice, in no real sense, differs from practices normally followed by governments;

or

(a)(2) there is any form of income or price support in the sense of Article XVI of GATT 1994;

and

(b) a benefit is thereby conferred.

1.2. A subsidy as defined in paragraph 1 shall be subject to the provisions of Part II or shall be subject to the provisions of Part III or V only if such a subsidy is specific in accordance with the provisions of Article 2.

APPENDIX D. AGREEMENT ON SUBSIDIES AND COUNTERVAILING MEASURES; PART III: ACTIONABLE SUBSIDIES; ARTICLES 5 AND 6

Part III: Actionable Subsidies

Article 5: Adverse Effects

No Member should cause, through the use of any subsidy referred to in paragraphs 1 and 2 of Article 1, adverse effects to the interests of other Members, i.e.:

(a) injury to the domestic industry of another Member ;
(b) nullification or impairment of benefits accruing directly or indirectly to other Members under GATT 1994 in particular the benefits of concessions bound under Article II of GATT 1994 ;
(c) serious prejudice to the interests of another Member.

This Article does not apply to subsidies maintained on agricultural products as provided in Article 13 [the 'Peace Clause'] of the Agreement on Agriculture.

Article 6: Serious Prejudice

6.1. Serious prejudice in the sense of paragraph (c) of Article 5 shall be deemed to exist in the case of:

(a) the total ad valorem subsidization of a product exceeding 5 per cent ;
(b) subsidies to cover operating losses sustained by an industry;
(c) subsidies to cover operating losses sustained by an enterprise, other than one time measures which are non recurrent and cannot be repeated for that enterprise and which are given merely to provide time for the development of long term solutions and to avoid acute social problems;
(d) direct forgiveness of debt, i.e. forgiveness of government held debt, and grants to cover debt repayment.

6.2. Notwithstanding the provisions of paragraph 1, serious prejudice shall not be found if the subsidizing Member demonstrates that the subsidy in question has not resulted in any of the effects enumerated in paragraph 3.

6.3. Serious prejudice in the sense of paragraph (c) of Article 5 may arise in any case where one or several of the following apply:

(a) the effect of the subsidy is to displace or impede the imports of a like product of another Member into the market of the subsidizing Member;
(b) the effect of the subsidy is to displace or impede the exports of a like product of another Member from a third country market;
(c) the effect of the subsidy is a significant price undercutting by the subsidized product as compared with the price of a like product of another Member in the same market or significant price suppression, price depression or lost sales in the same market;
(d) the effect of the subsidy is an increase in the world market share of the subsidizing Member in a particular subsidized primary product or commodity as compared to the average share it had during the previous period of three years and this increase follows a consistent trend over a period when subsidies have been granted.

6.4. For the purpose of paragraph 3(b), the displacement or impeding of exports shall include any case in which, subject to the provisions of paragraph 7, it has been demonstrated that there has been a change in relative shares of the market to the disadvantage of the non subsidized like product (over an appropriately representative period sufficient to demonstrate clear trends in the development of the market for the product concerned, which, in normal circumstances, shall be at least one year). "Change in relative shares of the market" shall include any of the following situations: (a) there is an increase in the market share of the subsidized product; (b) the market share of the subsidized product remains constant in circumstances in which, in the absence of the subsidy, it would have declined; (c) the market share of the subsidized product declines, but at a slower rate than would have been the case in the absence of the subsidy.

6.5. For the purpose of paragraph 3(c), price undercutting shall include any case in which such price undercutting has been demonstrated through a comparison of prices of the subsidized product with prices of a non subsidized like product supplied to the same market. The comparison shall be made at the same level of trade and at comparable times, due account being taken of any other factor affecting price comparability. However, if such a direct comparison is not possible, the existence of price undercutting may be demonstrated on the basis of export unit values.

6.6. Each Member in the market of which serious prejudice is alleged to have arisen shall, subject to the provisions of paragraph 3 of Annex V, make available to the parties to a dispute arising under Article 7, and to the Panel established pursuant to paragraph 4 of Article 7, all relevant information that can be obtained as to the changes in market shares of the parties to the dispute as well as concerning prices of the products involved.

6.7. Displacement or impediment resulting in serious prejudice shall not arise under paragraph 3 where any of the following circumstances exist during the relevant period: (a) prohibition or restriction on exports of the like product from the complaining Member or on imports from the complaining Member into the third country market concerned; (b) decision by an importing government operating a monopoly of trade or state trading in the product concerned to shift, for non commercial reasons, imports from the complaining Member to another country or countries; (c) natural disasters, strikes, transport disruptions or other force majeure substantially affecting production, qualities, quantities or prices of the product available for export from the complaining Member; (d) existence of arrangements limiting exports from the complaining Member; (e) voluntary decrease in the availability for export of the product concerned from the complaining Member (including, inter alia, a situation where firms in the complaining Member have been autonomously reallocating exports of this product to new markets);

(a) failure to conform to standards and other regulatory requirements in the importing country.

6.8. In the absence of circumstances referred to in paragraph 7, the existence of serious prejudice should be determined on the basis of the information submitted to or obtained by the Panel, including information submitted in accordance with the provisions of Annex V.

6.9. This Article does not apply to subsidies maintained on agricultural products as provided in Article 13 [the 'Peace Clause'] of the Agreement on Agriculture.

APPENDIX E. AGREEMENT ON AGRICULTURE, KEY PROVISIONS OF ANNEX 2 (THE GREEN BOX)[86]

1. Domestic support measures for which exemption from the reduction commitments is claimed shall meet the fundamental requirement that they have no, or at most minimal, trade-distorting effects or effects on production. Accordingly, all measures for which exemption is claimed shall conform to the following basic criteria:

(a) the support in question shall be provided through a publicly-funded government program (including government revenue foregone) not involving transfers from consumers; and,
(b) the support in question shall not have the effect of providing price support to producers; plus policy-specific criteria and conditions as set out below.

5. Direct Payments to Producers

Support provided through direct payments (or revenue foregone, including payments in kind) to producers for which exemption from reduction commitments is claimed shall meet the basic criteria set out in paragraph 1 above, plus specific criteria applying to individual types of direct payment as set out in paragraphs 6 through 13 below. Where exemption from reduction is claimed for any existing or new type of direct payment other than those specified in paragraphs 6 through 13, it shall conform to criteria (b) through (e) in paragraph 6, in addition to the general criteria set out in paragraph 1.

6. Decoupled Income Support

a. Eligibility for such payments shall be determined by clearly-defined criteria such as income, status as a producer or landowner, factor use or production level in a defined and fixed base period.
b. The amount of such payments in any given year shall not be related to, or based on, the type or volume of production (including livestock units) undertaken by the producer in any year after the base period.
c. The amount of such payments in any given year shall not be related to, or based on, the prices, domestic or international, applying to any production undertaken in any year after the base period.
d. The amount of such payments in any given year shall not be related to, or based on, the factors of production employed in any year after the base period.
e. No production shall be required in order to receive such payments.

7. Government Financial Participation in Income Insurance and Income Safety-Net Programs

a. Eligibility for such payments shall be determined by an income loss, taking into account only income derived from agriculture, which exceeds 30 per cent of average gross income or the equivalent in net income terms (excluding any payments from the same or similar schemes) in the preceding three-year period or a three-year average based on the preceding five-year period, excluding the highest and the lowest entry. Any producer meeting this condition shall be eligible to receive the payments.
b. The amount of such payments shall compensate for less than 70 percent of the producer's income loss in the year the producer becomes eligible to receive this assistance.
c. The amount of any such payments shall relate solely to income; it shall not relate to the type or volume of production (including livestock units) undertaken by the producer; or to the prices, domestic or international, applying to such production; or to the factors of production employed.

d. Where a producer receives in the same year payments under this paragraph and under paragraph 8 (relief from natural disasters), the total of such payments shall be less than 100 per cent of the producer's total loss.

12. Payments under Environmental Programs

   a. Eligibility for such payments shall be determined as part of a clearly-defined government environmental or conservation program and be dependent on the fulfilment of specific conditions under the government program, including conditions related to production methods or inputs.
   b. The amount of payment shall be limited to the extra costs or loss of income involved in complying with the government program.

REFERENCES

[1] Agreement on Agriculture, Article 13.

[2] For more information, see CRS Report RS22187, *U.S. Agricultural Policy Response to WTO Cotton Decision*, by Randy Schnepf.

[3] For a recent discussion of the legal context for WTO challenges before and after the expiration of the Peace Clause, see Terence P. Stewart and Amy S. Dwyer, "Doha's Plan B: the Current Pause and Prospects for the WTO," paper presented to the Global Business Dialogue, Inc., September 13, 2006; hereafter referred to as Stewart and Dwyer (2006).

[4] Remarks by Agriculture Secretary Mike Johanns at the Cato Institute's Center for Trade Policy Studies, Washington, DC, USDA News Release No. 0333.06, August 31, 2006.

[5] For more information and the U.S. response, see CRS Report RS22187, *U.S. Agricultural Policy Response to WTO Cotton Decision*, by Randy Schnepf.

[6] For more information and the U.S. response, see CRS Report RL33853, *U.S.-Canada WTO Corn Trade Dispute*, by Randy Schnepf.

[7] For more information and a general discussion of trade remedies, see CRS Report RL32371, *Trade Remedies: A Primer*, by Vivian C. Jones.

[8] For more information, see CRS Report RL32916, Agriculture in the WTO: Policy Commitments Made Under the Agreement on Agriculture, by Randy Schnepf.

[9] For more information on WTO AA liberalization commitments as well as notification requirements, special treatment of developing countries, and related issues, see CRS Report RL32916, *Agriculture in the WTO: Policy Commitments Made Under the Agreement on Agriculture*, and CRS Report RL30612, *Agriculture in the WTO: Member Spending on Domestic Support*, both by Randy Schnepf.

[10] For all official WTO legal texts (including those mentioned here), see *The Legal Texts: The Results of the Uruguay Round of Multilateral Trade Negotiations* (Cambridge University Press, ©World Trade Organization, 1999); available at [http://www.wto.org/english/docs_e/legal_e/legal_e.htm].

[11] Each member's schedule of concessions is publicly available at the WTO website at [http://www.wto.org/english/tratop_e/schedules_e/goods_schedules_e.htm].
[12] For more information, see CRS Report RS20088, *Dispute Settlement in the World Trade Organization: An Overview*, by Jeanne Grimmett.
[13] Specific WTO domestic support commitments in dollar values, as well as country-specific notifications of support by program, are presented in CRS Report RL30612, *Agriculture in the WTO: Member Spending on Domestic Support*, by Randy Schnepf.
[14] AMS is defined in the AA, Article 1 (a) and (h). Calculation of the AMS is described in Annex 3 of the AA.
[15] AA Articles 6 and 7.
[16] See Attachment 4, "Agreement on Agriculture, Key Provisions of Annex 2 (the green box)" for criteria for inclusion in the green box.
[17] AA Article 6.5.
[18] AA Article 6.4.
[19] See CRS Report RL32916 for more information on WTO notification requirements.
[20] Discussed in more detail in section "Brazil's WTO Case Against the U.S. Cotton Program."
[21] Export subsidies are specifically dealt with in Articles 8-12 of the AA. For more information on U.S. agricultural export programs see USDA, Foreign Agricultural Service, "Programs and Opportunities," at [http://www.fas.usda.gov/programs.asp].
[22] AA Article 8.
[23] AA Article 4 treats market access, and AA Article 5 treats Special Safeguard Provisions.
[24] GATT 1994 Article 28.
[25] SCM Article 3.
[26] AA Article 3.1.
[27] See later section "Brazil's WTO Case Against U.S. Cotton Program" for details.
[28] SCM Article 4.7.
[29] SCM Article 5.
[30] The evaluation of WTO legal provisions and their potential relevance to future DSU challenges of agricultural support programs relies heavily on the analysis done in Richard H. Steinberg and Timothy E. Josling, "When the Peace Ends: the Vulnerability of EC and US Agricultural Subsidies to WTO Legal Challenge," *Journal of International Economic Law*, Vol. 6, No. 2, pp. 369-417, July 2003; hereafter referred to as Steinberg and Josling (2003).
[31] See annotated version of AA Article 13 appended to this memo as Appendix B.
[32] Based on CRS review of WTO dispute settlement cases listed chronologically at [http://www.wto.org/english/tratop_e/dispu_e/dispu_status_e.htm].
[33] Refer to WTO case number DS267 for official documentation; available at [http://docsonline.wto.org/gen_home.asp?language=1 and _=1].
[34] For more information, see CRS Report RS22187, *U.S. Agricultural Policy Response to WTO Cotton Decision* by Randy Schnepf.
[35] Chad E. Hart, "The WTO Picture After the Cotton Ruling," *Iowa Ag Review*, Vol. 11, No. 2, Spring 2005, pp. 10-11, available at [http://www.card.iastate.edu/iowa_ag_review/spring_05/]; and Daniel A. Sumner, *Boxed In: Conflicts between U.S.*

Farm Policies and WTO Obligations, CATO Institute Trade Policy Studies, No. 32, December 5, 2005, available at [http://www.freetrade.org/pubs/ pas/pas.html].

[36] WTO, Panel Report, *United States — Subsidies on Upland Cotton*, paras. 8.3 (b), (c), WT/DS267/R, (September 8, 2004); hereafter referred to as *WTO Upland Cotton Panel Report*.

[37] The United States has scheduled export subsidy reduction commitments for the following thirteen commodities: wheat, coarse grains, rice, vegetable oils, butter and butter oil, skim milk powder, cheese, other milk products, bovine meat, pigmeat, poultry meat, live dairy cattle, and eggs. For more information on the EEP program and U.S. export subsidy commitments see CRS Report RS20399, *Agricultural Export Programs: The Export Enhancement Program (EEP)*. See also *Export Enhancement Program*, Foreign Agricultural Service, USDA at [http://www.fas.usda.gov/excredits/eep.html].

[38] WTO Upland Cotton Panel Report, paras 7.857-7.869.

[39] For more information on USDA market development programs, see [http://www.fas.usda.gov/programs.asp], and CRS Report RL33553, *Agricultural Export and Food Aid Programs*, by Charles Hanrahan.

[40] WTO, Recourse to Article 21.5 of the DSU by Brazil, *United States — Subsidies on Upland Cotton*, WT/DS267/30 (August 21, 2006). For more information, see CRS Report RS22187, *U.S. Agricultural Policy Response to WTO Cotton Decision*, by Randy Schnepf.

[41] WTO, Dispute Settlement Body, "DSB Sets Up Compliance Panel to Review U.S.

[42] Implementation of 'Cotton' Rulings," 2006 News Item, September 28, 2006.

[43] For a recent discussion, see Stewart and Dwyer (2006) p. 6; supra note 2.

[44] Steinberg and Josling (2003), p. 371.

[45] SCM Article 6.3 (italics added by CRS).

[46] Steinberg and Josling (2003), p. 389.

[47] Sumner, Daniel A. *A Quantitative Simulation Analysis of the Impacts of U.S. Cotton Subsidies on Cotton Prices and Quantities*, Paper presented to the WTO Cotton Panel (DS267). October 26, 2003; available at [http://www.fao.org/es/esc/common/ecg/47647_en_ sumner.pdf].

[48] WTO Upland Cotton Panel Report, paras 7.1348-7.1353.

[49] For more information see CRS Report RL30612, *Agriculture in the WTO: Member Spending on Domestic Support*, by Randy Schnepf.

[50] USDA, Farm Service Agency, Budget Division, "Table 35, CCC Net Outlays by Commodity and Function," available at [http://www.fsa.usda.gov/dam/bud/bud1.htm].

[51] For more information see CRS Report RL33412, *Agriculture and Related Agencies: FY2007 Appropriations*, Jim Monke coordinator.

[52] For more information on U.S. farm programs, see CRS Report RS21999, Farm Commodity Policy: Programs and Issues for Congress, and CRS Report RL33271, Farm Commodity Programs: Direct Payments, Counter-Cyclical Payments, and Marketing Loans, both by James Monke.

[53] For more information on market loss payments, see CRS Report RL31095, Emergency Funding for Agriculture: A Brief History of Supplemental Appropriations, FY1989-FY2006, by Ralph Chite.

[54] See USDA, Risk Management Agency's Summary of Business searchable database for crop-specific data; available at [http://www3.rma.usda.gov/apps/sob/].
[55] FAPRI, *2006 U.S. and World Agricultural Outlook*, FAPRI Staff Report 06, January 2006.
[56] For more information on USDA's Section 32 program, see CRS Report RS20235, *Farm and Food Support Under USDA's Section 32 Program*, by Geoffrey Becker.
[57] FY2000 subsidy payments are compared with calendar year 2001 cash receipts.
[58] SCM Article 3(a), footnote 4.
[59] Neto, Pedro Camargo, "An End to Dumping through Domestic Agricultural Support," *Bridges*, No. 8, August 2005, pp. 3-4.
[60] Ibid., p. 4.
[61] For more information see CRS Report RL33037, *Previewing a 2007 Farm Bill*, Jasper Womach coordinator.
[62] See Attachment 4, "AA, Key Provisions of Annex 2" for the specific WTO criteria.
[63] Ibid., see Annex 2, provisions 1, 5, and 6 for specific detail.
[64] Bruce A. Babcock and Chad Hart, *Judging the Performance of the 2002 Farm Bill*, Iowa Ag Review, Spring 2005; available at [http://www.card.iastate.edu/iowa_ag_review].
[65] See Attachment 4, Annex 2, provision 7 (a)-(d) for specific details.
[66] For a potential redesign of U.S. revenue insurance programs to fit within WTO limits, see Bruce A. Babcock and Chad Hart, *How Much "Safety" is Available under the U.S. Proposal to the WTO?*, Center for Agri. and Rural Dev., ISU, Briefing Paper 05-BP 48, November 2005; available at [http://www.card.iastate.edu/publications].
[67] For more information see CRS Report RL32624, *Green Payments in U.S. and European Union Agricultural Policy* by Charles Hanrahan and Jeffrey Zinn.
[68] See Attachment 4, Annex 2, provision 12 (a) and (b) for specific details.
[69] USDA News Release No. 0020.07, "Johanns Unveils 2007 Farm Bill Proposals," January 31, 2007; available at [http://www.usda.gov].
[70] For more information, see USDA Farm Bill Fact Sheet, Release No. 0019.07, available at [http://www.usda.gov/].
[71] For examples, see David Orden, "Feasibility of Farm Program Buyouts," background paper on U.S. farm program buyouts, January 23, 2007; available at [http://farmpolicy.typepad.com/farmpolicy/files/orden_buyouts.pdf]; and Sallie James and Daniel Griswold, *Freeing the Farm: A Farm Bill for All Americans*, Trade Policy Analysis No. 34, Cato Institute, April 16, 2007; available at [http://www.freetrade.org/node/609].
[72] For more information, see European Commission, Agriculture and Rural Development, CAP Reform, "Sugar;" at [http://ec.europa.eu/agriculture/capreform/index_en.htm].
[73] WTO Upland Cotton Panel Report, para. 7.1207.
[74] Sumner, Daniel A. *Boxed In: Conflicts between U.S. Farm Policies and WTO Obligations*, CATO Institute Trade Policy Studies, No. 32, December 5, 2005; available at [http://www.freetrade.org/pubs/pas/pas.html].
[75] Ibid., p. 23.
[76] Ibid.
[77] Ibid.
[78] Ibid.

[79] Ibid., p. 24.
[80] Ibid.
[81] Ibid.
[82] FAPRI, Potential Impacts on U.S. Agriculture of the U.S. October 2005 WTO Proposal, FAPRI-UMC Report #16-05, December 15, 2005.
[83] FAPRI applies a repetitive, stochastic estimation technique to its simulation model that generates 500 outcomes for each scenario. It is these outcomes that are evaluated to ascertain scenario effects. Based on this approach, FAPRI reduced target prices and loan rates for major program crops until the incidence of the stochastic outcomes violating the aggregate spending limit occurred in 5% or less of each scenario's 500 outcomes.
[84] ABARE, *U.S. Agriculture Without Farm Support* by Daniel McDonald, Roneel Nair, Troy Podbury, Belinda Sheldrick, Don Gunasekera, and Brian S. Fisher, Research Report 06.10, September 2006.
[85] Ibid., p. 20.
[86] Abridged and annotated by CRS. For the official WTO text, see WTO Legal Texts at [http://www.wto.org/english/docs_e/legal_e/legal_e.htm]. For WTO terminology, refer to CRS Report RL32916, *Agriculture in the WTO: Policy Commitments Made Under the Agreement on Agriculture*, by Randy Schnepf.
[87] AA, Annex 2 is available in full at [http://www.wto.org/english/docs_e/legal_e/14-ag_02_e.htm#annII].

In: The World Trade Organization: Another Round
Editor: Harold B. Whitiker, pp. 87-120

ISBN: 978-1-60021-816-3
© 2007 Nova Science Publishers, Inc.

Chapter 3

WTO DOHA ROUND: THE AGRICULTURAL NEGOTIATIONS[*]

Charles E. Hanrahan and Randy Schnepf

ABSTRACT

On July 24, 2006, the WTO's Director General announced the indefinite suspension of further negotiations in the Doha Development Agenda or Doha Round of multilateral trade negotiations. The principal cause of the suspension was that a core group of WTO member countries — the United States, the European Union (EU), Brazil, India, Australia, and Japan — known as the G-6 had reached an impasse over specific methods to achieve the broad aims of the round for agricultural trade: substantial reductions in trade-distorting domestic subsidies, elimination of export subsidies, and substantially increased market access for agricultural products.

The WTO is unique among the various fora of international trade negotiations in that it brings together its entire 149-country membership to negotiate a common set of rules to govern international trade in agricultural products, industrial goods, and services. Agreement across such a large assemblage of participating nations and range of issues contributes significantly to consistency and harmonization of trade rules across countries. Regarding agriculture, because policy reform is addressed across three broadly inclusive fronts — export competition, domestic support, and market access — WTO negotiations provide a framework for give and take to help foster mutual agreement. As a result, the Doha Round represents an unusual opportunity for addressing most policy-induced distortions in international agricultural markets.

Doha Round negotiators were operating under a deadline effectively imposed by the expiration of U.S. Trade Promotion Authority (TPA), which permits the President to negotiate trade deals and present them to Congress for expedited consideration. To meet congressional notification requirements under TPA, an agreement would have to have been completed by the end of 2006. That now appears unlikely. TPA expires on June 30, 2007, and most trade experts and officials think that the authority would not be renewed.

As a result of the suspension of the negotiations, a major source of pressure for U.S. farm policy change will have dissipated. The current farm bill expires in 2007, and many were looking to a Doha Round agreement to require changes in U.S. farm subsidies to

---

[*] Excerpted from CRS Report RL33144, dated dated September 12, 2.

make them more compatible with world trade rules. The option of extending the current farm law appears strengthened by the indefinite suspension of the Doha talks. The United States must still meet obligations under existing WTO agricultural agreements, which limit trade-distorting spending to $19.1 billion annually. Some trade analysts think that, now that the Round has been suspended, there could be an increase in litigation by WTO member countries that allege they are harmed by U.S. farm subsidies.

This article assesses the current status of agricultural negotiations in the Doha Round; traces the developments leading up to the December 2005 Hong Kong Ministerial; examines the major agricultural negotiating proposals; discusses the potential effects of a successful Doha Round agreement on global trade, income, U.S. farm policy, and U.S. agriculture; and provides background on the WTO, the Doha Round, the key negotiating groups, and a chronology of key events relevant to the agricultural negotiations.

INTRODUCTION

This article discusses the indefinitely suspended World Trade Organization (WTO) multilateral trade negotiations — the so-called Doha Round or the Doha Development Agenda (DDA). The focus initially is on the implications for future trade negotiations and the next U.S. farm bill of the suspension of negotiations in July 2006. The article discusses the agreements reached at the December 13-18, 2005, Hong Kong Ministerial meeting and reviews the agricultural negotiating developments that occurred in the second half of 2005 leading up to the Ministerial. Briefly discussed also are the role of the U.S. Congress; the major negotiating issues and proposals at play in the Doha Round; the historical development of agricultural trade negotiations since the Uruguay Round; and the potential economic benefits estimated to ensue from a successful trade agreement according to several recent studies.

CURRENT STATUS: THE INDEFINITE SUSPENSION OF DOHA ROUND NEGOTIATIONS

On July 24, 2006, the Director General of the WTO, Pascal Lamy, announced the indefinite suspension of further negotiations in the Doha Development Agenda or Doha Round. The principal cause of the suspension was that a core group of WTO member countries — the United States, the European Union (EU), Brazil, India, Australia, and Japan — known as the G-6 had reached an impasse over specific methods to achieve the broad aims of the round for agricultural trade: substantial reductions in trade-distorting domestic subsidies, elimination of export subsidies, and substantially increased market access for agricultural products. The United States maintained that it had made an ambitious offer of reductions in trade supporting domestic support (discussed below) that had not been matched by agricultural tariff reductions by the EU or by market opening for agricultural and industrial products by Brazil and India, both large developing countries. The EU and Brazil argued that the U.S. offer on domestic support did not go far enough in reducing trade-distorting support and would in fact leave the United States in a position to spend more on such subsidies than under the current WTO (Uruguay Round) Agreement on Agriculture.

Doha Round negotiators were operating under a deadline effectively imposed by the expiration of U.S. Trade Promotion Authority (TPA), which permits the President to negotiate trade deals and present them to Congress for an up or down vote without amendment. To meet congressional notification requirements under TPA legislation, an agreement would have to have been completed by the end of 2006. TPA expires on June 30, 2007, and most trade experts and officials think that the authority would not be renewed. Some, however, think that Congress might extend TPA temporarily if a Doha Round agreement seemed imminent, as was the case in 1994 for the Uruguay Round Multilateral Trade Agreements.

A number of agreements had already been reached in the Doha Round agricultural negotiations, but they are contingent on a comprehensive agreement in the single undertaking ("nothing is agreed until everything is agreed") that is the round and will now be put on hold. Those include an agreement by the EU to eliminate its agricultural export subsidies by the end of 2013 and an agreement by developed countries to extend duty and quota free access to 97% of the exports of the least developed countries. The agreement at Hong Kong to provide early and ambitious subsidy reduction for cotton also is dependent on there being a comprehensive Doha round agreement. The WTO will continue to provide aid for trade funds to help developing countries participate more fully in the world trade system. Aid for trade discussions were conducted outside the framework of Doha Round negotiations.

As a result of the suspension of the negotiations, a major source of pressure for U.S. farm policy change will have dissipated. The current farm bill (P.L.107-171) expires in 2007, and many were looking to a Doha Round agreement on curbing trade-distorting domestic support to require changes in U.S. farm subsidies to make them more compatible with world trade rules. The option of extending the current farm law appears strengthened by the indefinite suspension of the Doha talks. Legislation (H.R. 4332, H.R. 4775, and S. 2696) already had been introduced in the 109th Congress to extend the 2002 farm bill by one year.

The United States must still meet obligations under existing WTO agricultural agreements, which limit its trade-distorting spending to $19.1 billion annually. Some trade analysts think that there could be an increase in litigation by WTO member countries that allege they are harmed by U.S. farm subsidies.[1] The expiration of the "peace clause" (Article 13 of the 1994 Uruguay Round Agreement on Agriculture) means that WTO member countries are no longer bound by an agreement to refrain from challenging each other's agricultural subsidy programs so long as commitments under the agreement are being met. Brazil's successful challenges of U.S. cotton subsidies and EU sugar subsidies in WTO dispute settlement are cited as illustrations of the possible kinds of legal actions that WTO members might take.[2]

Another consequence of the suspension of Doha Round negotiations is that the United States may pursue more aggressively bilateral and regional free trade agreements (FTAs). Currently, the United States is negotiating nine FTAs. Agreements with larger economies will be particularly attractive to U.S. agricultural interests. The U.S. Trade Representative has indicated that in the near term priority will be given to negotiating FTAs with such larger U.S. trading partners as Korea, Malaysia, and Thailand.[3] TPA procedures also will apply to legislation to implement bilateral FTAs, lending some urgency to the completion of ongoing negotiations in time to meet TPA deadlines for congressional notification. Congress also could choose to extend TPA for bilateral trade agreements.

Restarting negotiations before the expiration of TPA seems unlikely, but some WTO member countries have been holding discussions with trading partners to explore the possibility of completing the Doha Round. The U.S. Trade Representative has held bilateral discussions with Australia, Brazil, China, the EU, India, and Japan where resuming the Round has been a topic for discussion. No agreements, however, that would break the negotiating impasse on agriculture have been announced. Members of the G-20 developing country negotiating group, led by Brazil and India, have called for resumption of the negotiations, but make no specific proposals for breaking the current deadlock.[4] The Cairns Group[5] of agricultural exporting countries (both developed and developing) are expected to call for resumption of the Round at their September 20-22, 2006, meeting in Australia.

THE HONG KONG MINISTERIAL DECLARATION

On December 18, 2005, in Hong Kong, WTO member countries reached agreement on a broad outline of negotiating objectives for liberalizing global trade in agriculture, manufactures, and services in the Doha Round of multilateral trade negotiations.[6] However, only limited progress was made in reaching agreement on precise numerical formulas or targets (termed "modalities") for liberalizing agricultural trade, the original aim of the Hong Kong (HK) Ministerial.

The Hong Kong agreement set new deadlines for completing the Round in 2006 (see Appendix Table 1). None of these deadlines were met prior to the July 2006 announcement that the negotiations had been suspended indefinitely. According to the HK agreement, modalities for cutting tariffs on agricultural products, eliminating export subsidies, and cutting trade-distorting domestic support would be agreed to by April 30, 2006. Based on these modalities, member countries would then submit comprehensive draft schedules by July 31, 2006. The Doha Round would be concluded in 2006. Completing negotiations by year-end would allow enough time to submit an agreement to Congress before the expiration of the President's TPA authority in mid-2007.

Incremental Progress on Agriculture in the Hong Kong Declaration

The Hong Kong (HK) declaration (adopted on December 18, 2005) deals with all three pillars of the agricultural negotiations — export competition, domestic support, and market access — and also with the controversial issue of the nature and pace of reform of trade-distorting cotton subsidies in the United States and other developed countries. Most progress was made in negotiations on the export competition pillar with an agreement on a specific end date for the elimination of export subsidies, but difficult negotiations remained on establishing new disciplines for other forms of export competition. Detailed negotiations were not carried out for domestic support and market access.

As throughout the Doha agricultural negotiations, market access, and especially how to deal with access for import-sensitive products, remains the thorniest issue, not least because of EU intransigence on this pillar. Some agreement was reached on how to deal with export subsidies and market access for cotton, but this issue still pits the United States, which argues for handling the reduction of trade-distorting support for cotton within the domestic support pillar, against the cotton-producing African countries who insist on an early harvest of reductions in cotton support.

Export Competition

The most concrete outcome of the Hong Kong Ministerial was an agreement to eliminate agricultural export subsidies by the end of 2013. The European Union (EU), the largest user of export subsidies, had opposed setting an end date, maintaining that WTO members needed to determine first how other forms of subsidized export competition — export credit programs, insurance, export activities of State Trading Enterprises (STEs), and food aid — would be disciplined. The United States and Brazil, among others, had been demanding an end to such export subsides by 2010 to be followed by negotiations on other forms of export completion. As a compromise, the HK declaration calls for the parallel elimination of all forms of export subsidies and disciplines on measures with equivalent effect by the end of 2013. The end date will be confirmed, however, only after the completion of modalities for the elimination of all forms of export subsidies.

With respect to other forms of export competition, the HK declaration included the following.

- Export credit programs should be "self-financing, reflecting market consistency, and of a sufficiently short duration so as not to effectively circumvent real commercially-oriented discipline;"
- On exporting STEs, disciplines will be such that their "monopoly powers cannot be exercised in any way that would circumvent the irect disciplines on STEs on export subsidies, government financing, and the underwriting of losses."
- On food aid, a "safe box" will be established for "bona fide" food aid "to ensure there will be no impediment to dealing with emergency situations." However, disciplines will be established on in-kind food aid, monetization, and re-exports to prevent loopholes for continuing export subsidization leading to elimination or displacement of commercial sales by food aid.

Domestic Support

On trade-distorting domestic support, WTO members agreed to three bands for reductions, with the percentages for reducing support in each band to be decided during the modalities negotiations. The EU would be in the highest band and be subject to the largest reduction commitments, while Japan and the United States would be in the middle band. (The U.S. proposal would have subjected Japan to a higher percentage cut of its domestic support.) All other WTO members, including developing countries, would be in the bottom band.

The HK declaration states further that "the overall reduction in trade-distorting domestic support will still need to be made even if the sum of the reductions in the three categories of trade-distorting support — amber box, blue box, and de minimis — would otherwise be less than the overall reduction requirement.[7] (This appears intended at ensuring that the United States does not engage in box shifting to maintain its current spending levels.)

Market Access

The HK declaration calls for four bands for structuring tariff cuts, with the relevant band thresholds and within-band reduction percentages to be worked out during modalities negotiations. The treatment of sensitive products (those to be exempted from formula tariff reductions) was also left to modalities negotiations. A preliminary draft of the declaration would have required WTO member countries to ensure that, for sensitive products, the greater the deviation from agreed tariff reduction formulas, the greater would be the increase in tariff rate quotas. The extent to which tariff rate quotas for sensitive products are expanded remains a key determinant of the market access gains that would result from the Round.

The HK declaration also ensured that developing countries would have two privileges not otherwise available to developed countries: (1) the right to self-designate a number of tariff lines to be treated as special products (with lower cuts in tariffs) based on certain criteria — food security, livelihood security, and rural development; and (2) the ability to impose a special safeguard mechanism (SSG) on imports based on both import quantity and price triggers.[8]

Cotton

On cotton, the HK declaration reaffirms the commitment (made in the July 2004 framework agreement discussed below) to ensure an explicit decision on cotton "within the agriculture negotiations and through the Sub-Committee on Cotton expeditiously and specifically." The HK declaration calls for developed countries to eliminate all forms of export subsidies on cotton in 2006. This coincides with the United States's elimination of its Step 2 program for cotton by August 1, 2006, as contained in the pending 2006 budget reconciliation act (S. 1932, Deficit Reduction Act of 2005). Step 2, which compensates U.S. millers and exporters for using high-priced American cotton, was declared in violation of WTO rules in the Brazil-U.S. cotton case.[9]

On cotton market access, the HK declaration calls on developed countries to give duty and quota free access to cotton exports from least-developed countries (LDCs) from the beginning of the implementation of a Doha Round agreement. Not agreed to, but certain to be revisited during the modalities negotiations in 2006, was a provision that "trade-distorting domestic subsidies for cotton should be reduced more ambitiously than under whatever general formula is agreed and that it should be implemented over a shorter period of time" than for other commodities.

Agriculture, NAMA, and LDCs

Two other provisions in the HK declaration touch on agriculture. One is a provision in the declaration calling for balance between agricultural and non-agricultural market access (NAMA) modalities. The HK declaration recognizes that it is important to advance the development objectives of the Round through enhanced market access for developing countries in both agriculture and NAMA. As a result, the HK declaration calls for a "complementary high level of ambition" in market access for both these components of the round. Second, in a departure from special and differential treatment, the HK declaration calls for all developed countries, and developing countries in a position to do so, to provide duty-free and quota-free market access for products originating from LDCs, with some exceptions, by 2008 or no later than the beginning of the implementation period.

AGRICULTURAL NEGOTIATING DEVELOPMENTS PRECEDING THE HONG KONG MINISTERIAL

Overview

On October 10, 2005, the United States offered a detailed proposal with specific modalities (i.e., schedules, formulas, and other criteria for implementing tariff and subsidy reduction rates and other aspects of the reform) for the adoption of new disciplines on the three major agricultural reform pillars — export competition, domestic support, and market access — in the ongoing round of WTO multilateral trade negotiations. The U.S. proposal appeared to break a negotiations log-jam as it was followed closely in mid-October, by separate proposals for agricultural modalities from three other major negotiating participants — the EU, the G-20 developing countries, and the G-10, a group of mainly developed countries that are net importers of agricultural products. These negotiating proposals revealed that wide differences exist, especially between the United States and the EU, in the modalities proposed for market access, the most difficult issue encountered by negotiators. (The proposals are examined below. See the Appendix Tables 1-3 at the end of this chapter for a schedule of key events, a description of the various negotiating groups, and a brief list of key WTO terms.)

As part of its oversight and consultation with the Administration on the Doha Round agriculture negotiations, Chairmen of both House and Senate Agriculture Committees have expressed their views on the kind of WTO agricultural agreement that would garner their support.[10] According to the chairmen, the four principles that should guide any WTO agreement are:

- Substantial improvement in real market access.
- Greater harmonization in trade-distorting domestic support.
- Elimination of export subsidies; and
- Greater certainty and predictability regarding WTO litigation.

Negotiations on the agricultural modalities in U.S. and other country proposals continued in preparation for the Hong Kong WTO Ministerial during November and December, but as the meeting approached, the negotiations appeared to have reached another impasse. The United States, the G-20, and the CAIRNS group called for the EU to improve and resubmit its offer on market access because it was not as extensive as its current reform proposals for domestic support and export competition, and thus provided insufficient bargaining room. The EU (with at least partial backing from the G-10 and India) claimed that it was unable to improve its market access offer without some formal proposals from other countries on reform in the non-agricultural trade sectors — primarily services and industrial goods.

With the prospect of little movement at Hong Kong under prevailing circumstances (e.g., limited time to bridge U.S.-EU-developing country differences and internal EU-country disagreements over the nature of the EU's offer), news reports surfaced about scaled-back ambitions for the Hong Kong Ministerial.[11] In the draft ministerial declaration for the Hong Kong meeting, the WTO Director General Pascal Lamy suggested that, rather than agreeing on modalities, trade ministers set deadlines for establishing modalities and agreeing to schedules of concessions, both before the end of 2006.[12]

Comparison of Major Agricultural Negotiating Proposals

The four major DDA negotiating proposals for agricultural modalities are from the United States, EU, G-20, and the G-10. Each proposal (described below) varies in terms of its degree of specificity for each of the three negotiating pillars. Tables 1 and 2 summarize domestic policy reforms and market access reforms, respectively, under each of the negotiating proposals.

Export competition negotiations were facilitated by the EU's July 2005 pledge to end export subsidies (conditioned on parallel treatment of other forms of export subsidies). Domestic support disciplines hinge primarily on commitments by three countries: the United States, the EU, and Japan. In contrast, market access has been the most difficult issue, especially for the EU and the G-10, but also for the G-20. The EU's latest offer on market access (October 27, 2005) — average tariff cuts of 35%-60% coupled with extensive protection for "sensitive products" — falls short of the "level of ambition" of the G-20 proposal which proposes tariff cuts of 45%-75% and limited protection for "sensitive products."

The U.S. Proposal

The U.S. modalities proposal of October 10, 2005, is credited with unblocking stalled modalities negotiations. It addressed domestic support and market access with specifics for the first time, and put the EU on the defensive especially on market access. It proposes a three-stage reform: five years of substantial reductions in trade-distorting support and tariffs, followed by a five-year pause; then five more years to phase-in total elimination of all remaining trade-distorting domestic measures and import tariffs.

Export Competition
- Eliminate all agricultural export subsidies.
- Establish disciplines for export credit guarantees, STEs, and food aid.

Domestic Support
- Cut the U.S. amber box bound by 60% based on 1999-2001 period.
- Reduce the EU and Japanese amber box bounds by 83%.
- Reduce overall level of trade-distorting support by 75% for EU, and by 53% for the United States and Japan.
- Cap blue box spending at 2.5% of value of production.
- Cut *de minimis* exemptions to 2.5% of value of production (for both total and for specific products).
- Maintain green box criteria without caps.
- Establish a new peace clause to protect domestic supports against WTO litigation.

Table 1. Comparison of Proposals for Domestic Policy Reform: U.S., G-20, EU, and G-10

	Highest Tier	2nd Tier	3rd Tier	Developing Countries	LDCs
U.S. Proposal[a]	EU, Japan	U.S.	Other Developed		
Amber Box Cuts	83%	60%	37%	n.s.	n.s.
— De Minimis cuts	Bound at 2.5% of TVP	Bound at 2.5% of TVP	Bound at 2.5% of TVP	n.s.	n.s.
— Blue Box Ceiling	Bound at 2.5% of TVP	Bound at 2.5% of TVP	Bound at 2.5% of TVP	n.s.	n.s.
Overall Ceiling Cuts	75% (53% Japan)	53%	31%	n.s.	n.s.
G-20 Proposal	EU, Japan	U.S.	Other Developed		
Amber Box Cuts[b]	80%	70%	60%	n.s.	n.s.
Overall Ceiling Cuts[b]	80%	75%	n.s	n.s.	n.s.
EU Proposal	EU (Japan?)	U.S. (Japan?)	Other Developed		
Amber Box Cuts[c]	70%	60%	50%	n.s	No cuts
Overall Ceiling Cuts	70%	60%	50%	n.s	No cuts
— De Minimis cuts	Bound at 1% of TVP	Bound at 1% of TVP	Bound at 1% of TVP	n.s	No cuts
— Blue Box Ceiling	Bound at 5% of TVP	Bound at 5% of TVP	Bound at 5% of TVP	n.s	No cuts
G-10 Proposal	EU, Japan ($25 +)	U.S. ($15 - $25)	Other Developed ($0 - $15)		
Amber Box Cuts	80%	70%	60%	n.s.	n.s.

Source: Assembled by CRS from various news releases of the USTR and World Trade Online.

n.s. = not specified

a. The U.S. proposes different value ranges for amber box and overall ceilings: however, the within-tier country composition remains unchanged under the different ranges: 1st tier: EU and Japan; 2nd tier: U.S.; 3rd tier: rest-of-world.

b. The G-20 is also calling for product-specific caps both in the overall AMS and the Blue Box.

c. The EU also proposes commodity-specific amber box spending limits.

Table 2. Doha Round Negotiations Market Access Proposals: G-10, G-20, EU, and U.S

Developed Countries	G-10			G-20		EU		United States [a]	
Tiers % and Within-Tier Cuts	Tiers %	Linear	flexibility	Tiers %	Linear	Tiers %	Linear	Tiers %	Progressive
1	0 ≤ 20	27%	32% ± 7%	0 ≤ 20	45%	0 ≤ 30	35% (20%–45%)[b]	0 ≤ 20	55-65%
2	> 20 ≤50	31%	36% ± 8%	> 20 ≤ 50	55%	> 30 ≤60	45%	> 20 ≤ 40	65-75%
3	> 50 ≤70	37%	42% ± 9%	> 50 ≤ 70	65%	> 60 ≤ 90	50%	> 40 ≤ 60	75-85%
4	> 70	45%	50% ± 10%	> 70	75%	> 90	60%[c]	> 60	85-90%
Tariff Cap %	No Cap			100%		100% (no cap for sens. prod.)		75%	
Estimated Average Tariff Cut	25-30%			54%		46% (39%)[d]		75%	
Sensitive Products	15% w/linear cuts; 10% w/flex cuts			1% of total tariff lines and subject to capping		8% of tariff line[e]		1% of total tariff lines	
Sensitive Products & TRQs				Minimum access level = 6% of annual domestic cons in base period[f]		Small TRQ expansion on small # of products[g]		Expanded TRQs	
Special Products	Not defined			Not defined		Not defined		Not defined	
Special Safeguard Mechanism (SSM)				Limited to developing countries		Available for all members for selected commodities			
Geographical Indicators (GIs)						Extend TRIPS, Art 23 to all products[h]		Existing trademark laws are sufficient.	
Developing Countries	G-10			G-20		EU		United States [a]	
Special & Differential Treatment (SDT)	More flexibility on sensitive products.			2/3 treatment in tiers. ≤2/3 treatment in cuts		Higher thresholds for top tiers; 2/3 lower in cuts		Slightly smaller cuts and longer phase-in periods	
	Tiers %	Linear	flexibility	Tiers %	Linear	Tiers %	Linear	Tiers %	Progressive
1	0 ≤30	27%	32% ± 7%	0 ≤30	< 30%	0 ≤ 30	25% (10-40%)[b]	0 ≤20	TBD
2	> 30 ≤ 70	31%	36% ± 8%	> 30 ≤ 80	< 40%	> 30 ≤ 80	30%	> 20 ≤ 40	TBD
3	> 70 ≤ 100	37%	42% ± 9%	> 80 ≤ 130	< 50%	> 30 ≤ 80	30%	> 40 ≤ 60	TBD
4	> 100	45%	50% ± 10%	> 130	< 60%	> 80 ≤ 130	35%	> 60	TBD

Table 2. (Continued).

Developed Countries	G-10	G-20	EU	United States[a]
Tariff Cap %	No Cap	150%	>130	100%
Sensitive Products	Not defined	1.5% of total tariff lines	Not defined	Not defined
Least-Developed Countries	G-10	G-20	EU	United States[a]
LDC Treatment	Not defined	Same as EU plus exemption from tariff reduction commitments.	All developed countries should allow full duty-free access for EBA.	Not defined

Source: Assembled by CRS from USTR, EC, and World Trade Online news releases. Data are as of October 28, 2005

[a] The U.S. has proposed applying the set of tiered tariff cuts described below during the 1st five-year period of implementation; to be followed by a period of stability during the next (2nd) five years; then totally eliminating tariffs during the 3rd five-year period. This same reduction-stability-elimination sequence would be applied to trade-distorting domestic support as well.

[b] The EU proposes additional FLEXIBILITY be given for tariff cuts within the lowest tier (0-30%) such that the tier's overall average cut of 35% (25% for developing countries) is still respected, but that within tier cuts may vary between 20% to 45% (10% to 40%).

[c] The EU has expressed a willingness to consider 70% cuts for the top tier of tariffs.

[d] The EU estimates the average tariff cut, according to its proposed tier/tariff reduction formula, would be 46% across all tariff lines. However, USTR suggests that a more accurate estimate would be 39%. Since the average tariff cut across all tariff lines must also consider the level of protection provided by TRQs for sensitive products, it would appear that the EU's estimated average tariff cut of 46% grossly overstates the true average as it apparently ignores the large degree of protection provided by allowing 8% of tariff lines to hide behind TRQs. (See next footnote.)

[e] The EU has approximately 2,200 8-digit tariff lines. An 8% limit on sensitive products would imply a maximum of about 176 sensitive products to be subject to TRQs with expanded market access. The EU currently has 300 to 400 tariff lines covered by TRQs under the Uruguay Round Agreement. The EU suggests that such a large number of sensitive products is necessary to achieve both protection for its agricultural sector while allowing for substantial tariff cuts across unprotected tariff line items. Furthermore, the EU states that its sensitive products, although numerous, would be structured to allow for "substantial increases in market access that would nonetheless still be lower than that granted by the result of the full tariff cut."

[f] The G-20 proposes that no new tariff-rate quotas (apart from existing TRQs agreed to under the Uruguay Round's Agreement on Agriculture) be created for products designated as sensitive, and it calls for a maximum deviation from the tariff reduction formula of 30%. It said existing TRQs on developed country sensitive products should at least be expanded so that a minimum access level is increased to a level equivalent to 6% of annual domestic consumption.

[g] The EU proposal calls for the possibility of new TRQs. In addition it recommends a TRQ formula linking the quota increase to the level of tariff reduction, proposing that the quota increase is: [(Normal tariff cut) - (applied cut)] / [(import price) + (ad valorem for that tariff line)] * (0.8). At the same stage there should be a minimum tariff reduction in each of the bands of 5%, 10%, 15%, and 20%, respectively.

[h] EU proposes that GIs receive the same protection as a trade mark in line with protection currently available for wine and spirits under Article 23 of TRIPS agreement. For products with existing trade mark protection that would otherwise be invalidated by GI protection elsewhere, Article 24 of TRIPS would be adjusted such that existing trade marks would not be affected. The EU considers this a major concession.

Definitions:
EBA = Everything But Arms (i.e., all products except weaponry and munitions)
TBD = To Be Determined
TRQ = Tariff Rate Quota. This involves a quota level (TBD) within which all imports enter duty-free or subject to a minimal tariff duty (TBD). All over-quota imports are subject to a higher (often prohibitive) duty (TBD). Greater market access (or greater TRQ) is achieved by raising the quota level and reducing the over-quota tariff rate

Table 3. U.S. Domestic Spending Limits and Outlays: Current Status, Framework Agreement, and U.S. Reform Proposal

Category	Current Outlays 1995-2001[a] US$ Billion	Current Outlays 2005[b]	Current WTO Limits Status	Current WTO Limits US$ Billion	Framework Status	Framework US$ Billion	U.S. Proposal Status	U.S. Proposal US$ Billion
Total Overall Ceiling	$16.3	$19.1	Unbound (due to blue box)	—	20% initial cut: further cuts implemented gradually. Final total cut TBD	~$45.4	Bound and subject to cuts that vary based on level of domestic support (Table 3)	~$23
Amber box (Bound AMS)	$11.0	$12.7	Separate Bound for each country	$19.1	20% initial cut: further cuts implemented gradually; with product-specific AMS caps TBD.	$15.4[c]	Tiered: subject to substantial cuts during 1st five years; stable for 2nd five years, then eliminated in 3rd five-years.[d]	$7.6
Blue box	$1.0	$0.0	Unbound	—	Bound TBD but < 5% of TVP	~$10	Bound at 2.5% of TVP	~$5
De Minimis aggregate	$4.2	$6.2	Bound at 5% of TVP	~$10	Bound TBD but < 5% of TVP	~$10	Bound at 2.5% of TVP	~$5
De Minimis commodity specific	$0.1	$0.1	Bound at 5% of SCVP	~$10	Bound TBD but < 5% of SCVP	~$10	Bound at 2.5% of SCVP	~$5
Green Box	$49.9	—	Unbound	—	Unbound	—	Unbound	—

Source: Assembled by CRS from news releases of various sources. For a detailed description of U.S. domestic spending by category for both commitments and actual outlay notifications, see CRS Report RL30612, *Agriculture in the WTO: Member Spending on Domestic Support*, by Randy Schnepf.

a. Average for 1995-2001 period for which official WTO notification data is available.
b. Estimate for 2005 period based on CRS calculations from various USDA projections.
c. Reflects only the 20% initial cut.
d. The three five-year period phase out would apply to all trade-distorting domestic support and tariffs (including safeguard mechanisms).

Definitions:
AMS — Aggregate Measure of (trade-distorting domestic) Support as defined in the Agreement on Agriculture.
TBD — To Be Determined.
TVP — Total Value of agricultural Production for all commodities.
SCVP — Total Value of agricultural Production for a Specific Commodity.

Market Access
- Cut highest tariffs by 90%; cut other tariffs in a range of 55%-90%.
- Cap the maximum agricultural tariff at 75%.
- Limit sensitive products to 1% of tariff lines.
- Expand TRQs: i.e., larger quotas with lower tariffs.
- SDT for developing countries (TBD), but cap maximum developing country agricultural tariff at 100%.

Conditions

U.S. domestic support commitments are conditioned on "ambitious" market access proposals especially from the EU and the G-20.

The EU Proposal

Under pressure from France and 12 other EU countries (but not a qualified majority) not to improve its offers, the EU made a new market access proposal on October 27 and provided additional detail on its proposal for domestic support, export competition, and Geographical Indications (GIs are place names associated with particular products). The EU's "level of ambition" in market access does not reach that of the G-20 or the United States. A major criticism of the EU's agricultural proposal is that its market access offer does not provide an inducement for developing countries like Brazil, Thailand, or other G-20 members to make concessions in non-agricultural market access or services. The United States and G-20 countries continue to pressure the EU to offer further concessions on agricultural market access.

Export Competition
- Eliminate all agricultural export subsidies, contingent on "parallel" disciplines for export credits, food aid, and STEs by 2012.
- Establish a "short-term self-financing principle" for credits: programs must demonstrate that they charge adequate premiums to ensure self-financing.
- STEs: eliminate price-pooling, anti-trust immunity, direct and indirect preferential financing, and preferential transport services; and eliminate single-desk selling.
- Food Aid: phase out food aid that leads to commercial displacement but maintain commitments to adequate food aid levels; move gradually to untied and in-cash food aid; permit in-kind food aid only in exceptional, emergency situations under agreed criteria.

Domestic Support
- Reduce the EU's amber box ceiling by 70% (in line with already established EU spending limits); reduce the U.S. amber box ceiling by 60%.
- Base amber box product-specific caps on the Uruguay Round implementation period of 1986-88.
- Reduce the *de minimis* exemptions ceiling by 80% of the Framework's proposed 5% cap (i.e., establish a cap of 1% of the value of total production).
- Blue box: freeze the existing price difference between linked price support prices and limit the price gap to a percentage of the base price difference.

- Reduce overall trade-distorting support in three bands: 70% (EU), 60% (U.S.), and 50% (rest-of-world).
- Maintain the green box without limits.

Market Access
- Reduce the highest tariffs by 60%; cut other tariffs in a range of 35%-60%.
- Reduce the number of sensitive products to 8% of tariff lines (given the EU's approximately 2,200 tariff lines this would result in about 176 protected tariff lines for the EU).
- Apply both tariff cuts and expanded TRQs to sensitive products.
- Cap the maximum agricultural tariff for developed countries at 100% (but with no cap for sensitive products).

Special Safeguard Mechanism (SSG)
- Keep the SSG available for both developed and developing countries. Specifically, the EU wants the SSG to be available for beef, poultry, butter, fruits and vegetables, and sugar.

Geographical Indications (GIs)
- Extend protection available to wines and spirits under Article 23 of TRIPS to all products, while leaving existing trademarks unaffected.
- Establish a multilateral system of notification and registration of GIs, open to all products, with legal effect in all Member countries not having lodged a reservation to the registration.
- Use of well-known GIs on a short list should be prohibited, again subject to existing trademark rights.

Special And Differential Treatment (SDT) for Developing Countries
- Establish higher tariff bands, lower tariff cuts, and a maximum tariff of 150% for developing countries.
- No tariff cuts for the 32 WTO-member LDCs.

Conditions
- *NAMA*: agreement before Hong Kong on a progressive formula that cuts into applied tariffs for manufactured products.
- *Services*: agreement at Hong Kong to establish mandatory country targets for services trade liberalization.
- *Rules*: Negotiate before the Hong Kong Ministerial meeting a list of issues to be resolved including antidumping.
- *Development*: prepare for Hong Kong a Trade Related Assistance package for developing countries and extend tariff and quota free access to all LDCs no later than the conclusion of the DDA.

The G-20 Proposal

The G-20 proposal on market access reflects differences between Brazil, an agricultural exporter, and India, an agricultural importer.

Export Competition
- Eliminate all forms of export subsidies over five-year period.
- New food aid disciplines should not compromise emergency humanitarian assistance.

Domestic Support
- Cut the bound for overall trade-distorting domestic support in three bands: >$60 billion, 80%; $10-$60 billion, 75%; and $0-$10 billion, 70%.
- Cut the amber box ceiling in three bands: >$25 billion, 80%; $15-$25 billion, 70%; and $0-$15 billion, $60%.
- Reduce *de minimis* exemption allowances so as to meet the cut in the overall bound.
- Address the cotton issues no later than the Hong Kong Ministerial meeting.

Market Access
- Cut developed country tariffs by 45%-75%; cut developing country tariffs by 25%-40%.
- Cap the developed country maximum agricultural tariff at 100%, developing country maximum tariff at 150%.
- Limit the number of sensitive products; compensate for designation as sensitive with a combination of tariff cuts and expanded TRQs.
- Maintain Special Safeguard Mechanism (SSG) for developing countries; eliminate SSG for developed countries.
- Address issue of preference erosion for developing countries with expanded access for LDCs and trade capacity building.
- Special and Differential Treatment (SDT): exempt LDCs from reduction commitments.

The G-10 Proposal

The G-10 is a group of mainly developed, net-agricultural importing countries led by Japan, Norway, and Switzerland. The G-10 has tabled proposals on market access and domestic support, but not on export competition. The G-10 takes a relatively "defensive" posture on market access that calls for lower tariff reductions and a larger number of sensitive products than do other proposals.

Market Access
- Reduce agricultural tariffs by 27% to 45% for most products.
- The number of sensitive products would be 10% of tariff lines with linear cuts within tiers, 15% of tariff lines would have flexibility for within-tier adjustments.
- There would be no cap on the highest agricultural tariff allowed.

Domestic Support
- Reduce the amber box ceiling by 80% for support >$25 billion; by 70% for support in the $15-$25 billion range; and by 60% for support <$15 billion.
- Reduce the overall support ceiling by 80% for support >$60 billion; 75% for $10-$60 billion; and 70% for support <$10 billion.
- Blue box and *de minimis* spending are not addressed.

The G-33 Proposal for Special Products

The G-33 is an alliance of 42 developing countries including larger countries like China and India, but also least-developed countries like Benin and Zambia. The G-33 calls for the following.

- 20% of tariff lines of developing countries to be designated as Special Products (those deemed essential for food security, rural development, and other factors).
- 50% of the tariff lines so designated would be exempt from any tariff reduction commitment.
- An additional 15% of designated tariff lines would be exempted from tariff reductions if there are "special circumstances" (e.g., low bound tariffs, high ceiling bindings, high proportion of low income or resource poor producers.
- A further 25% of designated special products would be subject only to a 5% reduction in bound tariff rates while the remaining tariff lines would be subject to cuts no greater than 10%.

The Cotton Issue: Background

Among the unresolved issues going into the Hong Kong Ministerial was the so-called African Cotton Initiative. Four least-developed African countries — Benin, Burkina Faso, Chad, and Mali — proposed (May 2003) a sectoral initiative for cotton that would entail the complete elimination of export subsidies and trade-distorting domestic support by all WTO members.[13] Although not specifically mentioned in the Doha Round negotiating mandate, cotton was identified as a key to a successful conclusion of the Doha Round following the Cancun Ministerial in September 2003. A preliminary agreement on a "framework" for the Doha Round negotiations reached in July 2004 (see detailed discussion below) also recognized the importance of cotton for certain developing countries and stated that cotton will be "addressed ambitiously, expeditiously, and specifically" within the agriculture negotiations.[14] In addition, the Framework called for the establishment of a "Cotton" SubCommittee (established on November 19, 2004) to deal with the initiative.

Going into the Hong Kong meeting, there were two main proposals for dealing with the trade-related aspects of the sectoral initiative on cotton.[15] One was a revised proposal from the African group and the second was an EU proposal. Both called for decisions to be made at the Hong Kong Ministerial. The African proposal called for export subsidies on cotton to be eliminated by the end of 2005. Trade-distorting domestic support would be completely eliminated by January 1, 2009, with 80% eliminated by the end of 2006 and 10% each in 2007 and 2008. The market access aspects of the initiative would be addressed by duty-free and quota-free access for cotton and cotton products from least-developed countries. An emergency fund would be established to deal with depressed international prices. Additionally, this proposal called for technical and financial assistance for the cotton sector in African countries.

The EU proposal called for the Hong Kong Ministerial to endorse more ambitious and faster commitments on cotton than for agriculture as a whole. The EU provided details of its proposal for cotton, but without assigning numerical targets, which is consistent with its position that Hong Kong should not be about deciding numbers (i.e., actual modalities). For export subsidies, the EU proposed an earlier end date for elimination. As to market access, the EU indicated its willingness to eliminate all duties, quotas and other quantitative restrictions on imports from all countries. For domestic support, the EU would eliminate all trade-distorting subsidies for cotton. The EU indicated that all its cotton commitments "will already be in place, as far as the EU is concerned, from 2006."

The U.S. position on the cotton initiative has been that cotton should be dealt with as an integral part of the agriculture negotiations. Thus cotton subsidy reductions or market access commitments would be made as part of an overall agreement on agriculture. A more ambitious result for cotton, then, would depend on the underlying agriculture agreement. According to the WTO summary of the cotton subcommittee meeting in which the initiative was discussed most recently, the U.S. Deputy Trade Representative indicated that the United States agreed that the outcome for cotton should be "more than the average" (i.e., the general outcome for agriculture).[16]

Role of Developing Countries

The active participation of developing countries in the Doha Round distinguishes it from previous multilateral trade rounds held under the auspices of the General Agreement on Tariffs and Trade (GATT), the predecessor of the WTO. During the Uruguay Round, an agreement between the United States and the EU on agricultural issues at Blair House in 1992 paved the way for a successful conclusion of this last GATT round. However, a U.S.-EU joint proposal on agriculture during the 2003 Cancun Ministerial meeting was greeted with strong opposition from a group of developing countries.[17] This group, led by Brazil, India, and China, known as the G-20, has remained together since Cancun and is playing a key role in the Doha agricultural negotiations. The G-20 was first among the major players in the Doha Round to offer a proposal on agricultural modalities in advance of the Hong Kong meeting, and its proposal became a benchmark for evaluating other, developed country proposals.

Not only the more advanced developing countries like the G-20 members, but also the least developed countries (LDCs) are participating actively in the Doha negotiations. The African Cotton Initiative (discussed above) is an example of the LDCs attempting to use multilateral trade negotiations to accomplish their policy objectives. The LDCs also were instrumental in blocking an overall agreement at Cancun when they rejected an EU proposal to enlarge the negotiating agenda to include discussion of the so-called "Singapore issues" of trade facilitation, competition policy, investment, and transparency in government procurement. Subsequent agreement to limit negotiations of Singapore issues to just one — trade facilitation — was a victory for the LDCs.

Other Negotiating Issues

A number of other issues are on the agenda of the Doha Round.[18] These include negotiations to reduce tariff and non-tariff barriers to trade in industrial products (referred to as non-agricultural market access or NAMA negotiations), liberalization of trade in the services sector, reviews of anti-dumping and countervailing duty measures and dispute settlement procedures, a number of specific issues of interest to developing countries (for example, access to patented medicines, implementation of existing WTO agreements, and changes in special and differential treatment provisions), and trade facilitation (which refers generally to harmonizing and streamlining customs procedures among WTO members).

ROLE OF CONGRESS: TRADE PROMOTION AUTHORITY AND THE FARM BILL

If DDA negotiations result in a trade agreement, then Congress would presumably take up legislation to implement it under trade promotion authority (TPA), or fast-track, procedures (Title XXI of P.L. 107-210). Under fast-track, if the President meets the trade negotiating objectives established in the legislation and satisfies consultation and notification requirements in P.L. 107-210, then Congress would consider legislation to implement a trade agreement with limited debate, no amendments, and with an up-or-down vote. However, unless it is extended by Congress TPA only covers trade agreements signed by July 1, 2007. As such, TPA expiration is the effective deadline for U.S. participation in the Doha Round and for congressional consideration of implementing legislation. That time frame also coincides with the expiration of the 2002 farm bill (P.L. 107-171) on September 30, 2007. Farm bill changes may be needed to meet U.S. commitments in a final DDA agreement on agriculture.

BACKGROUND ON THE DOHA ROUND

Agricultural Negotiations: Doha to Cancun

The previous round of multilateral trade negotiations — the Uruguay Round — which spanned 1988 to 1994 was the first international trade agreement to include agricultural policy reform. The Uruguay Round's Agreement on Agriculture (AA) was the first multilateral agreement dedicated entirely to agriculture. The AAs implementation period lasted six years (1995-2000) for developed countries and 10 years (1995-2004) for developing countries. Article 20 of the AA included a provision for the continuation of the agricultural policy reform process.

At the WTO's Fourth Ministerial Conference (held in Doha, Qatar, on November 9-14, 2001), WTO member countries agreed to launch a new round of multilateral trade negotiations, including negotiations on agricultural trade liberalization.[19] This new round, because it emphasized integrating developing countries into the world trading system, was called the Doha Development Agenda (DDA). The new round incorporates agriculture into a comprehensive framework that includes negotiations on industrial tariffs, services, anti-dumping and countervailing duty measures (referred to as rules), dispute settlement, and other trade issues.

The Doha Ministerial (DM) Declaration mandate for agriculture called for comprehensive negotiations aimed at substantial improvements in market access; reductions of, with a view to phasing out, all forms of export subsidies; and substantial reductions in trade-distorting domestic support. These topics — domestic support, export subsidies, and market access — have become known as the three pillars of the agricultural negotiations. The DM declaration also provided that special and differential treatment (SDT) for developing countries would be an integral part of all elements of the negotiations. The DM declaration took note of non-trade concerns reflected in negotiating proposals of various member countries and confirmed that they would be taken into account in the negotiations. March 31, 2003 was set as the deadline for reaching agreement on "modalities" (targets, formulas, timetables, etc.) for achieving the mandated objectives, but that deadline was missed. During the rest of 2003, negotiations on modalities continued in preparation for the fifth WTO Ministerial Conference held in Cancun, Mexico September 10-14, 2003.

While the United States and the EU reached agreement on a broad framework for negotiating agricultural trade liberalization before the Cancun meeting, a group of developing countries, the G-20 which includes Brazil, China, India, and South Africa, among others, made a counter-proposal. The G-20 proposal emphasized agricultural subsidy and tariff reduction for developed countries with fewer demands on developing countries. The Chairman of the Cancun ministerial circulated a draft declaration at the meeting that attempted to reconcile differences between developed (especially the United States and the EU) and developing countries (especially the G-20) on the agricultural issues. Neither the proposals made by the United States and the EU, the G-20, nor the Chairman's draft declaration proposed specific modalities (formulas, targets, or timetables) for reducing tariffs and trade-distorting support and for phasing out export subsidies.

The Cancun Ministerial Conference thus failed to reconcile differences on agricultural issues as well as differences between developed and developing countries over expanding the negotiating agenda to include such issues as competition and investment policy. The Cancun Ministerial ended without an agreement on modalities or a framework for continuing multilateral negotiations on agricultural trade liberalization. The inconclusive end of the Cancun ministerial largely eliminated the prospect that the DDA would conclude by its scheduled end date, January 1, 2005.

July 2004 Framework Agreement for Agriculture

On July 31, 2004, WTO member countries reached an agreement on a work program for completing the DDA negotiations. The July 31 work program includes annexes that lay out negotiating frameworks for agriculture and other DDA issues.[20] The agricultural framework (referred throughout this report as the Framework) set the stage for negotiations to determine modalities (i.e., the specific targets, formulas, timetables, etc.), for curbing trade-distorting domestic support, reducing trade barriers and eliminating export subsidies. Negotiators set for themselves a deadline of July 2005 for completing a first draft of the agricultural modalities, another deadline that was subsequently missed. The following three subsections describe what was agreed to in the July 31 Framework, and the issues that remained to be negotiated for each of the three negotiating pillars.

Pillar 1 — Export Competition

Although 36 WTO members are permitted to use export subsidies as listed in their country schedules, only 24 countries have actually used export subsidies. Most countries with permissible export subsidies have used them very sparingly. During the 1995-2001 period for which WTO notification data are available, the EU accounted for nearly 90% of all export subsidies used by WTO members.[21]

What Was Agreed to in the Framework

Under the Framework, WTO members agreed to establish detailed modalities ensuring the parallel elimination of all forms of export subsidies and disciplines on all export measures with equivalent effect by a credible end date. The following will be eliminated by the end date to be determined (TBD):

1. Export subsidies.
2. Export credits, export credit guarantees or insurance programs with repayment periods beyond 180 days.
3. Terms and conditions — e.g., interest payments, minimum interest rates, minimum premium requirements, and any other subsidy elements — relating to export credits, export credit guarantees or insurance programs with repayment periods of 180 days or less which are not in accordance with disciplines TBD.
4. Trade distorting practices of exporting State Trading Enterprises (STEs) including elimination of export subsidies they receive and government financing and underwriting of losses.
5. Provision of food aid not in conformity with disciplines TBD.
6. Developing countries will benefit from longer implementation periods TBD for eliminating all forms of export subsidies.

Export Competition Issues to Be Resolved

1. Schedule for eliminating export subsidies.
2. Nature of "parallel treatment" of export credit programs.
3. Rules for exporting STEs.
4. New disciplines for food aid to prevent commercial displacement.
5. An assessment of whether and to what extend food aid should be provided in grant form.
6. A review of the role of international organizations in providing food aid.

Pillar 2 — Domestic Support

Only 35 out of 149 members have notified use of trade-distorting domestic subsidies in their country schedules. During the 1995-2001 period for which notification data are available, three countries — the EU, the United States, and Japan — accounted for 91% of all domestic subsidies used by WTO members.[22]

What Was Agreed to in the Framework

1. General Concepts a. Doha Ministerial Declaration calls for *substantial reductions in trade-distorting domestic support*. b. Special and Differential Treatment (SDT) remains an integral component of domestic support: developing countries to be given *smaller cuts with a longer implementation period* and continued access to AA, Article 6.2 — special exemptions for investment and input subsidies. c. There will be a strong element of harmonization in the reductions made by Developed Members. A tiered, progressive formula TBD will be used for implementing all reductions.
2. Amber Box — Current bounds are detailed in country schedules.
   (a) Substantial reductions (TBD) from bound levels
   (b) Limits (TBD) will be placed on supports for specific products in order to avoid shifting support between different products.
3. De Minimis exemptions — The current bound for non-product-specific support is 5% of the total value of agricultural production (TVP); for product-specific support it is 5% of the value of production for each specific product (PVP). Developing countries are bound at 10% for both measures. a. Substantial reductions, TBD, that take into account SDT.
4. Blue Box — Currently unbound; includes only production limiting direct payments. a. "Members recognize the role of the Blue Box in promoting agricultural reforms." b. To be bound at no more than 5% of TVP (or PVP for individual products) during an historical period TBD. c. Will be expanded to include direct payments that do not require production under certain conditions (e.g., U.S. counter-cyclical payments (CCP)). d. Criteria TBD will be added to ensure that blue box payments are less trade distorting than AMS measures.
5. Overall Ceiling for Trade-Distorting Domestic Support — The sum of amber box, blue box, and de minimis is currently unbound. a. Substantial reductions (TBD) including an initial 20% cut enacted in the first year, with further cuts to be negotiated. b. If the sum of bound ceilings for amber box, de minimis, and blue box is still above the Overall Ceiling, then additional cuts in at least one of them must be made to comply with the Overall Ceiling commitment.
6. Green Box — Criteria will be reviewed and clarified to ensure that Green Box measures have no, or at most minimal, trade-distorting effects on production.

Domestic Support Issues to Be Resolved.

1. Formula for reductions in bounds for Overall and Amber Box: -Levels and number of tiers.
   - Rate and formula for within-tier cuts encompassing greater harmonization. -Levels for individual commodity limits within the amber box.
2. Blue box disciplines:
   - Formula for establishing bound levels as a share of production value. -Base period against which to measure bounds.
3. De Minimis disciplines:
   - Formula for establishing bound levels as a share of production value. -Base period against which to measure bounds.

Pillar 3 — Market Access

All countries have market access barriers, whereas only some have export subsidies or Amber or Blue Box domestic support. Therefore, the range of interest in market access reform is more complex and is proving more difficult to achieve.

What Was Agreed to in the Framework
1. All members must improve market access substantially for all products.
2. The Framework gives no tariff reduction formula, but provides direction: a. All members except LDCs must improve market access. b. Tiered and progressive: larger within-tier cuts for higher tiers. c. Reductions to be made from "bound" rate, not (generally lower) applied rate. d. Special and Differential Treatment (SDT) for developing countries: i. Smaller formula commitments in tariff reductions. ii. Greater access to and treatment of sensitive products. iii. A longer implementation period. iv. Designation of a number of products as Special Products, eligible for more flexible tariff treatment, based on criteria of food security, livelihood security, and rural development need. e. Sensitive Products: i. Principle of substantial improvement in market access TBD. ii. Appropriate number of permissible sensitive products TBD.

Market Access Issues to Be Resolved
1. Harmonized tariff reduction scheme:
   a. Levels and number of tariff tiers.
   b. Rate and formula for within-tier tariff cuts.
   c. Tariff caps, i.e., a bound maximum tariff rate.

2. Parameters governing Sensitive Products:
   a. Limit on sensitive products (how many and what treatment?).
   b. Tariff rate quota (TRQ) formula for linking quota to reduced tariff via: (1) MFN-based tariff quota expansion required of all sensitive products; (2) within and over-quota tariff reductions.
   c. Improved administration of TRQs.
   d. Reducing or eliminating tariff escalation associated with increasing stages of value-added products.

3. Exact nature of SDT for developing countries:
   a. Lesser commitments; longer implementation period; greater flexibility for sensitive products
   b. Special products (i.e., related to food or livelihood security, or rural development) given additional flexibility.
   c. Special Safeguard Mechanism (SSG) — to deal with surges in imports or falling prices — are to be available for developing countries. Their status is TBD with respect to developed countries.
   d. Special treatment of agricultural product alternatives to illicit narcotic crops.
   e. Erosion of trade preferences when the WTO agreement supercedes bilateral or regional trade agreements.

4. Treatment of Least-Developed Countries (LDCs): should LDCs be given a "free" round with no new market access commitments TBD?
5. Geographical Indications (GIs): will GIs be a part of any final agreement and, if so, how will they be defined and implemented?

POTENTIAL EFFECTS OF A SUCCESSFUL DOHA ROUND

The economic and policy implications of trade liberalization are briefly reviewed at three levels: analysis of global trade and income effects; existing U.S. policy context; and analysis of U.S. domestic agricultural income and policy effects.

In estimating the economic benefits to the U.S. and world from a new round of trade liberalization, two points must be kept in mind. First, based on the current proposals for reforming the domestic and trade policy of WTO members, any agreement from the Doha Round will institute only a "partial" liberalization, i.e., it will allow countries to maintain some policies (whether domestic subsidies or border measures) that continue to distort agricultural trade. Second, current proposals deal with setting limits on aggregate spending categories. If adopted, each individual member country will ultimately decide how to implement their domestic policies so as to achieve the aggregate spending limits agreed to under a new trade agreement.

Global Trade and GDP

According to the several recent economic analyses of the potential economic benefits from global trade liberalization, the following common conclusions emerge.[23]

- Policies that distort agricultural trade account for roughly two-thirds of all policies that distort trade in goods of any kind.
- Of policies that distort world agricultural trade, tariffs and tariff-rate quotas are by far the most costly — accounting for 80% to 90% of the cost — with domestic support and export subsidies comprising the remainder.
- A significant gap between bound and applied tariff rates for most products in most countries suggests that substantial tariff cuts in bound rates (those affected by Doha Round negotiations) will have to be realized before applied rates are actually lowered.
- Similarly, a significant gap between bound and actual domestic spending levels suggests that substantial cuts in bound domestic spending limits (those affected by Doha Round negotiations) will have to be realized before actual spending levels are lowered.
- Much of the eventual market access gains will be determined by the treatment of sensitive products, i.e., their number and the extent to which they are exempted from reform.

A 2005 World Bank study to measure the effects of a partial trade liberalization (using cuts to tariff and subsidy bounds similar to those contained in the G-20 proposal, but with no special treatment for "sensitive" or "special" products) found that such reform would produce annual welfare benefits to the world (in 2001 dollars) of $74.5 billion once fully implemented.[24] This compares with a potential annual benefit of $182 billion under full trade liberalization and suggests both the potential economic importance of a successful Doha Round as well as the extent of remaining policy reform needed to achieve full liberalization.

However, the World Bank study also found that if developed countries are allowed to select 2% of their tariff lines (4% for developing countries) as sensitive products and provide them with special TRQ protection that includes very high above-quota tariffs, then annual economic benefits from trade liberalization would fall to $17.7 billion.[25] In other words, nearly 80% of the potential economic gains would be eliminated. The same study also found that a substantial portion of the potential economic benefits could be preserved, even with a 2% sensitive product threshold, if above-quota tariffs are capped at 200%. Under this scenario the annual economic benefits from trade liberalization are estimated at $44.3 billion.

U.S. Farm Policy Implications

Current Doha reform proposals suggest that substantial changes will be needed for several phases of existing U.S. agricultural policies. These are briefly reviewed below.

Export Competition
The United States uses export subsidies and export credit guarantees to support some of its commodity exports, and is a major donor of international food aid. As a result, changes in these programs will have some impacts on U.S. commodity markets and trade policy.

Elimination of Export Subsidies
Although the United States has the second-largest level of permissible export subsidies under current WTO limits, it uses only a very small share of its allowable level.[26] Milk and milk products are the principal beneficiaries of U.S. export subsidies.

Reform of Agricultural Export Credit Guarantees
The United States is the world's leading user of export credit guarantees.[27] In FY2004, nearly $3.7 billion worth of U.S. agricultural exports (out of a total of $62.4 billion) were facilitated with agricultural export credit guarantees. Current Doha reform proposals would likely reduce the effectiveness of traditional export credit guarantees at supporting U.S. commodity exports into price-competitive markets. However, on-going U.S. changes in its export credit guarantee program, made in response to a WTO dispute settlement ruling against certain features of the U.S. cotton program,[28] are likely to bring them into compliance with Doha reform proposals, thereby necessitating little if any further changes.

Changes in Food Aid Programs
The United States is among the world's leading food aid donors. In FY2004, nearly $2.2 billion worth of U.S. agricultural exports (out of a total of $62.4 billion) were made under some form of U.S. food aid program (including PL480, Food-For-Peace, and McGovern-Dole

International Food for Education and Child Nutrition Program). Since most of U.S. food aid is in the form of commodity donations rather than cash, U.S. food aid donations will likely be reduced to the extent that reforms to food aid limit or restrict the donation of actual commodities.[29]

Domestic Support

The United States together with the EU and Japan account for nearly 90% of global agricultural domestic support subsidies.[30] As a result, these three countries are most likely to bear the brunt of the economic consequences associated with new disciplines on domestic support. Table 1 contains information on U.S. domestic support and various Doha Round reform proposals.

Reductions to Bound Level of Amber Box Spending

Under the U.S. proposal for reform of domestic support (Table 3), the U.S. amber box ceiling would be lowered by 60% to approximately $7.6 billion. This compares with current amber box spending in FY2005 of an estimated $12.7 billion and an amber box ceiling of $19.1 billion. As a result, U.S. domestic support programs would require some redesign (with likely box shifting) to be able to meet such a lower ceiling. Although there are many ways that such changes could be achieved, a likely candidate would include shifting away from market-distorting programs such as loan deficiency payments (LDP) or marketing loan gains (MLG) and towards greater use of green box programs such as decoupled direct payments, conservations payments, or rural infrastructure development.

Tightening of De Minimis Bounds

Under the U.S. proposal for reform of domestic support (Table 4), the *de minimis* exemptions, both non-product specific and product specific, would be bound at 2.5% of the value of relevant production (i.e., either aggregate or commodity specific). For non-product specific *de minimis*, this would result in a ceiling of about $5 billion, compared with estimated exemptions of $6.2 billion in FY2005. However, shifting the counter-cyclical payments (CCP) to the blue box (see below) would bring spending under the *de minimis* exemptions back into line with their proposed commitments.[31]

Establishment of Bound on Blue Box

Under both the framework agreement and the U.S. proposal for reform of domestic support, CCPs would be eligible for the blue box. The U.S. proposal also recommends establishing a blue box ceiling of 2.5% of the total value of national agricultural production (TVP). For the United States, 2.5% of TVP would be approximately $5 billion. The U.S. currently has no spending in the blue box, however, CCP outlays are estimated at $4.2 billion in FY2005.[32]

Market Access

There is substantial potential for U.S. agricultural exports to expand under an international system of improved market access based on lower tariffs and increased quotas. In contrast, further reductions in tariff levels are unlikely to produce significant increases in imports for most U.S. agricultural commodities since U.S. agricultural tariffs are already very low relative to most other nations and relatively few commodities receive tariff-rate quota (TRQ) protection.

Dairy products, beef, and sugar are three of the major U.S. beneficiaries of TRQ protection. Each of these products are likely to continue to receive protection as "sensitive" products under a new DDA agreement (although no specific information concerning the identification of sensitive products has yet been made by the United States or any other negotiating country). Expanded quota levels would likely result in increased imports for each of these commodities.

The U.S. proposal does not provide any specificity regarding the administration of TRQs; however, the G-20 proposal recommends that minimum access quotas be set at 6% of domestic consumption for some undefined base period. Australia recommended a higher access quota level of 8-10% of domestic consumption.

Potential Economic Impact on U.S. Agriculture

In response to a request by the Chairman of the Senate Agriculture Committee, Senator Chambliss, the Food and Agricultural Policy Research Institute (FAPRI) analyzed the potential impacts on U.S. agriculture of the U.S. proposal (see Tables 1-3 for details of the U.S. proposal).[33] Under the U.S. proposal, the amber box (AMS) annual limit falls to $7.6 billion (representing a 60% cut from the previous $19.1 billion limit). To achieve this lower spending limit, FAPRI had to make specific assumptions about U.S. farm policy reform (see Table 4).[34] In particular, loan rates for grain, oilseed, and cotton, and the dairy support price were reduced by 11%; sugar loan rates were reduced by 16% (to avoid excessive stock accumulation); and CCP payments were redirected from the amber box to the redefined blue box. For all non-sensitive products, tariff reductions are made in accordance with the tiers described in Table 2. In addition, for each designated sensitive product TRQs were increased by 7.5% of the 1999-2001 level of domestic consumption. Finally, export subsidies are eliminated by 2010.

In addition to the above program changes, two scenarios were evaluated: an "uncompensated" scenario where all target prices were reduced by 7%; and a "compensated" scenario where instead of lowering target prices, direct payment rates were increased by 7%. CCP payments equal the target price minus the per unit direct payment rate minus the higher of the loan rate or the market price. Thus, both of these scenarios have the effect of lowering CCP payments by 7%. The difference is that in the "compensated" scenario government outlays are increased to offset the lower CCP payment. Replacing non-product specific CCP payments with decoupled direct payments represents shifting from the capped blue box to the unlimited green box. A summary of the net effect of these changes is presented in Table 4 and are described briefly below.

Under the Uncompensated Scenario

Annual net government outlays are reduced by 22.5% but net farm income is still up by $1.3 billion (2.4%) as increases in prices resulting from increased exports offsets at least some of the reduction in payments. Rice producers experience a sharp jump (5.7%) in combined market returns plus government payments. However, returns plus payments remain below baseline levels for corn, soybeans, and cotton.

Under the Compensated Scenario

Annual net farm income is up by $3.4 billion (6.5%) as the increase in direct payments further offsets reductions in CCPs and loan benefits. For rice, wheat, corn, and soybeans, average estimated returns plus payments exceed the baseline levels. Of the five major program crops, only for cotton do returns plus payments remain below baseline levels.

Table 4. Summary of FAPRI Analysis of U.S. Proposal

	Baseline[a]	Absolute Changes		Percent Changes	
		Uncompensated[b]	Compensated[c]	Uncompensated[b]	Compensated[c]
Policy change					
Sugar loan rates				-16%	-16%
Milk support price				-11%	-11%
Target prices (TP)				-7%	-7%
Direct payment rates				0%	7%*TP[d]
WTO Indicators		$ billion			
AMS limit	19.1	7.6	7.6	-60%	-60%
Product-Specific AMS	9.4	4.7	4.7	-50%	-50%
Blue box limit	9.5	4.8	4.8	-50%	-50%
CCPs	3.1	1.5	1.5	-50%	-50%
Net Govt Outlays	16.5	12.5	16.0	-24%	-3%
Crop Returns + Govt payments		$ per acre			
Corn	424	418	434	-1.3%	2.4%
Soybeans	254	247	257	-2.5%	1.5%
Wheat	177	179	187	0.8%	5.1%
Upland Cotton	582	545	571	-6.3%	-1.8%
Rice	768	812	841	5.7%	9.5%
Farm Income		$ billion			
Crop Receipts	125.1	127.1	127.1	1.6%	1.6%
Livestock Receipts	112.2	116.4	116.4	3.8%	3.7%
Govt payments	16.7	12.9	16.4	-22.5%	-1.8%
Production Costs	237.7	239.1	240.5	0.6%	1.2%
Net Farm Income	53.1	54.4	56.5	2.4%	6.5%

Source: Abridged from Table 1 of FAPRI (2005). The reported data for all categories represent averages for the three-year period, 2012-2014, where all program reforms have been fully implemented.
a. Baseline assumes the elimination of the Step 2 program for cotton, but no other program reforms.
b. The uncompensated scenario assumes program reforms commensurate with the U.S. proposal including a 7% cut in all target prices to achieve a reduction in CCP outlays.
c. The compensated scenario is similar to the uncompensated but uses a 7% increase in per-unit direct payments, instead of a 7% cut in target prices, to achieve a reduction in CCP outlays.
d. Direct payment rates are increased by 7% of the target price for each commodity.

Under Both Scenarios

Crop and livestock receipts are up by about $2 billion and $4.2 billion, respectively. Livestock receipts increase in response to higher prices for cattle, hogs, poultry, and milk, due to increased U.S. meat and poultry exports. Higher crop receipts result from both increased feed demand and exports. Key drivers behind the higher international commodity prices and higher U.S. exports include the following.[35]

- Removal of export subsidies raises prices in the international wheat, barley, rice, sugar, beef, and dairy markets.

- Expansion of TRQs, in general, increase trade in those protected commodities by exposing highly protected markets to lower international prices.
- Tariff reductions, in general, raise the demand for traded products, while reductions of domestic support reduce competition from more inefficient producers.
- Expansion of rice TRQs in Japan and South Korea, in particular, push international rice prices higher by 8% on average.
- Tariff reductions and the removal of the Special Safeguard Mechanism in Japan raise both demand and prices for pork and beef.

In the FAPRI study, U.S. farm real estate values experience small, but significant changes. Under the uncompensated scenario, average U.S. farm land values decline by 1.4% as the reduction in government payments (-22.5%) more than offsets higher market returns. Factors other than net market returns and payments affect land values, but changes in profitability play an important role and (in the uncompensated scenario) translate into lower projected future revenue streams to the land. Under the compensated scenario, farm real estate values increase by 1.7% as slightly lower projected government payments (-1.8%) are more than offset by expected market returns suggesting improved long-run returns to the land.

APPENDIX

Table 1. Chronology of Key Events

Dates	Key Events
1986-1994	Uruguay Round of multilateral trade negotiations.
1994	Uruguay Round culminated in the establishment of the World Trade Organization (WTO). The Agreement on Agriculture was one of 29 legal texts underwriting the WTO and its administration of rules governing international trade.
Nov. 9-13, 2001	Current Doha Development Agenda (DDA) or Doha Round of multilateral negotiations was initiated in Doha, Qatar.
July 31, 2004	WTO Doha Round negotiations produce an interim guideline document, the *Framework Agreement*, to solidify existing commitments and to guide negotiations of details for final agricultural agreement.
Jan. 1, 2005	Current Doha Round of multilateral negotiations was scheduled to end, but several 2003 and 2004 deadlines were missed. As a result, DDA negotiations continue with no formal schedule, but subject to several looming deadlines.
Summer 2005	USDA initiates farm bill listening sessions around the country.
Oct. 10-14, 2005	Series of position papers released by major negotiations participants including the U.S., EU, G-10, and G-20.
Oct. 27, 2005	EU released updated proposal in response to concerns about the inadequacy of its first proposal's market access offerings.
Dec. 13-18, 2005	WTO Hong Kong Ministerial.
July 24, 2006	Indefinite Suspension of Doha Development Agenda Negotiations
July 1, 2007	U.S. Trade Promotion Authority expires
Sept. 30, 2007	2002 farm bill expires.

Source: Compiled by CRS from various sources.

APPENDIX

Table 2. Key Players in the WTO DDA Negotiations

Group	Members
Big Two	U.S. and EU.
Big Three	U.S., EU, and Japan.
New Quad	U.S., EU, India, and Brazil.
C-4	The group of 4 African cotton-producing countries — Benin, Burkina Faso, Chad, and Mali — that have proposed a sectoral Doha Round initiative for cotton.
FIPS	Five Interested Parties: U.S., EU, Brazil, India, and Australia.
FIPS Plus	FIPS plus Argentina, Canada, Switz., Japan, China, and Malaysia
G-5	Group of Five: U.S., EU, Japan, India, and Brazil.
G-6	G-5 plus Australia.
G-7	A group of 7 nations — U.S., Japan, Canada, Britain, France, Germany, and Italy — whose finance ministers and/or Heads of State meet to discuss political and economic developments.
G-8	G-7 plus Russia.
(G-8)+5	G-8 plus 5 countries — Brazil, India, Mexico, China, and South Africa — with major emerging economies.
G-10	Group of 10 developed, net importing countries that subsidize domestic agriculture: Bulgaria, Iceland, Israel, Japan, South Korea, Liechtenstein, Mauritius, Norway, Switzerland, and Chinese Taipei.
G-20	Group of some 20+ major developing countries whose members vary but essentially includes Argentina, Bolivia, Brazil, Chile, China, Colombia, Costa Rica, Cuba, Ecuador, Egypt, El Salvador, Guatemala, India, Mexico, Nigeria, Pakistan, Paraguay, Peru, Philippines, South Africa, Thailand, and Venezuela.
G-33	Group of 33 (now expanded to 42) developing countries otherwise called the "friends of special products" including China, Turkey, Indonesia, India, Pakistan, plus some African, Caribbean, South American, and Asian countries.
G-90	Group of Least-Developed Countries (LDCs).
Cairns Group	Members are generally free-market oriented and supportive of increased trade liberalization. Members include Argentina, Australia, Bolivia, Brazil, Canada, Chile, Colombia, Costa Rica, Guatemala, Indonesia, Malaysia, New Zealand, Paraguay, Philippines, South Africa, Thailand, and Uruguay.
LDCs	The WTO recognizes as least-developed countries (LDCs) those countries which have been designated as such by the United Nations. There are currently 50 LDCs on the U.N. list, 32 of which to date have become WTO members. A complete listing is available at [http://www.wto.org/english/thewto_e/whatis_e/tif_e/org7_e.htm].

Note: For more information, see the WTO trade negotiations background report, *WTO Agriculture Negotiations: The Issues, and Where We Are Now,* "Key to Groups," Dec. 1, 2004, pp. 83-84; available at [http://www.wto.org/english/tratop_e/agric_e/agnegs_bkgrnd_e.doc].

APPENDIX

Table 3. Key Terms From the WTO Agreement on Agriculture and the DDA

1. The *Agreement on Agriculture* (AA)
Text of agricultural policy reform commitments agreed to under the Uruguay Round (1986-1994) of WTO multilateral trade negotiations.
2. The *Three Pillars* of agricultural policy reform
    a. Export competition
        i. Export subsidies
        ii. Export credit
        iii. Food Aid
        iv. State Trading Enterprises
    b. Domestic Support
        i. Aggregate Measure of Support (AMS): summary measure of a country's total level of trade-distorting domestic subsidies.
        ii. Amber box: non-exempt trade-distorting subsidies; individual members' amber box bounds are listed in their country schedules.
        iii. Blue box: production-limited subsidies; unbound.
        iv. De Minimis-non-product specific: bound <5% of total production. value.
        v. De Minimis-product specific: bound <5% of specific prod. value.
        vi. Green Box: minimally distorting subsidies; unbound.
    c. Market Access
        i. Bound and Applied Tariffs
        ii. Sensitive Products Treatment
        iii. Tariff Rate Quotas (TRQs) administration
        iv. Special Safeguard Mechanisms (SSMs)
3. *Special and Differential Treatment (SDT)* for developing countries
    a. Smaller commitments and longer implementation periods
    b. Other flexibilities and privileges
4. *Least-Developing Countries* a. Free Round: no new commitments
5. *WTO Framework Agreement* (referred to as the "Framework")
    a. The Framework provided agreement on a general framework for reform within each of the three main "pillars" of agricultural trade with details to be worked out in subsequent negotiations.
    b. The Framework touched on several "non-pillar" issues: including cotton subsidies and geographical indications.

Source: For detailed definitions see "CRS Reports" listed in Information Sources, above.

INFORMATION SOURCES

CRS Reports

CRS Report RL32060, World Trade Organization Negotiations: The Doha Development Agenda, by Ian F. Fergusson.

CRS Report RS21905, Agriculture in the WTO Doha Round: The Framework Agreement and Next Steps, by Charles E. Hanrahan.

CRS Report RL33553, Agricultural Export and Food Aid Programs, by Charles E. Hanrahan.

CRS Report RL32278, Trends in U.S. Agricultural Export Credit Guarantee Programs and P.L. 480, Title I, FY1992-2002, by Carol Canada.

CRS Report RL32916, Agriculture in the WTO: Policy Commitments Made Under the Agreement on Agriculture, by Randy Schnepf.

CRS Report RL30612, Agriculture in the WTO: Member Spending on Domestic Support, by Randy Schnepf.

CRS Report RS20840, Agriculture in the WTO: Limits on Domestic Support, by Randy Schnepf.

CRS Report RS21569, Geographical Indications and WTO Negotiations, by Charles E. Hanrahan.

CRS Report RS21712, The African Cotton Initiative and WTO Agriculture Negotiations, by Charles E. Hanrahan.

Other Sources

Anderson, Kym, and Will Martin, Eds., *Agricultural Trade Reform and the Doha Development Agenda*, (New York: Palgrave Macmillan and the World Bank, 2006); available at [http://web.worldbank.org/WBSITE/EXTERNAL/TOPICS/TRADE/ 0,,contentMDK:20517767~menuPK:207652~pagePK:148956~piPK:216618~the SitePK:239071,00.html].

Congressional Budget Office (CBO), *The Effects of Liberalizing World Agricultural Trade: A Survey*, Dec. 2005; available at [http://www.cbo.gov/ftpdocs/69xx/ doc6909/12-01-TradeLib.pdf].

European Commission, Agriculture, International Trade Relations, [http://europa.eu.int/comm/agriculture/external/wto/index_en.htm].

Food and Agricultural Policy Research Institute (FAPRI), *Potential Impacts on U.S. Agriculture of the U.S. October 2005 WTO Proposal*, FAPRI-UMC Report #16-05, Dec. 15, 2005; available at [http://www.fapri.missouri.edu/outreach/publications/2005/FAPRI_UMC_Report_16_05.pdf].

FAPRI, *U.S. Proposal for WTO Agricultural Negotiations: Its Impact on U.S. and World Agriculture*, CARD Working Paper 05-WP 417, December 2005; available at [http://www.card.iastate.edu/publications/DBS/PDFFiles/05wp417.pdf].

Office of the U.S. Trade Representative (USTR), Online information on U.S. trade negotiations and agreements, available at [http://www.ustr.gov/].

Polaski, Sandra, *Winners and Losers: Impact of the Doha Round on Developing Countries*, Carnegie Endowment Report, March 2006. [http://www.carnegieendowment.org/publications/index.cfm?fa=view and id=18083 and prog=zgp and proj=zted].

USDA, FAS, *International Trade Policy Division*, Online information on U.S. trade negotiations and agreements, [http://www.fas.usda.gov/itp/policy/tradepolicy.asp].

USDA, ERS, *World Trade Organization Briefing Room*, [http://www.ers.usda.gov/briefing/WTO/].

WTO, *Agriculture Negotiations: Backgrounder: The Issues and Where We Are Now*, [http://www.wto.org/english/tratop_e/agric_e/negs_bkgrnd00_contents_e.htm].

REFERENCES

[1] For discussions of the potential for WTO legal challenges to U.S. farm subsidies, see "When the Peace Clause Ends: The Vulnerability of EC and US Agricultural Subsidies to WTO Legal Challenges," by Richard H. Steinberg and Timothy Josling, *Journal of International Economic Law*, vol. 6, No. 2 (July 2003), available at [http://papers.ssrn.com/ sol3/papers.cfm?abstract_id=413883]; and "Why the EU and the USA must reform their subsidies, or pay the price," *Oxfam Briefing Paper 81*, November 2005, available at [http://www.oxfam.org/en/policy/briefing papers/bp81_truth].

[2] For an analysis of the Brazil-U.S. cotton dispute, see CRS Report RL32571, *Background on the U.S.-Brazil WTO Cotton Subsidy Dispute*, by Randy Schnepf; and CRS Report RS22187, *U.S. Agricultural Policy Response to WTO Cotton Decision*, by Randy Schnepf.

[3] Statement of U.S. Trade Representative, Susan C., Schwab, at her joint press conference with Malaysian Minister of Commerce and Industry, Datuk Rafidah Aziz, Kuala Lumpur, Malaysia, August 25, 2006, viewed on August 30, 2006, at [http://www.insidetrade.com/ secure/pdf9/wto2006_5220.pdf.]

[4] "G_20 meeting Unlikely to Provide Breakthrough for Doha Round," *Inside U.S. Trade*, Sept. 8, 2006; available at [http://www.insidetrade.com/secure/ dsply_nl_txt.asp?f= wto2002. ask and dh=61120272 and q=]

[5] Information about the Cairns Group is available at [http://www.cairnsgroup.org/].

[6] The declaration of the WTO's Sixth Ministerial Conference in Hong Kong, hereafter referred to as the Hong Kong (HK) declaration is available at [http://www.wto.org/english/ thewto_e/ minist_e/min05_e/final_text_e.pdf].

[7] See Appendix Table 3 for definitions of these terms.

[8] SSGs are presently available to all WTO members (not just developing countries) that have them listed in their country schedules. See CRS Report RL32916 *Agriculture in the WTO: Policy Commitments Made Under the Agreement on Agriculture*.

[9] See CRS Report RS22187, U.S. Agricultural Policy Response to the WTO Cotton Decision.

[10] Letter to the Honorable Rob Portman, U.S. Trade Representative, Oct. 6, 2005, from Senator Saxby Chambliss, Chairman of the Senate Committee on Agriculture, Nutrition

and Forestry, and Representative Bob Goodlatte, Chairman, House Committee on Agriculture.
[11] "A Less Ambitious Hong Kong Conference," *Washington Trade Daily*, vol. 14, no. 222, Nov. 9, 2005.
[12] The draft ministerial text is available at [http://www.wto.org/english/thewto_e/minist_e/min05_e/draft_text_e.htm].
[13] For a detailed discussion of the initiative, see CRS Report RS21712, The African Cotton Initiative and WTO Agriculture Negotiations, by Charles E. Hanrahan. The original proposal, WTO Negotiations on Agriculture, Poverty Reduction: Sectoral Initiative in Favour of Cotton: Joint proposal by Benin, Burkina Faso, Chad, and Mali, Committee on Agriculture, Special Session, TN/AG/GEN/4, May 16, 2003, was revised in WTO, General Council, Poverty Reduction: Sectoral Initiative on Cotton: Wording of Paragraph 27 of the Revised Draft Cancun Ministerial Text: Communication from Benin, WT/GC/W/516, October 7, 2003. These documents can be retrieved from [http://www.wto.org].
[14] Paragraph 1(b) of the July Framework agreement addresses the cotton issue.
[15] These two proposals are reviewed at the WTO website at [http://www.wto.org/english/news_e/news05_e/cotton_18nov05_e.htm].
[16] The African and EU proposals for a sectoral initiative on cotton as well as the U.S. reaction are also discussed in "U.S. Links Cotton-Specific Moves on Overall Agriculture Deal," *Inside U.S. Trade*, November 18, 2005.
[17] See CRS Report RL32053, *Agriculture in the WTO*, by Charles E. Hanrahan.
[18] See CRS Report RL32060, *World Trade Organization Negotiations: The Doha Development Agenda*, for an overview of Doha Round negotiating issues.
[19] The Doha Ministerial Declaration launching the DDA negotiations is at [http://www.wto.org/english/tratop_e/dda_e/dda_e.htm#dohadeclaration]. Paragraphs 13 and 14 of the Doha declaration set out the agricultural negotiating mandate.
[20] See CRS Report RS21905, Agriculture in the WTO Doha Round: The Framework Agreement and Next Steps, by Charles E. Hanrahan. The framework agreement known as the Doha Work Programme: Decision Adopted by the General Council on August 1, 2004 is at [http://www.wto.org/english/tratop_e/dda_e/ddadraft_31jul04_e.pdf].
[21] USDA, Economic Research Service, WTO Agricultural Trade Policy Commitments Database, WTO Export Subsidy Notifications, "Total export subsidies by country, 1995-2001" available at [http://www.ers.usda.gov/db/Wto/ExportSubsidy_database/Default.asp?ERSTab=2].
[22] See Appendix Table 4 of RL30612 as listed in Information Sources below.
[23] The Congressional Budget Office (CBO) examined several economic studies of global trade liberalization completed during the 2001 to 2005 period and have summarized the results in its report, *The Effects of Liberalizing World Agricultural Trade: A Survey*, Dec. 2005; available at [http://www.cbo.gov/ftpdocs/69xx/doc6909/12-01-TradeLib.pdf].
[24] Ibid., p. 9.
[25] Ibid., p. 10.
[26] See footnote 12 for source.
[27] For more information, see CRS Report RL32278, *Trends in U.S. Agricultural Export Credit Guarantee Programs and P.L. 480, Title I, FY1992-2002*; and USDA, Foreign

Agricultural Service, Export Programs at [http://www.fas.usda.gov/ exportprograms.asp].

[28] For more information, see CRS Report RL32014, WTO Dispute Settlement: Status of U.S. Compliance in Pending Cases; and CRS Report RS22187, U.S. Agricultural Policy Response to WTO Cotton Decision.

[29] For more information, see CRS Report RL33553, *Agricultural Export and Food Aid Programs*.

[30] For more information, see CRS Report RL30612, Agriculture in the WTO: Member Spending on Domestic Support.

[31] The CCP program was first authorized under the 2002 farm bill. U.S. notification to the WTO of its domestic spending is complete through 2001. As a result, the U.S. has not yet notified CCP spending as pertaining to a specific box. However, its design and operation suggest that CCP spending would qualify as a non-product specific AMS outlay.

[32] See CRS Report RS21970, *The Farm Economy*.

[33] FAPRI, *Potential Impacts on U.S. Agriculture of the U.S. October 2005 WTO Proposal*, FAPRI-UMC Report #16-05, Dec. 15, 2005, hereafter referred to as FAPRI (2005); available at [http://www.fapri.missouri.edu/outreach/publications/2005/FAPRI_UMC_Report_16_05.pdf]. The Center for Agricultural and Rural Development (CARD) conducted supporting analysis of the effects on global markets in *U.S. Proposal for WTO Agricultural Negotiations: Its Impact on U.S. and World Agriculture*, CARD Working Paper 05-WP 417, Dec. 2005, hereafter referred to as CARD (2005); available at [http://www.card.iastate.edu/ publications/DBS/PDFFiles/05wp417.pdf].

[34] The program changes were selected so as to restrict violation of WTO limits to less than 5% of the stochastic outcomes from 500 simulations runs. See FAPRI (2005) for details.

[35] For more details see CARD (2005).

In: The World Trade Organization: Another Round
Editor: Harold B. Whitiker, pp. 121-127

ISBN: 978-1-60021-816-3
© 2007 Nova Science Publishers, Inc.

Chapter 4

U.S. AGRICULTURAL POLICY RESPONSE TO WTO COTTON DECISION[*]

Randy Schnepf

ABSTRACT

In a dispute settlement case (DS267) brought by Brazil against certain aspects of the U.S. cotton program, a WTO Appellate Body (AB) recommended in March 2005 that the United States remove certain "prohibited subsidies" by July 21, 2005, and remove the adverse effects resulting from certain "actionable subsidies" by September 21, 2005. When the United States failed to meet these deadlines, Brazil claimed the right to retaliate against $3 billion in U.S. exports to Brazil based on the prohibited subsidies, and proposed $1 billion in retaliation based on the actionable subsidies. The United States objected to these retaliation amounts and requested WTO arbitration on the matter. However, in mid-2005 the United States and Brazil reached a procedural agreement to temporarily suspend retaliation proceedings.

On August 21, 2006, Brazil submitted a request for a WTO compliance panel to review whether the United States has fully complied with panel and AB rulings. The United States blocked the WTO's Dispute Settlement Body (DSB) from approving Brazil's request on August 31, 2006; however, Brazil is expected to make a second request (which the United States will be unable to block) at the DSB meeting set for September 28, 2006. If a compliance panel finds that the United States has not fully complied with the AB rulings, Brazil could ask the WTO arbitration panel to resume its work. Although the United States has already complied with a portion of the AB's recommendation by eliminating the Step 2 program (August 1, 2006), additional permanent modifications to U.S. farm programs may still be needed to fully comply with the WTO ruling on "actionable subsidies."

---

[*] Excerpted from CRS Report RS22187, dated September 8, 2006.

INTRODUCTION

The United States is the world's largest cotton exporter. During the 2001-2003 period, U.S. exports accounted for 40% of world trade, on average, while government domestic subsidies averaged $3 billion per year. In late 2002, Brazil — a major cotton export competitor — expressed its growing concerns about U.S. cotton subsidies by initiating a WTO dispute settlement case (DS267) against specific provisions of the U.S. cotton program. On September 8, 2004, a WTO dispute settlement panel ruled against the United States on several key issues (WT/DS267/R). On March 3, 2005, a WTO Appellate Body (AB) upheld the panel's ruling on appeal (WT/DS267/AB/R). On March 21, 2005, the panel and AB reports were adopted by the WTO membership, initiating a sequence of events, under WTO dispute settlement rules, whereby the United States is expected to bring its policies into line with the panel's recommendations or negotiate a mutually acceptable settlement with Brazil.[1]

THE WTO DISPUTE SETTLEMENT PANEL'S RECOMMENDATION

In their ruling against the United States, the WTO panel and AB recommended that the United States withdraw those support programs identified as "prohibited" subsidies within six months of adoption of the panel's and AB's reports by the WTO membership or by July 1, 2005, whichever was earlier; and that it remove the prejudicial effects of those programs identified as "actionable" subsidies by September 21, 2005. Each of these subsidy types — prohibited and actionable — involves a different type of response and a different timetable for implementing that response.[2]

Prohibited Subsidies

Two types of prohibited subsidies were identified by the WTO panel: unscheduled export subsidies (i.e., subsidies applied to commodities not listed on a country's WTO schedule or made in excess of the value listed on the schedule);[3] and import substitution subsidies, which refers to subsidies paid to domestic users to encourage the use of domestic products over imported products. Both Step 2 export payments and export credit guarantees were found to operate as prohibited export subsidies. Step 2 domestic user payments were found to operate as prohibited import substitution subsidies. Under the WTO's Agreement on Agriculture, prohibited subsidies are treated with greater urgency than actionable subsidies — in particular, they are given a shorter time frame for compliance.

Step 2 Program
Step 2 payments were part of special cotton marketing provisions authorized under U.S. farm program legislation to keep U.S. upland cotton competitive on the world market.[4] Step 2 payments were made to exporters and domestic mill users to compensate them for their purchase of U.S. upland cotton, which tends to be priced higher than the world market price.

Export Credit Guarantee Programs

USDA's export credit guarantee programs (GSM-102, GSM-103, and SCGP) underwrite credit extended by private U.S. banks to approved foreign banks for purchases of U.S. food and agricultural products by foreign buyers.[5] GSM-102 covers credit terms up to three years, while GSM-103 covers longer credit terms up to 10 years. The Supplier Credit Guarantee Program (SCGP) insures short-term, open account financing designed to make it easier for exporters to sell U.S. food products overseas. The WTO panel found that all three export credit programs effectively functioned as export subsidies because the financial benefits returned to the government by these programs failed to cover their long-run operating cost. Furthermore, the panel found that this export-subsidy aspect of export credit guarantees applies not just to cotton but to all recipient commodities that benefit from U.S. commodity support programs. In other words, so long as the credit guarantees act as an implicit export subsidy, only U.S. program crops that have scheduled export subsidies (in accordance with the U.S. WTO country schedule) are eligible for U.S. export credit guarantees.[6]

Actionable Subsidies

Any subsidy may be challenged in the WTO (i.e., is "actionable") if it fulfills the WTO definition of a subsidy[7] and is alleged to cause adverse effects to the interests of other WTO members. Actionable U.S. subsidies were identified as contributing to serious prejudice to the interests of Brazil by depressing prices for cotton on the world market during the marketing years 1999-2002. Specifically, this involved those U.S. subsidy measures singled out as price-contingent (i.e., dependent on changes in current market prices) — marketing loan provisions, Step 2 payments, market loss payments, and counter-cyclical payments.[8] The panel recommended that, upon adoption of its final report, the United States take appropriate steps to remove the adverse effects of these subsidies or to withdraw the subsidies entirely.[9] Such subsidies were previously afforded some protection under the so-called "peace clause" (Article 13) of the WTO's Agreement on Agriculture.[10]

BRAZIL'S RESPONSE

Prohibited Subsidies

Because the prohibited export subsidies had not been removed by July 1, 2005, Brazil requested (July 4, 2005) authorization from the WTO to impose countermeasures against U.S. cotton subsidies. According to WTO rules, trade sanctions are limited to a value not to exceed the level of lost benefits. Brazil proposed to suspend tariff concessions as well as obligations under the WTO Agreement on Trade-Related Intellectual Property Rights and the General Agreement on Trade in Services until the United States withdrew the exports subsidies identified by the WTO, in an amount estimated at $3 billion, corresponding to (1) Step 2 payments made in the most recently concluded marketing year (2004/05) and (2) the total of exporter applications received under the three export credit guarantee programs, for all unscheduled commodities and for rice, for the most recent fiscal year (2004).[11] The United

States objected to the amount of Brazil's proposed sanctions, and requested WTO arbitration (July 19, 2005; WT/DS267/24). However, the United States and Brazil reached a procedural agreement (Aug. 18, 2005; WT/DS267/25) temporarily suspending arbitration proceedings insofar as the prohibited subsidies are involved.

Actionable Subsidies

To date, the Administration has not announced any specific initiative to address the programs deemed to cause prejudicial impact to Brazil's trade interest. Because the prejudicial effects of the price-contingent actionable subsidies had not been removed by September 21, 2005, Brazil requested authorization from the WTO to impose additional countermeasures valued at $1 billion as retaliation against the programs causing serious prejudice. Once again, the United States requested WTO arbitration (Oct 18, 2005; WT/DS267/27) over the level of the proposed sanctions. However, the United States and Brazil reached another procedural agreement (Dec. 7, 2005; WT/DS267/29) suspending further retaliation proceedings insofar as the actionable subsidies are involved.

U.S. RESPONSE

With respect to the "prohibited subsidies," the Step 2 cotton program, which was authorized by the 2002 farm act (P.L. 107-171; Sect. 1207), was eliminated on August 1, 2006, by a provision (Sec. 1103) in the Deficit Reduction Act of 2005 (P.L. 109-171). As for export credit guarantees, user fees for GSM-102, the primary export credit program, presently are capped at 1% of the value of the export product. Higher fees are needed to ensure that the financial benefits returned by these programs fully cover their long-run operating costs; thereby eliminating their subsidy component. On July 1, 2005, USDA instituted a temporary fix whereby the Commodity Credit Corporation (CCC) would use a risk-based fee structure for the GSM-102 and SCGP programs.[12] The new structure responds to a key finding by the WTO that the fees charged by the programs should be risk-based. In addition, the CCC stopped accepting applications for payment guarantees under GSM-103. On July 5, 2005, USDA Secretary Johanns proposed that Congress implement statutory changes to comply with the prohibited subsidy ruling that included the removal of the 1% cap on fees that can be charged under the GSM-102 program and termination of the GSM-103 program.[13] According to Secretary Johanns the proposed changes were worked out in collaboration with U.S. industry groups.

Additional permanent modifications to U.S. farm programs may still be needed to fully comply with the "actionable subsidies" portion of the WTO ruling. The National Cotton Council (NCC) has been watching the U.S. policy response to this case very closely. The NCC is an industry group representing cotton producers, ginners, warehousers, merchants, cottonseed processors/dealers, cooperatives and textile manufacturers. While the NCC has expressed interest in working with Congress in effecting a "fair and appropriate" response to the WTO case, in previous testimony to Congress the NCC leadership has also expressed interest in participating in the WTO's rules-based international trading system and in maintaining an effective U.S. cotton program that complies with WTO rules.[14]

RECENT DEVELOPMENTS

Brazil continues to undertake the procedural steps necessary to preserve its authority under the auspices of the WTO to retaliate in the event of noncompliance by the United States. However, Brazil has shown a willingness to permit the U.S. legislative process to make the changes needed to bring its farm programs into compliance with the WTO ruling, even if this process extends well beyond the deadlines established under the WTO dispute settlement ruling. For example, Brazil agreed to suspend retaliation arbitration for both the prohibited and actionable subsidy cases, partly because the U.S. proposal to eliminate the Step 2 cotton program signaled U.S. intentions to fully remove the prohibited subsidies, and partly due to the expectation that further changes to the actionable subsidy component of the U.S. cotton program would be reached as part of a negotiated solution under the Doha Round of WTO trade negotiations and that such changes would then be incorporated as part of the next U.S. farm bill.

In July 2006, the Doha Round talks were suspended indefinitely. Shortly thereafter, on August 21, 2006, Brazil submitted a request for a WTO compliance panel to review whether the United States has fully complied with panel and AB rulings. The United States blocked the WTO's Dispute Settlement Body (DSB) from approving Brazil's request on August 31, 2006; however, Brazil is expected to make a second request (which the United States will be unable to block) at the DSB meeting set for September 28, 2006. Under Article 21.5 of the Understanding on Rules and Procedures Governing the Settlement of Procedures, a compliance panel would have 90 days to reach a decision with the possibility of requesting an extension. A decision by the compliance panel could also be appealed and the AB also would have 90 days to reach a decision. If the compliance panel found that the United States has not fully complied with the AB rulings, Brazil could ask the WTO arbitration panel to resume its work, with a decision within 60 days, according to the U.S.-Brazil agreement on prohibited subsidies.[15]

U.S. failure to comply could result in WTO-sanctioned trade retaliation by Brazil against the United States. The U.S. response to the WTO cotton ruling is being watched closely by developing countries, particularly by a consortium of four African cotton-producing countries that has submitted its own proposal to the WTO calling for a global agreement to end all production-related support for cotton growers of all WTO-member countries.[16]

POTENTIAL EFFECTS TO U.S. AGRICULTURE OF PROPOSED CHANGES

Eliminating the Step 2 Program

The Step 2 program channeled $3 billion to the U.S. cotton industry during the 1996-2005 period.[17] In July 2005, USDA's chief economist, Keith Collins, suggested that ending the Step 2 program would result in slightly lower domestic prices — by two to three cents per pound — and higher export prices for U.S. cotton.[18] But he also anticipated that declines in producer prices would be likely to trigger an increase in counter-cyclical payments (CCP) to U.S. cotton farmers that would offset losses from lower prices. A December 2005 analysis by the Food and Agricultural Policy Research Institute (FAPRI) found a -1.3¢ decline in U.S. farm price and a 0.4¢ rise in international prices due to the elimination of Step 2 payments.[19]

Changing GSM-102 and Terminating GSM-103

In FY2004, about 11% of U.S. cotton exports were facilitated with export credit guarantees — FY2004 U.S. cotton exports were valued at $4.5 billion, of which $480 million were facilitated with GSM-102 export credit guarantees and another $8 million relied on SCGP guarantees. Redesign of export credit guarantees (as discussed above) would likely have a small but negative effect on U.S. cotton exports, thus reinforcing the results of removing Step 2.

ROLE OF CONGRESS

Ultimately, Congress is responsible for passing farm program legislation that complies with U.S. commitments in international trade agreements. The Step 2 program has already been permanently eliminated by a provision in the Deficit Reduction Act of 2005 (Sec. 1103, P.L. 109-171). Further statutory changes could be needed to eliminate the "subsidy" component of export credit guarantees as represented by the 1% cap on user fees. In addition, changes to those programs, specific to cotton, deemed part of the actionable subsidy ruling (i.e., CCP and marketing loan provision) would also necessitate legislative action. The legislation authorizing current farm programs is not set to expire until 2007. Senate Agriculture Committee Chairman Saxby Chambliss has said that he would review the Administration's proposal and work with industry and the Administration to identify the appropriate legislative solution for complying with the WTO ruling.[20]

REFERENCES

[1]   For a detailed discussion of the U.S.-Brazil WTO dispute settlement case, see CRS Report RL32571, *Background on the U.S.-Brazil WTO Cotton Subsidy Dispute*, by Randy Schnepf.

[2]   For disputes involving prohibited (or WTO-illegal) subsidies, the prescribed remedy compliance time is halved. For more information on WTO disputes, see CRS Report RL32014, *WTO Dispute Settlement: Status of U.S. Compliance in Pending Cases*, by Jeanne Grimmett.

[3]   For more information, see CRS Report RL32916, Agriculture in the WTO: Policy Commitments Made Under the Agreement on Agriculture, by Randy Schnepf.

[4] For more information on Step 2 payments, see CRS Report RL32442, *Cotton Production and Support in the United States*, by Jasper Womach.
[5] For information on these programs, see USDA, Foreign Agricultural Service, "Export Credit Guarantee Programs," at [http://www.fas.usda.gov/excredits/default.htm].
[6] For more information on country schedules, see CRS Report RL32916 *Agriculture in the WTO: Policy Commitments Made Under the Agreement on Agriculture*, by Randy Schnepf.
[7] As defined in Article 1 of the WTO's Agreement on Subsidies and Countervailing Measures.
[8] For more information on these programs, see CRS Report RL33271, Farm Commodity Programs: Direct Payments, Counter-Cyclical Payments, and Marketing Loans, by Jim Monke.
[9] *Report of the Panel*, WTO, WT/DS267/R, para. 7.1503, p. 354.
[10] For more information, see CRS Report RL32571, *Background on the U.S.-Brazil WTO Cotton Subsidy Dispute*, by Randy Schnepf.
[11] For details, see CRS Report RL32014, WTO Dispute Settlement: Status of U.S. Compliance in Pending Cases, by Jeanne J. Grimmett.
[12] USDA press release No. 0238.05, June 30, 2005. For more information on the implementation of USDA's risk-based fee structure, see [http://www.fas.usda.gov/excredits/default.htm].
[13] USDA press release No. 0242.05, July 5, 2005.
[14] Statement of Woody Anderson, then-chairman, National Cotton Council, before the U.S. Congress, House Committee on Agriculture, May 19, 2004; available at [http://agriculture.house.gov/hearings/108/10829.pdf].
[15] "Brazil to Ask for WTO Cotton Compliance Panel in September," *Inside U.S. Trade*, Aug. 18, 2006; available at [http://www.insidetrade.com].
[16] For more information, see CRS Report RS21712, *The African Cotton Initiative and WTO Agriculture Negotiations*, by Charles Hanrahan.
[17] USDA, Farm Service Agency, Table 35-CCC, *Net Outlays by Commodity and Function*; available at [http://www.fsa.usda.gov/dam/bud/bud1.htm].
[18] "More Cotton Program Changes," *Washington Trade Daily*, Vol.14, p. 131-132, Jul. 5-6, 2005.
[19] FAPRI, Potential Impacts on U.S. Agriculture of the U.S. October 2005 WTO Proposal, FAPRI-UMC Report #16-05, December 15, 2005.
[20] "USDA Calls for Repeal of Cotton Subsidy to Achieve WTO Compliance," *Inside U.S. Trade*, July 8, 2005.

In: The World Trade Organization: Another Round
Editor: Harold B. Whitiker, pp. 129-151

ISBN: 978-1-60021-816-3
© 2007 Nova Science Publishers, Inc.

Chapter 5

RUSSIA'S ACCESSION TO THE WTO[*]

William H. Cooper

ABSTRACT

In 1993, Russia formally applied for accession to the General Agreement on Tariffs and Trade (GATT). Its application was taken up by the World Trade Organization (WTO) in 1995, the successor organization of the GATT. Russia's application has entered into its most significant phase as Russia negotiates with WTO members on the conditions for accession.

Accession to the WTO is critical to Russia and its political leadership. President Vladimir Putin has made it a top priority. He views accession as an important step in integrating the Russian economy with the rest of the world and in fostering economic growth and development by attracting foreign investment and by lowering trade barriers. For the United States, the European Union (EU) and other trading partners, Russia's accession to the WTO could increase stability and predictability in Russia's foreign trade and investment regime.

The Russian accession process is moving forward, but differences over some critical issues remain, making the time for Russian accession to the WTO uncertain. The European Union and the United States have raised concerns about Russian energy pricing policies which allow natural gas, oil, and electricity to be sold domestically far below world prices providing, they argue, a subsidy to domestic producers of fertilizers, steel, and other energy-intensive goods. Russia counters that the subsidies are not illegal under the WTO. Concerns regarding Russian trade barriers in the services sector, high tariffs for civil aircraft and autos, and intellectual property rights have slowed down the process and made the original target of completion in 2003 unattainable. There were indications that Russia and its trading partners, including the United States, wanted to see the process completed in time for the July 15-17, 2006, G-8 summit meeting in St. Petersburg chaired by Russian President Putin. Russia and the United States could not reach agreement in the final bilateral negotiations.

Congressional interest in Russia's accession to the WTO is multifaceted. Members of Congress are concerned that Russia enters the WTO under terms and conditions in line with U.S. economic interests, especially gaining access to Russian markets as well as

---

[*] Excerpted from CRS Report RL31979, dated July 17, 2006.

safeguards to protect U.S. import-sensitive industries. Some Members also assert that Congress should have a formal role in approving the conditions under which Russia accedes to the WTO, a role it does not have at this time. A number of Members of Congress and members of the U.S. business community have advised the Bush Administration not to agree too quickly to Russia's accession to the WTO and to ensure that U.S. concerns are met. The Congress has a direct role in determining whether Russia receives permanent normal trade relations (NTR) status which has implications for Russia's membership in the WTO and U.S.-Russian trade relations. Without granting permanent NTR (PNTR) to Russia, the United States would not benefit from the concessions that Russia makes upon accession. Issues regarding Russia's accession to the WTO may arise during the second session of the 109th Congress.

In 1993, Russia formally applied for accession to the General Agreement on Tariffs and Trade (GATT). Its application was taken up by the World Trade Organization (WTO) in 1995, the successor organization of the GATT.[1] Russia's application has entered into its most significant phase as Russia negotiates with WTO members on the conditions for accession. The process is moving forward, but differences over some critical issues remain, making the time for Russian accession to the WTO uncertain.

Accession to the WTO is critical to Russia and its political leadership. President Vladimir Putin has made it a top priority. He views accession as an important step in integrating the Russian economy with the rest of the world and in fostering economic growth and development by attracting foreign investment and by lowering trade barriers. For the United States, the European Union (EU) and other trading partners, Russia's accession to the WTO could increase stability and predictability in Russia's foreign trade and investment regime. Presidents Bush and Putin have discussed Russia's accession to the WTO at their various bilateral meetings. At a September 2005 meeting in Washington, President Bush told the Russian leader that he was "very interested" in seeing Russia's negotiations for WTO accession completed by the end of the year, a deadline that went unmet.[2]

The United States remains the only WTO member out of 58 members that has not reached a bilateral agreement on Russia's accession. The two countries reportedly wanted to have the U.S.-Russian negotiations completed by the July 15-17, 2006 G-8 summit hosted by President Putin in St. Petersburg. Negotiators for the two sides were reportedly very close to reaching agreement. They conducted three days of intense negotiations led by United States Trade Representative Susan Schwab and Russian Economic Development and Trade Minister German Gref, but to no avail. Although the two sides made progress on key issues, the negotiations stopped short of completion because Russia insisted that its inspectors be able to audit U.S. facilities for beef and pork before those products are exported to Russia. Both countries indicated that they could reach an agreement by the end of October 2006.

Congressional interest in Russia's accession to the WTO is multifaceted. Members of Congress are concerned that Russia enters the WTO under terms and conditions in line with U.S. economic interests, especially gaining access to Russian markets as well as safeguards to protect U.S. import-sensitive industries. Some Members also assert that Congress should have a formal role in approving the conditions under which Russia accedes to the WTO, a role it does not have at this time. The Congress has a direct role in determining whether Russia receive permanent normal trade relations (NTR) status which has implications for Russia's membership in the WTO and U.S.-Russian trade relations. Without granting PNTR to Russia, the United States would not benefit from the concessions that Russia makes upon accession.

This article examines the issue of Russia's accession to the WTO, focusing on the implications for Russia, the United States, and the WTO. It begins with a short overview of the WTO accession process and reviews the history of the Soviet Union's relationship with the GATT/WTO. It provides a brief discussion of Russian economic conditions and the status of economic reforms as they are a major impetus for Russia's application to join the WTO. The focus of the article is the status of Russia's accession application and the outstanding issues. The article concludes with an analysis of the implications of Russia's accession to the WTO for Russia, the United States, the other WTO members and for the WTO itself and an analysis of the outlook for the Russia's application.

THE WTO AND THE ACCESSION PROCESS

The WTO's membership of close to 150 countries and customs areas spans all levels of economic development, from the least developed to the most highly developed economies. The WTO came into existence in January 1995 as a part of the agreements reached by the signatories to the General Agreement on Tariffs and Trade (GATT) at the end of the Uruguay Round negotiations. The WTO's primary purpose is to administer the roughly 60 agreements and separate commitments made by its members as part of the GATT (for trade in goods), the General Agreement on Trade in Services (GATS — for trade in services), and the agreement on trade-related aspects of intellectual property rights (TRIPS).

The membership in the GATT/WTO has grown exponentially. The GATT was originally founded in 1947 by 23 countries, and the WTO now has 148 members. Among the most recent entrants are China and Taiwan, which joined on December 11, 2001, and January 1, 2002, respectively, Armenia which joined on February 5, 2003, and the Former Yugoslavian Republic of Macedonia, who joined on April 4, 2003. Membership in the WTO commits its members to fundamental principles in trade with other members, including:

- Most-favored nation treatment (MFN): The imports of goods and services originating from one member country will be treated no less favorably than imports of goods and services from any other member country. MFN is to be unconditional. In practical terms, this means that in most cases a country cannot apply a higher import tariff to a good from one member country than it applies to like goods from any other member country.
- National treatment: Imports of goods and services are treated no less favorably than like goods and services produced domestically. In practical terms this means that governments cannot discriminate against imports in the application of laws and regulations, such as regulations to protect consumer safety or the environment.
- Transparency: Government laws and regulations that affect foreign trade and investment are to be published and available for anyone to see. Procedures to implement the laws and regulations are to be open.
- Lowering Trade Barriers Through Negotiations: Since the GATT's creation, its members have conducted eights rounds of negotiations to lower trade barriers. At first these negotiations focused on lowering tariffs. But over time, the rounds have broadened GATT/WTO coverage to include nontariff barriers, such as discriminatory government procurement practices, discriminatory standards, and trade-distorting government subsidies. The last completed round, the Uruguay Round (1986-94), resulted in the most ambitious expansion of rules to cover, for the first time, trade in agricultural products and services and government policies and practices pertaining

to intellectual property rights protection and foreign investment regulations that affect trade.
- Reliance on tariffs: In order to promote predictability and openness in commerce, the WTO requires member countries to use tariffs and avoid using quotas or other nontariff measures when restricting imports for legitimate purposes, such as on injurious imports.

As part of its function to administer the rules established under the agreements, the WTO provides a mechanism for the settlement of disputes between members where the dispute involves alleged violations of WTO agreements. Moreover, each member's trade regime is reviewed by the WTO Secretariat from time-to-time to ensure that it conforms to WTO rules. Trade among WTO members accounts for about 90% of total world trade. [3]

The collapse of the Soviet Union and its East European Bloc and the movement of many developing countries toward liberal trade policies have spurred interest in joining the WTO. Article XII of the agreement that established the WTO sets out the requirements and procedures for countries to "accede." "Any state or customs territory having full autonomy in the conduct of its trade policies is eligible to accede to the WTO on terms agreed between it and WTO members."

The accession process begins with a letter from the applicant to the WTO requesting membership. The WTO General Council, the governing body of the WTO when the Ministerial Conference is not meeting, forms a Working Party (WP) to consider the application. Membership on the WP is open to any interested member-country. More than sixty member countries, including the United States, are part of the WP. The U.S. delegation is led by the Assistant U.S. Trade Representative for WTO and Multilateral Affairs and includes representatives from the U.S. Departments of Commerce and Agriculture.

The applicant submits a memorandum to the WP that describes in detail its current trade regime. The applicant and the WP then negotiate to determine what legislative and structural changes the applicant must make to meet WTO requirements and to establish the terms and conditions for entry of the applicant into the WTO. The WP's findings are then included in a "Report of the Working Party" and are the basis for drawing up the "Protocol of Accession."

While it negotiates with the WP, the applicant must also conduct bilateral negotiations with each interested WTO member. During these negotiations the WTO member indicates what concessions and commitments on trade in goods and services it *expects* the applicant to make in order to gain entry, and the applicant indicates what concessions and commitments it is *willing* to make until the two agree and set down the terms. The terms of the bilateral agreements are combined into one document which will apply on an MFN basis to all WTO members once the applicant has joined the WTO. The accession package is conveyed to the General Council or Ministerial Conference for approval.

Article XII does not establish a deadline for the process. The length of the process depends on a number of factors: how many legislative and structural changes an applicant must make in its trade regime in order to meet the demands of the WP, how quickly its national and sub- national legislatures can make those changes, and the demands on the applicant made by members in bilateral negotiations and the willingness of the applicant to accept those demands. Because WTO accession is a political process as well as a legal process, its success depends on the political will of all sides — the WTO member countries and the applicant country. A formal vote is taken in the WTO that requires a 2/3 majority for accession, although in practice the WTO has sought to gain a consensus on each application. The process can take a long time: China's application took over 15 years.

THE SOVIET UNION AND THE GATT/WTO

The Soviet Union was not invited to become a contracting-party of the GATT in 1947 after it declined to join the International Monetary Fund (IMF) and the World Bank — the other two multilateral organizations that resulted from the Bretton Woods conference immediately following the end of World War II. In fact, Soviet trade and economic policy conflicted with the principles of the GATT. The GATT was based on removing barriers to trade and on developing economic interdependence among countries. Soviet foreign economic policy was largely based on the concept of self-sufficiency — the domestic economy would produce as much as possible for itself and import only those products which it could not produce. Exports were used merely to buy necessary imports, not to build markets. These economic policies helped to bring about the collapse of the Soviet Union. The Soviet Union modified the concept of self-sufficiency to include members of the Soviet Bloc- the East European countries, some Asian communist countries and Cuba, confining most of its trade with these countries in a system of limited international division of labor. Only a small amount of trade was conducted outside the Bloc. The Soviet Union spearheaded the formation of the Council for Mutual Economic Assistance (CMEA), what could be loosely described as the Soviet Bloc's version of the GATT.

In August 1986, the Soviet Union applied to take part in the Uruguay Round negotiations of the GATT as an observer with the intention of becoming a full member. The United States and other Western industrialized countries opposed the request because of the Soviet Union's central planning economic system.[4] In 1990, however, the Soviet Union received observer status to the Uruguay Round negotiations after GATT signatories, including the United States, concluded that the Soviet Union was moving toward becoming an open economy under President Mikhail Gorbachev.

After the collapse of the Soviet Union in 1991, Russia retained the observer status held by the Soviet Union and, in June 1993, it formally applied to accede to the GATT. On June 16, 1993, the GATT established a working party on Russia's accession and, in January 1995, the application was converted to an application to become a member of the WTO.

RUSSIAN ECONOMIC CONDITIONS AND REFORM: AN IMPETUS FOR JOINING THE WTO

Russia's motivation for and progress toward accession to the WTO are directly related to efforts to dismantle the Soviet economic system of central planning and replace it with a more market-based economy. President Putin has made entry into the WTO a top priority, because he sees it as a mechanism for overcoming the political hurdles that have impeded economic restructuring. The possibility of accession to the WTO has been an opportunity for him to get some significant economic reform legislation through the Russian parliament. Many Russian and foreign experts have argued that these reforms and more are necessary if Russia is to achieve long-term economic growth and development. At the same time, a number of economic interest groups that favor the status-quo, such as agriculture, the auto industry, and raw material producers, have fought against economic reforms and oppose Russian accession to the WTO.

Domestic Economic Conditions

Russia has enjoyed economic growth (measured in annual changes in GDP) since 1999. Russian GDP increased 5.4% in 1999, 9.1% in 2000, and 5.0% in 2001, 5.3% in 2002, 7.3 in 2003, 7.2 in 2004, and 6.4 in 2005.[5] But the growth occurred after a long period of economic stagnation during the final years of the Soviet Union and a deep recession/depression during the 1990s. Many specialists have attributed the economic growth to the depreciation of the ruble and to the rise in world energy prices at the end of the 1990s.

However, Russia has been plagued by economic problems including a high poverty rate and poor health conditions. In addition, economic growth has taken place unevenly throughout the country with the major cities of Moscow and St. Petersburg and regions well-endowed with marketable natural resources accounting for most of the economic growth, while less fortunate regions remained stagnant or have become poorer. Moreover, income distribution among the Russian population has become increasingly unequal as a small portion of the population acquires larger shares of wealth.

Russian Foreign Trade, Investment, and Debt

Since the collapse of the Soviet Union, the Russian economy has become more open to the rest of the world. The role of foreign trade in the Russian economy has grown. By 2005, Russian exports of goods and services were equivalent to 37.2% GDP and imports were equivalent to 21.6% of GDP.[6] Russian foreign trade has become more geographically diverse. In 2005, most of Russian foreign trade took place outside the former Soviet Union — only 14% of Russian exports and 15% of Russian imports were with former Soviet states.[7]

However, the commodity composition of Russian export markets has become less diverse. Russia is increasingly dependent on exports of fuels and raw materials. In 2005, fuels, including crude oil and natural gas, made up 61.1% of Russian exports, an increase from 51.2% in 2001.[8] This trend indicates that Russia's manufacturing sector has not been able to achieve global competitiveness to date. Therefore, Russia has been reluctant to make commitments in the WTO accession negotiations that would further expose its manufacturing sector to global competition.

Russia has enjoyed sizeable foreign trade surpluses over the past few years largely because of the rise in the value of Russian fuel exports resulting from higher world fuel prices and because of the import-substitution driven by the ruble. Russia had a current account surplus of $33.9 billion in 2001 increasing steadily to $84.2 billion in 2005.[9]

Russia's record on the capital account side of the balance of payments has not been as stellar, although it has improved in the last few years. From 1991 through 2005, about $63.2 billion in foreign direct investment *flowed into* Russia. In contrast, *in one year alone* (2005), $79.1 billion in foreign direct investment flowed into China.[10] Russia is substantially behind other former Communist states, such as Hungary, Poland, and the Czech Republic in terms of foreign direct investments on a per capita basis and is even behind such former and poor Soviet states as Armenia, Azerbaijan, and Kazakhstan.[11]

Russian Economic Policy and Restructuring

Russia's transition from central planning was bound to be more difficult and longer than that of the Central and East European states. The communist system was much more entrenched in the Soviet Union than it was in the rest of the Soviet Bloc. Furthermore, Russia does not have a legacy of a market economy to draw on as is the case with some of the Central and East European countries. Russia has had to deal with the legacy of a Soviet economy that was administered to meet the needs of the military while civilian production and investment were given low priority.

However, Russia's economic problems also were the result of policy failures during the transition. These failures included loose monetary and fiscal policies early in the transition period. They have also included structural problems such as poorly developed and executed privatization programs that have left many potentially productive assets in the control of enterprise mangers from the Soviet period or in the hands of a few politically-connected individuals ("oligarchs") who extracted the value from many of these assets rather than making them commercially viable for the long run. In addition, an inefficient banking system, the lack of private land ownership protection, the absence of adequate commercial laws, and an inefficient and corrupt government bureaucracy have inhibited economic growth and development.

Despite the setbacks, Russia has made some important strides:

- The government has eliminated price controls on most goods and services. This reform has been important because it allows the market forces of supply and demand to guide producers and consumers on purchasing, production and investment. Controls have remained on some important items, such as energy, housing, and transportation, but these, too, are to be removed eventually.
- The structure of Russian production more closely resembles that of an open economy than of a militarized economy. For example, the services sector, once a minor part of Soviet economy, has emerged in the post-Soviet Russian economy and now accounts for more than half of national output.
- The private sector has grown and accounts for roughly 3/4 of national output.

Since taking the reins of power, President Putin has forced Russia into a new phase of economic reform. Putin has enjoyed a high degree of popularity among the Russian people that has translated into overwhelming political clout in the Russian parliament. In addition, the continuing period of economic growth has provided a window of opportunity for Putin and his government to tackle economic restructuring. He has been able to push important economic legislation through the Russian parliament: tax reform; land reform; reform of government bureaucracy to make it more responsive to the needs of the economy rather than an impediment to development and growth; judicial reform; and improvement in corporate governance, especially the protection of minority shareholders' rights.

Still, the fragile basis of Russia's economic growth strongly suggests that Russia has far to go in economic reform. Analysts point to Russia's weak and underdeveloped financial sector, poorly developed system of commercial laws, and confusion over federal vs. regional and local responsibilities in important economic policy areas. Furthermore, even though Russian laws have been passed to restructure the economy, the success of their implementation remains to be seen. With parliamentary elections coming in December 2003, and with President Putin up for re-election in 2004, many observers question whether the Kremlin will push politically difficult reforms whose immediate costs could be substantial and whose benefits might be realized only in the long-run.

Russia's Foreign Trade and Investment Regimes and Policies

In determining the terms and conditions for Russia's accession to the WTO, WP members scrutinize Russia's foreign trade and investment regimes and policies to ascertain to what degree they conform to WTO rules and where Russia needs to change. Russia has made significant strides in that regard. It eliminated two important pillars of Soviet central planning in November 1991, the state monopoly on foreign trade and the ban on foreign investment in the Russian economy.

In October 1992, another legacy of central planning was eliminated when the Russian ruble was made convertible into foreign currencies and multiple exchange rates were eliminated. A dual exchange rate was briefly introduced in January 1999 as a result of the August 1998 financial crisis but was eliminated in June 1999. In the early to mid-1990s, the Central Bank imposed fixed or pegged exchange rates in an attempt to control ruble depreciation. Since the August 1998 crisis, the ruble has been allowed to float but the Central Bank of Russia intervenes by buying or selling rubles. The ruble has remained relatively stable since 1999.

In 1992, the Russian government adopted the Harmonized Tariff System that is used by WTO members, and it maintains a system of two-column tariff rates —MFN and non-MFN tariff rates. Tariff rates on non-agricultural products range from 0 to 30%. Some countries receive tariff advantages under Russia's Generalized System of Preferences(GSP) program in the form of tariff rates that are 25% below the MFN rate. A tariff-rate quota is applied to imports of sugar from countries receiving Russian GSP treatment.[12] Of the more than 11,000 commodity categories in the Russian tariff tables, only fifty have tariff rates above 30%.

Over time, the Russian government has lowered tariff rates. In 1995, the trade-weighted average tariff rate was 16.0%; by 2001 it was 11.1%.[13] Most products can be traded without restrictions, but the government requires exports and imports of some products, for example, pharmaceuticals, alcoholic beverages, precious metals and stones, to be licensed.[14] Russia also applies export tariffs on oil to ensure that domestic oil supplies are adequate and to compensate for the large differential between domestic and export oil prices. In 1998, the Russian government passed laws to provide for antidumping, countervailing, and safeguards measures against imports. Legislation is pending in the Russian parliament to revise them.

THE STATUS OF THE ACCESSION PROCESS AND OUTSTANDING ISSUES

In early 1995, Russia submitted to the working party(WP) the "Memorandum on the Foreign Trade Regime" which describes the structure of its foreign trade regime and also the structure, policies, and practices of its economy that would likely affect its conduct of trade.[15] Subsequently, the WP members submitted questions based on the memorandum, to which the Russian delegation replied. The process of submitting the original description of the trade regime, followed by a series of questions and replies established a benchmark on which the negotiations to determine the terms and conditions of Russia's accession would be based. The initial series of questions, replies and follow-up responses indicated strong concerns by the WP members in a broad range of areas including privatization, property rights, price controls, government financial support for business, and the structure and implementation of the tax regime.[16]

The Russian accession process is now at a critical stage. As with most negotiations, however, the last stages are the most difficult because negotiators now face the most contentious issues.[17] In November 2002, the WP released a draft report of the negotiations that indicates areas of agreement and bracketed text that indicates areas of continuing disagreement. According to the draft report and other reports of the negotiations, the United States, the European Union, and other participants have strong reservations about Russian policies and practices on intellectual property rights, energy pricing, agriculture, sanitary and phytosanitary regulations, trade in services, civil aircraft, and other issues. Russia's accession to the WTO will likely hinge on the resolution of these issues, which are examined below in more detail.

Energy Pricing

The energy sector dominates the Russian economy. Not only do oil, natural gas, and electricity drive industry and provide heat to residents, but energy is also the largest Russian export and hard currency earner. The current structure of Russia's energy sector is largely a legacy of the Soviet Union. The oil industry has been broken up into several privatized companies. Natural gas and electricity are largely monopolies run by Gazprom and United Energy Systems (UES), respectively, which are joint-stock companies with significant government ownership. The structures of these companies are now the subject of reform, but that process has proved politically controversial and therefore slow.

Domestic prices for Russian energy are regulated by the government while exports of energy products command world prices. Domestic prices are lower than world prices, in some cases significantly. The EU and the United States have pointed out that the gap between the world price for natural gas and the Russian domestic price has been as large as six to one, for electricity — five to one, and for oil — four to one.[18] The "dual pricing" is partially a result of a policy of providing affordable heating and electricity to residential customers regardless of ability to pay and providing favorable fuels rates to enterprises and to government agencies, such as the military.[19]

Some WP members, particularly the EU, and to a lesser extent the United States, have raised concern that dual energy pricing gives Russian manufacturers an unfair competitive advantage and would be illegal under the WTO subsidy agreement.[20]

WTO disciplines regarding subsidies are contained in the "Agreement on Subsidies and Countervailing Measures." Under the agreement, a subsidy is actionable only if it is a "specific subsidy," that is, it is a subsidy that is available only to an enterprise, an industry, a group of enterprises or industries in the country that gives the subsidy. The agreement defines three kinds of subsidies:

- Prohibited subsidies are ones that distort international trade, for example, subsidies that require recipients to meet exports targets or to use domestic products. These subsidies must be eliminated; otherwise, the country that complains about them can take countermeasures.
- Actionable subsidies are not prohibited unless it is determined that the subsidy causes injury. If such a determination is made, then the complaining country can impose a countervailing duty.
- Non-actionable subsidies are non-specific, or are specific subsidies for industrial research or development activity, for assistance to disadvantaged regions, or for adapting existing facilities to new environmental laws or regulations. They cannot be challenged in the WTO.[21]

European and U.S. fertilizer producers have been strong opponents of Russia's energy pricing policies because natural gas is a significant input in fertilizer production, accounting for 3/4 of the final price, according to one estimate.[22] The Russian government and Russian delegates to the WTO negotiations have strongly argued that Russian energy prices are not an actionable subsidy under WTO rules because they are available to all industries. They assert furthermore, that Russia's domestic energy prices reflect its comparative advantage in energy production. To date the dual energy pricing issue is still a huge roadblock, especially for the EU, in Russia's accession to the WTO.

Intellectual Property Rights Protection

WTO members are calling on Russia to be in full compliance with the WTO agreement on trade-related aspects of intellectual property rights (TRIPS) at the time of its accession, in terms of laws in place and enforcement. All WTO members are bound by the provisions of the TRIPS agreement, which was designed and ratified to introduce predictability and order to intellectual property rights (IPR) protection in all WTO members, because it has become an important factor in international trade. The TRIPS agreement requires WTO members to apply the fundamental principles of national treatment and most-favored-nation treatment in intellectual property rights protection. The agreement also requires WTO members to ensure protection of copyrights, trademarks, geographical indicators of products, and patents by imposing and enforcing appropriate laws.[23]

Russia has passed a number of laws on IPR protection and is a member of the major multilateral intellectual property rights conventions. Russia has committed to IPR protection in bilateral agreements with the United States and other trading partners. However, foreign investor and exporters have complained that the Russian government has not adequately enforced its laws allowing intellectual property piracy to continue and grow with impunity — culprits are either not caught, or if caught they are not punished.[24]

U.S. producers of copyrighted material have cited unauthorized Russian reproduction of American-made films, videos, sound recordings, books, and computer software as a source of lost revenues. Recently, Russian production of pirated DVDs has increased and has been a special source of concern. Losses due to intellectual piracy of U.S. products in Russia in 2002 are estimated at $755.8 million dollars.[25] The production of counterfeit American products has become so large that they now make up the vast majority of Russian purchases of these products.[26] Russia has argued that its enforcement of intellectual property rights is improving, and that it should not be singled out since intellectual piracy continues to take place in WTO member countries. IPR protection is of serious concern to the U.S. Congress. The House passed (421-2) and the Senate passed (voice vote) on November 16 and December 22, 2005, respectively, H.Con.Res. 230, calling on Russia to improve enforcement of IPR or face removal of its benefits under the U.S. Generalized System of Preferences (GSP) program.

Agriculture

Agriculture has been a sensitive part of the economy throughout Russian/Soviet history. Its political importance far outweighs its share of the Russian economy (7.2% of Russian GDP in 2001).[27] Agriculture has been severely affected by the transition to a market economy as much as, or more than, any other sector of the economy. According to one estimate, agricultural production declined around 40% in volume terms since 1991, much of the decline occurring in livestock production.[28]

Several factors have contributed to the downturn. One factor is Soviet agriculture policy. The Soviet government determined what and how much the economy should produce and directed resources accordingly. In the 1960s, the government decided that the Soviet people should eat more meat, and it subsidized animal feed production and imports of animal feed to fulfill this objective. The government set meat prices at a low level to make it affordable to consumers. However, after the collapse of the Soviet Union, market prices were instituted and state subsidies were dramatically cut, increasing the cost of meat production.[29] Furthermore, when the Russian government liberalized trade, Russian producers of poultry and other meats could not compete with foreign producers who could sell them more cheaply. While the Russian federal government has cut support, local and regional governments have continued to provide assistance in the form of equipment, favorable credits, and export subsidies. They are concerned about food security and unemployment and about maintaining the supply of housing, education, and other services that state farms provided to the rural communities during the Soviet period and continue to provide.

A second factor contributing to the decline in agricultural production has been the slow pace of restructuring of Russian farms. Despite the introduction of privatization, the vast majority of former state and collective farms remain intact as joint stock operations or cooperatives and operate in virtually the same inefficient manner as they did under the Soviet government.

The Russian federal government is under pressure from regional and local governments and from factions within the Russian parliament to protect agriculture from further erosion and to provide time and resources to permit it to become competitive. This pressure has translated into a difference in positions in the accession negotiations between Russia and agricultural exporting countries including the United States, Canada, and Australia over the level and longevity of government support to agriculture. The Russian government has argued for higher levels and longer phase-out periods for supports than its negotiating partners are willing to accept. Russian negotiators have also asserted that it should not be required to bind itself to dramatically lower support levels during the accession process while other WTO members are currently in the process of negotiating the agriculture subsidies in the current round of WTO negotiations, Doha Development Agenda (DDA). The WTO members have argued that the subsidies that Russia wants to maintain distort trade and are concerned that they give Russian agriculture producers an unfair advantage. The Russian side has argued that without government support, Russian agriculture could not compete with EU and U.S. agriculture, both of which receive sizeable government subsidies.[30]

Another controversy in agriculture has emerged over Russia's recent decision to restrict meat imports. On January 23, 2003, the Russian government announced it would impose a three-year quota on poultry imports effective May 1, 2003. At the same time the government announced tariff-rate quotas (TRQs) on imports of beef and pork effective April 1, 2003, and to remain in effect until 2010.[31] Meat exporting WTO member- countries, including the United States, Canada, Argentina, Australia, and New Zealand, have expressed stiff opposition, claiming that the restrictions may retard the process of Russia's accession to the WTO. They specifically argue that Russia has violated the "standstill" principle under which countries applying for WTO membership are to refrain from imposing new trade restrictions during the accession process. Russia counters that it is imposing the restrictions to protect its domestic meat producers from import surges, a right that is enjoyed by WTO members.[32]

During the Uruguay Round, WTO members agreed to expand disciplines over trade in agricultural products, and agricultural trade is on the agenda of the current round, the DDA. Under the Agricultural Agreement all WTO members, except least developed countries, are committed to reduce tariffs and subsidies on the production and export of agricultural goods.[33]

Sanitary and Phytosanitary Regulations

Some WP members have raised concerns over Russia's sanitary and phytosanitary (SPS) standards, that is standards and certification procedures that determine the safety of meats and other animal products, plants, and plant products. They argue that these procedures are not scientifically based and discriminate against imports thus violating WTO rules. Under the Agreement on Sanitary and Phytosanitary Measures (SPM), WTO members are permitted to apply controls on products in order to protect public health and safety, but those controls must be scientifically based and must not discriminate against imports.[34] Russia has argued that its SPS controls meet the requirements of the SPM agreement.

The United States has expressed particular concern about this issue. In March 2002, the Russian government imposed a ban on imports of U.S. poultry because of the possible presence of avian influenza. Russia had become the largest market for U.S. exports of chicken. After months of negotiations, the United States and Russia agreed in August 2002 on a new veterinary certificate for U.S. poultry that would include inspections by Russian veterinarians of U.S. processing and storage facilities, but technical issues remained that prevented the process from being implemented. On April 3, 2003, the two sides announced the resolution of the problems, allowing the inspection of the facilities to go forward and U.S. poultry exports to resume.[35] Nevertheless, the United States is concerned that Russia would impose similar restrictions in the future and has pressed Russia to adhere to the WTO requirements as part of the conditions of its accession.

Services

Services, especially financial services (banking, insurance, and securities), are a relatively new phenomenon in the Russian economy. Under the Soviet Union, services were government-owned and operated and were confined to personal services (for example, lodging, hair salons, restaurants). They were not well developed because they were not a government priority. Financial services were virtually non-existent in the Soviet Union because their function as intermediaries between savers and borrowers of capital had no role in the Soviet planned economy.

The services sector has grown rapidly during Russia's transition to a market economy but has not matured in most cases. The United States, the EU, and other advanced developed WTO members have argued that Russia needs an efficient financial services industry to promote economic growth and development and that opening the industry to foreign investment would introduce expertise and new capital.

Russian officials and business representatives claim that their service industries must have government protection as "infant industries," because they are too immature and would be wiped out if they had to face foreign competition too soon. An example is the fledgling Russian insurance industry. Private insurance companies have been developing since the government monopoly was removed after the collapse of the Soviet Union, but not sufficiently to meet demand. Foreign insurance companies that could help fill the gap and bring expertise and a wide range of products are restricted. For example, the government: limits total foreign capitalization to 15% of the domestic insurance industry; requires the general director and the chief accountant to be Russian citizens; restricts participation to foreign companies that have been in business no less than 15 years in their home country; and requires that foreign insurance companies operate as a minority shareholder in a Russian insurance company before they can be granted their own license. In addition, foreign providers are prohibited from underwriting and reinsuring mandatory insurance — auto and health insurance and insurance taken out by government entities — the fastest growing insurance market in Russia.[36] Russian negotiators assert that those restrictions should remain while U.S., EU, and other working party participants want them loosened or removed.

The Russian banking sector is similarly underdeveloped. About 30% of the volume of Russian banking activity is conducted by two banks — Sberbank and Vneshtorgbank, both of which are owned by the Central Bank of Russia. Sberbank holds roughly 70% of the Russian savings deposits. Foreign participation in the banking sector is restricted by government laws and regulations. Foreign banks may operate in Russia only as subsidiaries and not as branches of the parent bank. Foreign banks have cited the lack of an effective deposit insurance program as a disincentive for new, private banks to develop. The government in effect backs deposits of Sberbank 100%.[37] Russian negotiators claim that the government will establish a deposit insurance program for deposits in all banks but argues that the limit on foreign participation in Russian banking must be maintained to allow domestic banks to become competitive.[38] U.S. negotiators and negotiators from some of the other working party countries are requesting that Russia liberalize its banking sector to increase foreign participation, arguing that the foreign influence would increase, not undermine, the competitiveness of Russian banks by promoting stability and popular confidence. Furthermore, a liberalized banking sector would likely boost other sectors of the economy.

In telecommunications, Russia permits 100% foreign ownership of telecommunication services providers, but it has requested to be bound by a commitment of only 49% foreign ownership. U.S. and EU negotiators oppose such a ceiling because they view the Russian telecommunications market as potentially lucrative for its firms. The Russian government has also indicated it wants long distance and international telephone communications to remain in the control of a monopoly, Rostelcom, until 2010.[39]

WTO rules on trade in services, including financial services, are contained in the General Agreement on Trade in Services (GATS) which was agreed to during the Uruguay Round. In general, the GATS is designed to apply internationally accepted rules, such as most-favored-nation treatment, to trade in services that are similar to those applied to trade in goods. In important respects, however, the GATS is less comprehensive than the GATT. For example, WTO rules on goods trade contained in the GATT apply to all goods, but many of the rules, contained in the GATS, including, "national treatment," apply only to those services and the modes of delivery of those services on which that the member country has identified in its schedule of commitments.

Civil Aircraft

Russian aircraft manufacturers, as the case with the Russian defense-related industries in general, have seen demand for their production plummet after the government dramatically cut defense expenditures and after airlines from former Communist countries in Central and Eastern Europe and the former Soviet Union shifted to European and U.S. manufacturers for their aircraft. The Russian government wants to protect domestic aircraft manufacturers from further erosion of business. It imposes a 20% ad valorem tariff on imported aircraft. Russia argues that its aircraft industry is operating at only 0-15% of capacity and is in great need of modernization. For it to become competitive, it needs to be protected from foreign competition and therefore must apply high tariffs to imported aircraft. The United States and EU are pressing Russia to sign on to the plurilateral WTO Civil Aircraft Agreement (CAA) (only 26 members are currently signatories) which commits the signatories to eliminate tariffs on trade in civil aircraft and some related equipment. In an 1996 bilateral Memorandum of Understanding with the United States, Russia stated that it would sign the CAA but has backed off that commitment during the accession negotiations. Because its is a plurilateral agreement, a WTO member is not required to sign the CAA as part of its obligations.

Russia does grant some tariff waivers to allow domestic airlines to fulfill needs that cannot be accommodated by domestically manufactured aircraft. It has recently favored the

European firm, Airbus Industries in granting those waivers. The United States has demanded that the waivers should be granted without favoring any particular company.[40]

Other Issues

In addition to the above issues, the United States, the EU, and other working party members have raised other issues about Russia's trade and foreign investment regime and want Russia to make changes as part of the conditions for its accession to the WTO. They include:

- Tariffs: The Russian government has lowered tariffs on most categories of products in the tariff schedule. Nevertheless, it maintains high tariffs on some items to protect fledgling industries from foreign competition. High tariffs on autos, for example, have been a concern of U.S. manufacturers. Tariffs and excise taxes (that vary depending on the engine displacement) can add over 70% to the delivery cost of an imported new car. The Russian government also recently increased tariffs on used vehicles that are 3-7 years of age because they compete with Russian domestically produced new cars.[41] U.S., Japanese, and Korean delegations want Russia to lower tariffs on autos.[42] The Russian government asserts that the fledgling domestic auto industry requires some temporary protection from more developed foreign producers in order to become competitive.
- Customs regulations: Some WP members have argued that the implementation of federal customs regulations is inconsistent, leading to confusion and inhibiting trade. Some also raised problems with the policy of restricting trade of certain goods to specific ports, making it difficult for imported products to be delivered to customers. Legislation establishing a new customs code is pending in the parliament.
- Import licensing: The Russian government requires import licenses on certain products: pharmaceuticals, sugar (to implement a tariff-rate quota on sugar imported under Russia's Generalized System of Preferences program), precious metals and stones, and alcoholic beverages. Some WP members have expressed concern that Russia might impose additional licensing requirements that would further impede imports and are asking Russia to commit to removing import restrictions and not impose new ones that are not consistent with WTO requirements. Legislation to simplify the import licensing procedures is pending in the parliament.
- Government procurement: WP members have requested that Russia join the plurilateral Government Procurement Agreement which commits signatories to open contracts for government purchases to bids from other signatory countries.

U.S.-RUSSIAN ECONOMIC TIES AND WTO ACCESSION

The United States has strongly supported Russia's accession to the WTO since Russia first applied to join the GATT in 1993. The U.S. government has provided advice to the Russian government on how to make its trade and investment regime WTO compatible and to educate Russian firms on the implications of WTO accession. Because the United States is the world's largest economy, its support is critical to the success of Russia's application. However, the United States has also insisted that Russia enter the WTO on "commercial terms," that is, on terms that do not distort trade, and that Russia immediately adhere to WTO agreements upon accession.

U.S. support for Russian accession is just one part of post-Cold War U.S. trade and economic policy that has encouraged Russian endeavors to establish a market economy. And the trade and economic policy is itself part of a larger U.S. foreign policy strategy to anchor Russia in the world community and to reshape the U.S.-Russian relationship into one of cooperation.

U.S. support to Russia in the trade and investment areas has come in the form of technical assistance, trade preferences (including tariff preferences under the U.S. GSP program), and financial assistance to U.S. exporters to and investors in Russia through the U.S. Export-Import Bank and the Overseas Private Investment Corporation (OPIC). Since 1992, the United States has granted Russia conditional normal trade relations (NTR), or most-favored-nation (MFN), status, which means that lower tariffs are applied to imports from Russia than was the case when Russia did not have NTR status.

U.S.-Russian trade and investment flows have increased in the post-Cold War reflecting the changed U.S.-Russian relationship, although they remain lower than what many observers consider their potential. U.S. imports from Russia have increased substantially since the end of the Cold War from $0.5 billion in 1992 peaking at $15.3 billion in 2005. U.S. exports have increased but not as significantly, from $2.1 billion in 1992 peaking at $3.9 billion in 2005. Since 1994, the United States has incurred growing trade deficits with Russia, peaking at $11.3 billion in 2005. The large increase in U.S. imports may reflect not so much an increase in the volume of trade but the rise in world prices of raw materials, particularly oil, that comprise the bulk of those imports.

Table 1. U.S. Merchandise Trade with Russia, 1992-2005
(Billions of Dollars)

Year	U.S. Exports	U.S. Imports	U.S. Trade Balances	Year	U.S. Exports	U.S. Imports	U.S. Trade Balances
1992	2.1	0.5	1.6	1999	2.1	5.9	-3.8
1993	3.0	1.7	1.3	2000	2.1	7.7	-5.6
1994	2.6	3.2	-0.6	2001	2.7	6.3	-3.5
1995	2.8	4.0	-1.2	2002	2.4	6.8	-4.4
1996	3.3	3.6	-0.3	2003	2.4	8.6	-6.2
1997	3.4	4.3	-0.9	2004	3.0	11.9	-8.9
1998	3.6	5.7	-2.1	2005	3.9	15.3	-11.3

Source: Compiled by CRS from U.S. Department of Commerce Data. Bureau of the Census. FT900.

Slow Russian economic growth and the rapid depreciation of the ruble after 1998 constrained demand for imports from the United States. Russia's limited export base has constrained U.S. demand for imports from Russia. In 2004 close to 70% of U.S. imports from Russia consisted of precious metals, inorganic chemicals, fuels, and aluminum.[43]

Although the United States is the largest source of foreign direct investment in Russia, the level of the investment is far below most expectations and limited in scope. U.S. investors accounted for $4.08 billion in foreign direct investment as of the end of 2001, largely in the transportation, fuel, communications, and engineering industries.[44]

U.S. exporters and investors claim that a number of factors make them cautious about entering the Russian market: the lack of adherence to international standards of accounting; weak enforcement of intellectual property rights; the lack of protection of share- holders rights; burdensome taxation; and poor legal protection of contract sanctity. These concerns are largely mirrored in the demands the United States has made on Russia during its negotiations in the WTO.

For their part, Russian policymakers have asserted that U.S. trade policy has also been slow to adjust to the post-Cold War era. For example, they point out that the United States only recently removed the "nonmarket economy status" that was applied in antidumping duty cases against Russian imports.[45] Under U.S. antidumping laws, "fair value" for imports from nonmarket economies is calculated differently than for imports from other economies. That methodology leads to higher dumping margins and antidumping duties and, therefore, placed imports from Russia at a competitive disadvantage vis-a-vis other imports or U.S. domestic production. In response to requests from Russian steel producers, the U.S. Department of Commerce examined the possibility of no longer treating Russia as a nonmarket economy and removed the designation on June 7, 2002.[46]

More critical for Russia has been the U.S. government's continued application of the Jackson-Vanik amendment to trade relations with Russia. Russia's current conditional NTR status from the United States is governed by Title IV of the Trade Act of 1974, as amended. Section 401 of Title IV requires the President to continue to deny NTR status to any country that was not receiving such treatment at the time of the law's enactment on January 3, 1975. In effect, this meant all communist countries, except Poland and Yugoslavia. Section 402 of Title IV, the Jackson-Vanik amendment, denies the countries eligibility for NTR status as well as access to U.S. government credit facilities, such as the Export-Import Bank, as long as the country denies its citizens the right of freedom-of-emigration. These restrictions can be removed if the President determines that the country is in full compliance with the freedom-of-emigration conditions set out under the Jackson-Vanik amendment. For a country to retain that status, the President must reconfirm his determination of full compliance in a semiannual report (by June 30 and December 31) to Congress. His determination can be overturned by Congress via the enactment of a joint resolution of disapproval at the time of the December 31 report.

The Jackson-Vanik amendment also permits the President to waive full compliance with the free emigration requirement, if he determines that such a waiver would promote the objectives of the amendment, that is, encourage freedom of emigration. This waiver authority is subject to an annual renewal by the President and to congressional disapproval via a joint resolution. Before a country can receive NTR treatment under either the presidential determination of full compliance or the presidential waiver, both the United States and the country in question must have concluded and enacted a bilateral agreement that provides for, among other things, reciprocal extension of NTR (or MFN) status. The agreement and a presidential proclamation extending NTR status cannot go into effect until a joint resolution approving the agreement is enacted. In 1990, the United States and the Soviet Union signed a bilateral trade agreement. The agreement was subsequently applied to each of the former Soviet states. The United States first granted NTR treatment to Russia under the presidential waiver authority beginning in June 1992 and, since September 1994, under the full compliance provision. Presidential extensions of NTR status to Russia have met with virtually no congressional opposition.

Russian political leaders have continually pressed the United States to "graduate" Russia from Jackson-Vanik coverage entirely. They see the amendment as a Cold War relic that does not reflect Russia's new stature as a fledgling democracy and market economy. Moreover, Russian leaders argue that Russia has implemented freedom-of-emigration policies since the fall of the communist government, making the Jackson-Vanik conditions inappropriate and unnecessary.

While Russia remains subject to the Jackson-Vanik amendment, some of the other former Soviet republics have been granted permanent and unconditional NTR-Kyrgyzstan on June 29, 2000, and Georgia on December 29, 2000. Perhaps, what has particularly irked Russian leaders is that on January 1, 2002, the United States granted permanent and unconditional NTR status to China, which is ostensibly still a communist country.

Granting Russia permanent and unconditional NTR status will have little direct impact on U.S.-Russian trade, since Russian imports have entered the United States on a NTR basis since 1992. The initiative would be a political symbol of Russia's treatment as a "normal" country in U.S. trade, further distancing U.S.-Russian relations from the Cold War. For investors and other business people, PNTR may mean a more stable climate for doing business. But many observers have concluded that U.S.-Russian economic ties will grow only when Russia has undertaken sufficient economic reforms to improve the climate for trade and investment.

It has a direct bearing on the WTO accession issue since the WTO requires its members to extend mutual *unconditional* MFN status to one another's exports. If the United States does not extend permanent NTR to Russia, the United States would not benefit from the concessions, except tariff reductions, that Russia makes upon acceding to the WTO.

IMPLICATIONS OF RUSSIA'S ACCESSION TO THE WTO

Because the major trade powers — the United States, the EU, and Japan —strongly support Russia's entry into the WTO, the pending question is not whether Russia will accede but when. The answer to that question depends on when Russia and the more than sixty members of the working party can finish hammering out the conditions of accession. Negotiators have reportedly reached agreement on most issues, but disagreements on difficult issues of energy pricing, agriculture, services, civil aircraft, and intellectual property rights, have slowed down the process and the original goal of accession by the September 2003 WTO Ministerial Meeting in Cancun, Mexico unattainable. Several other desired deadlines have passed. There are indications that the United States and Russia would like to see the process completed by July 2006, when Russia chairs the G-8 meeting in St. Petersburg.

Implications for Russia

The stakes for Russia in joining the WTO are high. Russia's political leadership, led by Putin, has made a commitment to join the WTO. In his April 18, 2002 address to the Federal Assembly, the bicameral Russian legislature, Putin underscored his administration's priority to get Russia into the WTO. In the speech, Putin emphasized the need for the Russian government to establish the conditions to improve the economic well-being of the Russian people and linked that effort with joining the WTO:

> Tight competition is a norm in the international community and in the modern world, competition for markets, investments, economic and political influence. Russia must be strong and competitive in this fight.
> The world market is already here and our market has become part of the system...
> The WTO is an instrument. He who knows how to use it grows stronger; he who prefers to sit behind a fence of protectionist quotas, and duties — he is doomed, absolutely doomed strategically.
> Our country is still excluded from the process of making world trade rules. We are already in the world trade but we have no say in shaping the rules of trade. This tends to stunt the Russian economy and make it less competitive.[47]

In acceding to the WTO, Russia is making a *legally binding* commitment to conform to WTO rules. In so doing, it agrees to make its foreign trade and investment regimes open to the scrutiny of the WTO and its members. At the same time, the WTO provides a multilateral forum for Russia to settle trade disputes with other WTO members. As a WTO member, Russia will have a voice in how those rules are made and implemented. It would be a major step in integrating Russia within the international trade system.

But before it can accede to the WTO, Russia must satisfy WTO members that it is ready to meet its obligations. The working party negotiations and the bilateral negotiations to date suggest that those countries are not satisfied and require that Russia make major adjustments in policies and regulations.

The adjustments include reviewing and possibly changing more than 100 Russian laws and reviewing more than 1,000 international agreements that Russia has with various countries.[48] However, the overall impact of WTO accession on Russia will depend on the terms and conditions of accession that Russian and its trading partners in the WTO finally agree on. In general, Russia will likely have to reduce tariffs and other protective measures for import-sensitive industries such as autos and aircraft and will have to open up key financial service industries — banking and insurance — to foreign competition. In the short run, such adjustments could lead to the loss of jobs in those areas and the need for the Russian government to provide unemployment insurance and other adjustment assistance.

However, globally competitive industries, such as the raw material producers, could see markets abroad opening up and an increase in foreign investment as accession forces Russia to restructure its economy. In the long run, mainstream economic theory and the record of economies that have gone through similar transitions suggest that trade liberalization will lead to a more efficient Russian economy and to raising the living standard of the average Russian citizen.[49] New industries will probably emerge over time helping to diversify the Russian economy.

The Russian business community is divided on the issue of accession. Some have expressed skepticism if not out right opposition to accession. Among this group is Oleg Deripaska, an influential and powerful aluminum and auto business magnate. He is concerned that WTO accession will force Russia to eliminate protection and that the domestic auto industry will face competition from U.S., European, and Japanese manufacturers. He is also concerned that Russia would have to charge higher prices for energy, a major input in aluminum production. Similarly, representatives of aviation, furniture, financial services, telecommunications, and agriculture have asserted that Russia stands to lose more than it will gain from accession because Russia has not matured sufficiently to meet the competition.[50]

Views on accession cut across regions with support coming from regional political leaders in the major business centers of Moscow and St. Petersburg and in regions where raw material production is located. Political leaders in regions where fledgling import-sensitive manufacturers are located have been skeptical or opposed to accession. For most Russians, accession has not attracted much interest.[51]

Putin and the current Russian political leadership have made economic growth and development their highest priority and they view Russia's admission into the WTO as an essential part of the strategy to fulfill those goals. Putin appears to view the accession process as a way of forcing the government bureaucracy, the Duma, and Russian industry to confront the changes that are required if Russia is to attain long-term sustainable economic growth and development. While Putin's political future probably does not depend directly on whether Russia gets into the WTO, it will likely be evaluated on the basis to what degree economic life in Russia has improved.

WTO accession would be a further sign of Russia's acceptance and participation in the major multilateral economic institutions: the World Bank, the International Monetary Fund; and the G-8. In so doing, Russia would distance itself further from its Soviet past.

Implications for the United States

For U.S. exporters and investors, Russia's accession to the WTO may improve the business climate in Russia which has been unpredictable. The U.S. business community often cites poor intellectual property rights protection, inconsistent and opaque customs regulations, inconsistent enforcement of the regulations, and irrational SPS and technical trade barriers as among the impediments to trade and investment. Accession could bring more stability and openness in the business climate since Russia would have to adhere to WTO rules that promote these conditions.

The volume of U.S. imports from Russia has been low primarily because Russia's limited export-base. Nevertheless, some U.S. import-sensitive industries, for example steel, may face increased competition from Russian producers. These industries may press U.S. negotiators to include as part of the terms and conditions for Russia's accession, a special safeguard provision, beyond that provided in the WTO agreements, that would cushion the potentially adverse impact of a large increase in Russian imports upon accession. Such a provision was included in the conditions for China's accession to the WTO and was codified in U.S. law as section 421 of the Trade Act of 1974.

Similar to section 201 (escape clause) provision of the Trade Act of 1974, section 421 allows the United States to temporarily restrict fairly traded imports that cause or threaten to cause injury to the domestic injury. Unlike section 201, however, section 421 permits the restrictions to be applied solely to imports of like products from China, rather than requiring them to be applied on an MFN basis on imports of like products from all countries. In addition, the required thresholds of cause and level of injury to the domestic industry for relief under section 421 is lower than under section 201. Section 201 requires that imports be a "substantial" cause of "serious injury," whereas section 421 requires only that the imports be a "significant cause" of "material injury." For many in the U.S. business and agricultural community, the issue is not whether Russia should be allowed to join the WTO but one of assurance that Russia will enter under conditions that are commercially sound and will have minimal negative impact on U.S. industries.

Implications for other Countries and the WTO

Russia is the largest and most populous country that is not a member of the WTO. If Russia accedes, it would significantly expand the geographical coverage of WTO rules to all major economies leading to a larger degree of stability and transparency to the international trading system.

At the same time, Russia's entry into the WTO would continue a trend in which as the membership of the WTO becomes larger and more diverse, it becomes more difficult for that membership to reach a consensus on important issues. In addition, trade disputes between Russia and its trading partners will be brought to the WTO for resolution rather than addressed bilaterally, adding to the ever growing caseload of the WTO.

As an economy still in transition, Russia would bring its own perspective to WTO negotiations. For example, Russia could be expected to challenge the positions the United States and other countries have taken in the WTO on the role of subsidies in trade and the degree to which trade in services should be liberalized.

REFERENCES

[1] These agreements include the General Agreement on Trade in Services (GATS) and the agreement on Trade-Related Aspects of Intellectual Property Rights (TRIPS), among others.
[2] Washington Trade Daily, September 19, 2005.
[3] Based on WTO background information located at [http://www.wto.org].
[4] It should be noted that other nonmarket economies had acceded to the GATT, albeit under special conditions: Poland (1967); Hungary (1973); and Romania (1971). The United States was also concerned that the Soviet Union intended to use GATT membership for political purposes. The Soviet Union sought observer status once before in 1982. Kennedy, Kevin C, The Accession of the Soviet Union to the GATT, *Journal of World Trade Law,* April 1987, p. 23-39.
[5] The World Bank. *Russian Economic Report.* April 2006. p. 3.
[6] Calculations based on data found in Economist Intelligence Unit, *Country Report: Russia,* July 2006.

[7] Customs Committee of Russia.
[8] The World Bank. *Russian Economic Report.* April 2006. p. 24.
[9] The World Bank. *Russian Economic Report.* April 2006. p. 24.
[10] Economist Intelligence Unit. July 2006.
[11] Slay, p. 34.
[12] GSP is a program under which a country gives preferential tariff treatment to imports from developing countries. Many industrialized countries have GSP programs to encourage economic growth and development in developing countries.
[13] WTO, Draft Report of the Working Party, WT/ACC/SPEC/RUS/25/Rev.1 p. 124.
[14] Some working party members wanted to be assured that Russian traders were not favored over foreigner traders in license approval process. Ibid. p. 19-23.
[15] WTO L/7410.
[16] World Trade Organization, Accession of the Russian Federation: Questions and Replies to the Memorandum on the Foreign Trade Regime, Geneva, June 2, 1995. WT/ACC/RUS/2
[17] World Trade Organization, Draft Report of the Working Party on the Accession of the Russian Federation to the World Trade Organization, WT/ACC/SPEC/RUS/25/Rev.1.
[18] Ibid. p. 16.
[19] OECD, OECD Economic Surveys 2001-2002: Russian Federation, p. 125.
[20] Ibid. p. 17.
[21] The description of the agreement is taken from "What is the WTO?" located on the WTO website: [http://www.wto.org].
[22] International Trade Reporter, November 7, 2002, p. 1904.
[23] The description of the agreement is taken from "What is the WTO?" located on the WTO website: [http://www.wto.org].
[24] Office of the U.S. Trade Representative, *National Trade Estimate Report on Foreign Trade Barriers,* April 2003, p. 335.
[25] The estimates are according to the International Intellectual Property Rights Alliance (IIPA), a non-profit group representing copyright-based industries, [http://www.iipa.com].
[26] Office of the U.S. Trade Representative, p.335.
[27] Economist Intelligence Unit, *Country Profile 2002: Russia,* p. 58.
[28] Liefert, William, Agricultural Reform: Major Commodity Restructuring but Little Institutional Change, in Joint Economic Committee, p. 278.
[29] Ibid.
[30] Bush, Keith, *Russian Economic Survey,* April 2003, p. 25.
[31] USDA, Foreign Agricultural Service, Russian Federation Livestocks and Products, Gain Report # RS3006, February 20, 2003, p. 7; and USDA, Foreign Agricultural Service, Russian Federation Poultry and Products, *Gain Report,* #RS3001, February 10, 2003, p. 1. TRQs are restrictions in which a limited volume of a product can be imported at one tariff rate but imports above that limit can be imported only at another, usually much higher tariff rate.
[32] Inside U.S. Trade, March 14, 2003.
[33] WTO, op. cit.
[34] Ibid.
[35] Ibid., p. 332. *Washington Trade Daily,* April 7, 2003, p. 1.

[36] Vastine, Bob and Vladimir Gololobov, Moscow and the WTO: A Unique Chance to Modernize Russia, *European Affairs*, Winter 2003; and The Russian Ministry of Finance has proposed that the ban on foreign company issuance of compulsory insurance be lifted, EIU, *Country Report: Russia,* March 2003, p. 28.

[37] Coalition of Service Industries, CSI Background Paper on Russian Banking Services, May 22, 2002.

[38] Legislation to establish deposit insurance for other Russian banks is pending in the lower house of the Russian parliament, the Duma, but has not received action, *Reuters,* June 3, 2003.

[39] Washington Trade Daily, January 23, 2002.

[40] USTR, p. 340.

[41] USTR, p. 333.

[42] *Moscow Times,* March 4, 2002, p. 12.

[43] CRS calculations based on data from the Department of Commerce, Bureau of the Census.

[44] The island of Cyprus is the second largest source of foreign direct investments (considered largely the repatriation of offshore capital of Russian investors) with $3.72 billion and the Netherlands is the third largest source at $2.15 billion. U.S. Department of Commerce, International Trade Administration, *BISNIS Overview: U.S. Foreign Investment in Russia.*

[45] Washington Trade Daily, June 7, 2002.

[46] Ibid.

[47] Annual Address by President of the Russian Federation Vladimir Putin to the Federal Assembly of the Russian Federation Moscow, April 18, 2002, [http://www.russiaeurope.mid.ru].

[48] Likhachev, Aleksei Evgenievich (State Duma Committee on Economic Policy and Enterprise), Presentation at Adam Smith Institute International Congress on Russia's Accession to the WTO, October 16-17, 2002, Moscow.

[49] For an examination of the possible economic impact of accession see, Stern, Robert M., *An Economic Perspective on Russia's Accession to the WTO,* William Davidson Working Paper Number 472, June 2002, The William Davidson Institute at the University of Michigan Business School.

[50] *Financial Times,* April 15, 2002.

[51] EastWest Institute, *Regional Report,* vol 7, no. 22, July 10, 2002.

In: The World Trade Organization: Another Round
Editor: Harold B. Whitiker, pp. 153-172
ISBN: 978-1-60021-816-3
© 2007 Nova Science Publishers, Inc.

Chapter 6

WTO: ANTIDUMPING ISSUES IN THE DOHA DEVELOPMENT AGENDA[*]

Vivian C. Jones
Analyst in International Trade and Finance Foreign Affairs, Defense, and Trade Division

ABSTRACT

At the November 2001 Ministerial meeting of the World Trade Organization (WTO) in Doha, Qatar, WTO member countries launched a new round of trade talks known as the Doha Development Agenda (DDA). One of the negotiating objectives called for "clarifying and improving disciplines" under the WTO Antidumping and Subsidies Agreements. Since antidumping is the most frequently used trade remedy action worldwide, most of the discussion focused on changing ways that WTO members administer antidumping (AD) actions.

WTO negotiations in the DDA directly involve Congress since any trade agreement made by the United States must be implemented by legislation. In addition, Congress has an important oversight role in trade negotiations as provided in legislation granting presidential Trade Promotion Authority in the Trade Act of 2002 (P.L. 107-210).

The frequent use of antidumping actions by the United States and other developed nations has come under criticism by other WTO members as being protectionist. Many Members of Congress defend the use of U.S. antidumping actions brought as necessary to protect U.S. firms and workers from unfair competition. However, because the United States is also a leading target of antidumping actions by other countries, some U.S. export-oriented firms may support changes to the Antidumping Agreement.

The positions of major players in trade remedy talks are well-documented by position papers circulated through the WTO Negotiating Group on Rules. At the December 2005 WTO Ministerial in Hong Kong, rules negotiators were called upon to further "intensify and accelerate the negotiating process."

Most of the proposals on trade remedies focus on changing the Antidumping Agreement, currently a somewhat ambiguous document that gives broad guidelines for conducting AD investigations, in order to provide more specific definitions and stricter

---

[*] Excerpted from CRS Report RL32810, dated April 20, 2006.

procedures. The goal of many of the WTO members seems to be to lower the level of antidumping duties provided per investigation and/or to provide more restrictions on the ability of officials to grant relief to domestic industries. The gap between the U.S. position, where there is strong support in Congress to preserve the rights of WTO members to provide AD relief to domestic industries, and the viewpoints of other countries appears to be wide and may be difficult to narrow, but some countries see revision of the Antidumping Agreement and other WTO disciplines on trade remedies as a "make or break" issue if the DDA is to succeed.

This article examines antidumping issues in DDA negotiations by analyzing the issue in three parts. The first provides background information and contextual analysis for understanding why the issue is so controversial. The second section focuses on how antidumping issues fit into the DDA, and the third section provides a more specific overview of major reform proposals that are being considered.

INTRODUCTION

At the November 2001 Ministerial meeting of the World Trade Organization (WTO) in Doha, Qatar, WTO member countries launched a new round of trade talks known as the Doha Development Agenda (DDA). One of the negotiating objectives members agreed to address, in spite of opposition from U.S. negotiators, called for "clarifying and improving disciplines" on trade remedies. At the December 2005 WTO Ministerial in Hong Kong, the " high level of constructive engagement" in the trade remedy area was acknowledged, and negotiators were directed to "intensify and accelerate the negotiating process."[1]

Trade remedies are laws used by countries to mitigate the adverse impact of various trade practices on domestic industries and workers. Antidumping (AD) laws provide relief to domestic industries that have suffered material injury or are threatened with material injury as a result of competing imports being sold at prices shown to be less than their fair market value (LTFV). AD laws and actions are often controversial because many trade experts view them as protectionist. Others believe that they are an essential means of mitigating the adverse impact of unfair trade on domestic companies, workers, and the communities in which they are located.

Historically, multilateral negotiations on antidumping have been extremely contentious; in fact, some analysts claim that a failure to reach consensus on the Agreement on Implementation of Article VI of the General Agreement on Tariffs and Trade 1994 (Antidumping Agreement) was largely responsible for delaying the completion of the Uruguay Round negotiations by as long as two years.[2] In the DDA, a coalition of developed and developing nations known as the "Friends of Antidumping" are pushing for reforms that many in Congress oppose and U.S. negotiators are resisting. However, many WTO members regard trade remedy —especially antidumping — reform as a "make or break" issue in terms of their acceptance of any final DDA agreement. The gap between the U.S. position and that of other countries is wide and may be difficult to bridge.

Negotiations on antidumping in the DDA are taking place within the framework of the WTO Negotiating Group on Rules. In the initial phase of Rules negotiations, the major issues on antidumping and the positions of interested parties were established through position papers written by WTO members.[3] At this point in the negotiations, WTO members are suggesting changes to the text of the Antidumping Agreement that will be incorporated into a draft revision of the document. The chairman of the rules negotiations has requested that all of these changes be submitted by the end of April so that he has sufficient time to complete the draft by July.[4]

This report analyzes the issue in three parts. Section one provides background information and contextual analysis for understanding why the issue is regarded as controversial. It briefly discusses the Antidumping Agreement, U.S. antidumping laws and how they have worked in practice. Some U.S. stakeholders, including many U.S. industries and workers, believe that U.S. laws are effective and should not be changed or weakened. Others, including many foreign exporters to the U.S. market, U.S. exporters to international markets, U.S. manufacturers dependent on lower-cost inputs for their products, and other domestic importers of goods subject to AD actions, want to change the allegedly arbitrary way in which they are implemented.

The second section focuses on how antidumping issues fit into the DDA. The mandate to negotiate is explained and negotiating activity to date summarized. The nature of the reforms being considered is described in general terms.

Section three provides a more specific overview of major reform proposals. Many proposals attempt to regulate the manner by which countries assess dumping margins. Other submissions call for tightening rules or providing more specific definitions for terminology used in the WTO Antidumping Agreement. These proposals, if implemented, could significantly reduce the number of permissible AD investigations and/or the amount of duty margins assessed, thus reducing significantly the protective impact of the remedies.

BACKGROUND AND ANALYSIS

"Dumping" is defined in U.S. law as the actual or likely sale of merchandise imported into the United States at "less than its fair value" (LTFV) when these sales cause or threaten material injury to a U.S. industry manufacturing similar goods, or materially retard the establishment of a U.S. industry.[5] This practice is condemned in WTO rules as an unfair trade practice that can cause market disruption and injure producers of like products in the receiving market.[6] Antidumping laws are used by the United States and many U.S. trading partners in an effort to lessen the adverse impact of unfairly traded imports on domestic industries, producers and workers.

Trade remedy actions, particularly AD actions, continue to be a subject of intense debate within Congress, the WTO, and the international business community. Stakeholders in favor of preserving and strengthening AD laws include many U.S. import-competing industries vulnerable to the effects of increased trade liberalization. The steel and chemical industries have used antidumping measures frequently, but smaller industries (such as honey, candles, and crawfish) have also initiated successful AD petitions. Many in Congress have expressed a compelling interest in ensuring that the firms and workers they represent are able to compete on a "level playing field" in the face of increased global competition from firms that use unfair trade practices to gain greater U.S. market share, and believe that AD laws and actions are essential tools to that end.

Stakeholders in favor of eliminating or scaling back these actions include domestic retailers and U.S. consuming industry sectors, such as the automobile or construction industries, that import raw materials or other inputs to include in their downstream products. U.S. exporters have sometimes expressed support for relaxing AD laws because they face similar actions in other countries, and could bear the immediate effects of any trade retaliation if any U.S. laws are determined not to conform to WTO disciplines. Many multinational corporations also favor AD reform because they might have greater freedom to ship products at various stages of development across national boundaries for further transformation. These stakeholders, concerned about selling or producing goods at the lowest cost so that their end-use goods are also competitive, often accuse users of AD action of being protectionist and administrative officials of making arbitrary and politically motivated decisions.

WTO Antidumping Agreement

The General Agreement on Tariffs and Trade 1994 (GATT 1994) and the Antidumping Agreement set forth general governing principles applicable between WTO members, including the "most-favored-nation" principle and guidelines for market access and treatment of imported goods. Article VI of GATT 1994 authorizes WTO members to impose AD duties in addition to other tariffs if domestic officials find that (1) imports of a specific product are sold at less than normal value, and (2) the imports cause or threaten injury to a domestic industry, or materially retard its establishment.

The Antidumping Agreement clarifies and expands Article VI by laying out guidelines for determining if dumping has occurred, identifying the "normal value" of the targeted product, and assessing the dumping margin. The Agreement also provides specific rules for administrative authorities responsible for conducting injury investigations. Detailed methodology is set out for initiating anti-dumping cases, conducting investigations, and ensuring that all interested parties are given an opportunity to present evidence. Specific criteria are set for investigations, including a requirement that investigations must be dropped if authorities determine that the volume of the dumped imports is negligible (less than 3% of total product imports from any one country, or less than 7% for investigations involving several countries).

Antidumping measures must expire five years after the date of imposition, unless an investigation shows that ending the measure would continue to result in injury. According to the Antidumping Agreement, all WTO Member countries must inform the Committee on Antidumping Practices about anti-dumping actions, promptly and in detail, and must also report on all ongoing investigations.[7]

U.S. AD Laws

Although U.S. laws generally conform to the current WTO Antidumping Agreement, some U.S. laws and investigations have been successfully challenged through the WTO dispute settlement process. Recently, in response to an adverse WTO ruling, Congress repealed the Antidumping Act of 1916, which provided for criminal and civil penalties for any person importing goods in the U.S. market with the intent of destroying a domestic industry in the United States.[8] WTO dispute settlement panels and the WTO Appellate Body have also ruled against the Continued Dumping and Subsidy Offset Act (CDSOA), or

"Byrd Amendment," which requires that all duties collected pursuant to antidumping and countervailing investigations must be redistributed to qualified petitioners and interested parties that have been injured by the subject imports.[9] A U.S. administrative practice known as "zeroing" faces WTO challenges from a number of countries, and had been found in WTO dispute settlement proceedings to violate WTO obligations. This practice and the subsequent panel determinations are discussed in a later section.

In the United States, AD investigations generally begin with the filing of a petition by a domestic industry or representative (e.g. labor group, industry association) alleging that certain products are being imported into the country at less than fair value, thus causing material injury, or threat of material injury, to the petitioners.[10] Investigations are carried out by two agencies: the International Trade Administration (ITA) of the Department of Commerce, which investigates allegations of sales at less than fair value (LTFV); and the International Trade Commission (ITC), which investigates injury allegations. These agencies conduct preliminary and final investigations in a detailed administrative process with specific time lines.[11]

If affirmative final determinations are made by both agencies, an "AD duty order" imposing a duty equivalent to the "dumping margin"[12] is issued for the targeted product. This duty is intended to offset the effects of dumping by creating a "level playing field" for the domestic producer. According to current U.S. law, all duties collected as a result of AD duty orders are distributed to the petitioners and interested parties as provided by the CDSOA.[13]

U.S. law also allows the ITA to suspend an investigation at any point in favor of an alternative agreement to: (1) eliminate completely sales at less than fair value or to cease exports of the subject merchandise; (2) eliminate the injurious effect of the subject merchandise or; (3) limit the volume of imports of the subject merchandise into the United States, provided the foreign exporters agree to certain specific conditions.[14] In each case, the ITA must be satisfied that the agreement is in the public interest and that effective monitoring by the United States is practicable.[15]

All AD duty orders and suspension agreements are subject to annual review if requested by any interested party to an investigation or deemed necessary by the ITA.[16] "Changed circumstances" reviews may also be requested at any time, but the ITA must determine whether there is sufficient cause to conduct the review.[17] During the review process, the ITA recalculates the dumping margin for each exporter, thus the AD duties assessed on the subject merchandise may be raised or lowered depending on the price of sales transactions during the period of review (POR). In a changed circumstances review, the ITC also reviews whether a revocation of the order is likely to lead to continuation or recurrence of material injury, or whether a suspension agreement continues to eliminate completely the injurious effects of the imports of subject merchandise.[18]

"Sunset" reviews must be conducted on each AD order no later than once every five years.[19] The ITA determines whether dumping would be likely to continue or resume if an order were to be revoked or a suspension agreement terminated, and the ITC conducts a similar review to determine whether injury to the domestic industry would be likely to continue or resume. If both determinations are affirmative, the duty or suspension agreement remains in place. If either determination is negative, the order is revoked, or the suspension agreement is terminated.[20] In practice, sunset reviews of AD orders resulted in continuations about 53% of the time, according to ITA statistics, and several U.S. AD orders have been in effect since the mid-to-late 1970s.[21]

International AD Activity

Many WTO members are concerned about an apparent escalation of AD activity worldwide, especially since the implementation of the Antidumping Agreement in 1995. Another matter of concern is the apparent increase in these measures by developing countries — considered "nontraditional" users of AD measures. This is one of the reasons that led to the pressure for including WTO disciplines on antidumping in DDA negotiations.

Supporters of antidumping measures acknowledge that AD activity has increased (at least prior to 2003), but also point to a marked increase in the volume of international trade as a whole, suggesting that as overall trade increases the frequency of unfair trading practices, such as dumping, will also have a natural tendency to increase.[22]

WTO statistics on worldwide AD activity may help illustrate the scope and magnitude of the problem. According to antidumping statistics for January 1981 through June 2005 (see Figure 1), the total number of AD initiations rose steadily from 1990 to 1993, decreased sharply in 1994 and 1995 and peaked again in 1999, before reaching an all-time high of 366 in 2001.[23] However, AD activity has been declining since then. In fact, on November 1, 2004, the WTO Secretariat announced that from the period of January 1, 2004 to June 30, 2004 there were 52 final AD measures implemented (duties imposed as well as suspension agreements), as opposed to 114 during the same period in 2003.[24] The rapid decline has led some more skeptical observers to speculate that countries are curbing their appetite for antidumping activity due to the ongoing DDA negotiations. Since international activity seems to vary widely from year to year, it is unclear if the trend toward fewer measures will continue.

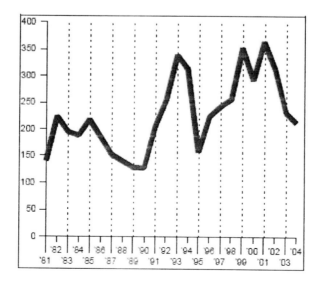

Figure 1. Worldwide Antidumping Initiations, 1981-2004.

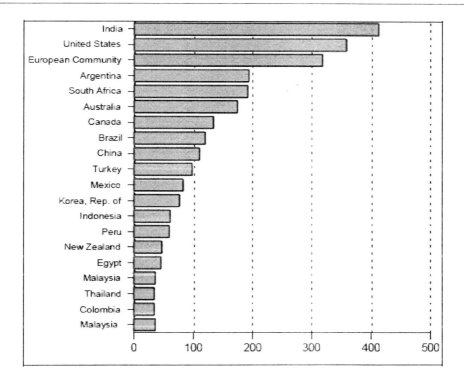

Figure 2. Leading Targets of Worldwide AD Initiations, January 1995 - June 2005.

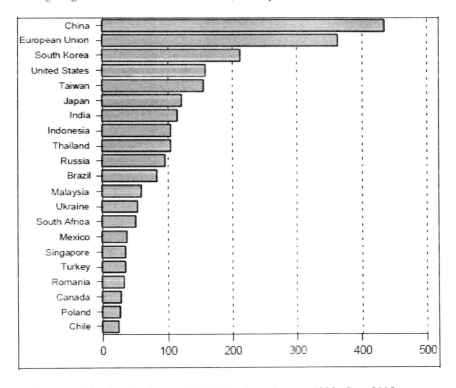

Figure 3. Antidumping Initiations by Selected WTO Members, January 1995 - June 2005.

Figures 2 and 3 illustrate the lead AD initiators and targets of AD initiations from the beginning of 1995 to the first six months of 2005 according to WTO statistics. Initiations were chosen to illustrate AD activity because, according to some economic studies, even the initiation of AD procedures has been shown to cause negative economic effects.[25] According to WTO statistics, India, a developing country who has had antidumping laws in place only since 1992, initiated the most AD petitions in the time period (412), followed by more "traditional" users of these actions, the United States (358) and the European Union (318). Other traditional users of antidumping were lower down on the list, including Australia (174), Canada (133), and New Zealand (46). Other developing countries that were leading initiators of AD actions include Argentina (193), South Africa (191), Brazil (119), China (110), and Turkey (97). Figure 3 illustrates the leading exporter targets of AD initiations from January 1995 to June 2005. China heads this list (434), followed by the European Union (363),[26] followed by Korea (212), the United States (158), Taiwan (155), and Japan (121).

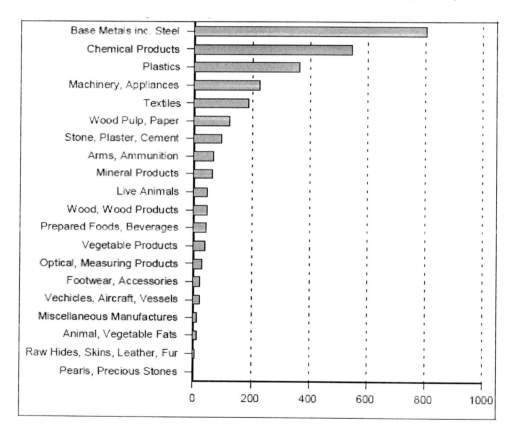

Figure 4. Worldwide Antidumping Initiations (WTO Members) by Sector, Jan. 1995 - June 1005.

Figure 4 illustrates worldwide antidumping initiations by sector. Most antidumping action is related to inputs used in the manufacturing process, including steel and chemical products.[27]

ANTIDUMPING NEGOTIATIONS IN DOHA

When the trade ministers of WTO member nations convened at the November 2001 Ministerial of the World Trade Organization in Doha, Qatar, many countries placed launching a new round of trade negotiations high on the agenda. Some observers believed that a new trade round would give the world economy a much-needed stimulus. U.S. officials wanted to negotiate expanded market access for U.S. exporters, especially in the agriculture and service sectors.[28]

As a result of mounting international concern on expanding trade remedy activity in general and about antidumping in particular, a coalition of developed and developing WTO member countries called the "Friends of Antidumping" — a group consisting of the European Union, Brazil, Chile, China, Colombia, Costa Rica, Hong Kong, India, Israel, Japan, Korea, Mexico, Norway, Singapore, Switzerland, Thailand, and Turkey — believed that any new framework for negotiations should include talks on improving WTO trade remedy rules.

The European Union may have joined the coalition of developing countries, in part, because it is a leading target of antidumping measures. EU trade officials expressed concern at Doha, primarily concerning major differences among countries in their interpretation and application of WTO rules in their domestic trade remedy procedures.[29] Many of the developing nations in the "Friends of Antidumping" group argued that trade remedy action disproportionately affects their economies, and that the Antidumping Agreement should require that developed nations provide some form of "special and differential treatment" when investigating products originating in developing nations.[30]

Then-U.S. Trade Representative (USTR) Robert B. Zoellick, aware of congressional interest in reserving the effectiveness of U.S. trade remedy laws, initially resisted efforts to open negotiations on the Antidumping Agreement. However, U.S. negotiators relented when it seemed evident that the new round of talks would not go forward without some concessions on antidumping. They were able, however, to include language in the Doha negotiating documents that limited radical change, and were also successful in injecting a certain amount of ambiguity in terms of the mandate. The final language of the Doha Ministerial Declaration regarding trade remedies read as follows:

> In light of experience and of the increasing application of these instruments by members, we agree to negotiations aimed at clarifying and improving disciplines under the Agreements on Implementation of Article VI of the GATT 1994 and on Subsidies and Countervailing Measures, while preserving the basic concepts, principles and effectiveness of these Agreements and their instruments and objectives, and taking into account the needs of developing and least-developed participants. In the initial phase of the negotiations, participants will indicate the provisions, including disciplines on trade distorting practices, that they seek to clarify and improve in the subsequent phase...[31]

Ambassador Zoellick later defended the decision to compromise on negotiations on trade remedies by stressing that the United States would push an "offensive agenda" on trade remedies in order to address the increasing "misuse" of trade remedy measures by other WTO Member countries against U.S. exporters.[32] He also said that since WTO dispute panels had gone against the United States in several cases involving trade remedy cases, U.S. negotiators were especially interested in tightening dispute panel and Appellate Body "standard of review" provisions so that panels do not add to the obligations of, nor diminish the rights of, WTO Member nations.[33] Many congressional supporters of trade remedy laws believe that Zoellick did not try hard enough to leave them off the table, and subsequently are concerned about the ability of the USTR to negotiate in this area in a manner that is favorable to their manufacturing constituents.[34]

RECENT DEVELOPMENTS

According to a report by the Chairman of the Negotiating Group on Rules prior to the Hong Kong Ministerial, work on trade remedies has taken place in three overlapping phases. First, negotiators presented formal written papers indicating the general areas in which the participants would like to see changes in the agreements. A compilation of the 141 proposals was published by the Chairman in August 2003, just prior to the Cancun Ministerial.[35] Second, after Cancun ministerial and through other ongoing negotiations, negotiators began discussing their positions in more detail, sometimes proposing legal drafts of suggested changes.[36] This phase helped negotiators develop a clearer idea of what proponents of specific changes are seeking, and "a realistic view of what may and may not attract broader support in the group."[37] The third phase consists of bilateral and plurilateral meetings for technical consultations, partly aimed at developing a possible standardized questionnaire which administering officials could use in AD investigations in order to reduce costs and increase transparency.[38]

The Chairman's report emphasizes "we are not dealing with ... big picture issues, but with a very large number of highly specific issues" and the result of discussions will be based on the "precise details of the drafting." Therefore, he said, traditional means of arriving at consensus in WTO discussions such as "modalities" may not work in this context.[39]

The Chairman of the Rules Committee further noted that any consensus on changing the ADA, SCM, or other trade remedy agreements is likely to involve internal trade-offs on trade remedies in exchange for external linkages — that is, perceived successes in other areas of DDA negotiations, such as improved agricultural market access or services trade.[40] Others agree, speculating, therefore, that any agreement on changes to trade remedies is not likely to take place until the end of the round. However, some speculate that, given the opposition expressed by many in Congress to any changes in the WTO agreements that would lead to lessening the effectiveness of U.S. trade remedy laws, some Members may not be willing to yield on such modifications *even if* major concessions were reached in other areas deemed critical to U.S. interests.[41]

Hong Kong Ministerial Text

In Appendix D of the Hong Kong Ministerial Declaration issued on December 18, 2005, WTO members reaffirmed that "achievement of substantial results on all aspects of the Rules mandate" is important to the further development of the rules-based multilateral trading system. The document recognized that negotiations, especially on antidumping procedures, have intensified and deepened and that "participants are demonstrating a high level of constructive engagement."[42] The Group was directed "to intensify and accelerate the negotiating process" and complete the process of analyzing proposals by Participants on the AD and SCM Agreements as soon as possible."[43] The Chairman was then directed to prepare consolidated texts of the Antidumping and Subsidies Agreements based on the previous negotiating papers which will become the "basis for the final stage of the negotiations."[44] This assertion is controversial given the opposition of many in Congress to any concessions that may weaken U.S. trade remedy laws.

The draft document also suggests that WTO members are committed to "enhancing the mutual supportiveness of trade and the environment, note that there is broad agreement that the Group should strengthen disciplines on subsidies in the fisheries sector" through prohibiting subsidies that lead to over-fishing and overcapacity.[45] In this context, the draft directs the Negotiating Group on Rules to intensify and accelerate the negotiating process.[46]

MAJOR ISSUES IN NEGOTIATIONS

The Antidumping Agreement, perhaps by design, is somewhat ambiguous. Many countries, especially the "Friends of Antidumping," would like to see more specific definitions and guidelines in order to provide some type of harmony in nations' implementation of trade remedy laws. However, most of the proposals, if implemented, could also lessen the ability of petitioners to obtain relief. Because the Agreement, in essence, is designed to provide general rules for various administrative officials in WTO member countries to follow when calculating dumping margins, determining injury, and granting relief, many of the proposals involve highly technical changes that are beyond the scope of this report. However, there are some specific discussion threads in presentations to date that can be explained in a very general way.

It is important to note that the DDA mandate specifies that negotiations on trade remedies are intended to "clarify and improve" the WTO Agreements rather than to eliminate them. With this in mind, many WTO members have identified key provisions they seek to address in future negotiations through proposals formally submitted to the WTO Negotiating Group on Rules.[47]

Because the United States is a large user, but also a large target, of AD actions, there is a trade-off between the costs and benefits of modifications to the Antidumping Agreement. The United States could benefit from some of the suggested modifications, especially if they enhance the transparency of trade remedy procedures in other WTO Member countries. However, other proposals could raise the threshold for domestic petitioners' ability to obtain relief, lower calculated dumping margin levels, or mandatorily limit the duration of antidumping orders.

In addition, all WTO negotiations are conducted on a consensus basis. Any proposal submitted by the United States would require the agreement of all other members, perhaps in conjunction with U.S. acceptance of other members' proposals. Thus, the submission of any proposal on trade remedies likely is accompanied by certain calculations on the part of the USTR on whether any consensus can be reached on the issues, and to what negotiating concessions the United States may have to agree. This calculation may be especially significant considering the generally defensive nature of U.S. negotiating positions at the rules talks.

This discussion of DDA negotiations on antidumping focuses on suggested changes (1) for which there seems to be broad support among WTO members, and (2) which could potentially result in significant amendment to U.S. laws or administrative procedures. Several of these recommendations could affect methodologies used by authorities to determine injury and calculate dumping margins. Another proposal seeks mandatory termination of AD orders after a specified period.

Antidumping Duty Assessment

Many WTO members believe that the methodology used by some countries to calculate dumping margins leads to highly inflated duties that are disproportionate to the amount needed to mitigate the injury to the domestic industry, as well as the level of dumping practiced by the exporters. Some Members have particularly criticized U.S. methodology, where ITA-calculated dumping margins typically average between 60 and 70 percent.[48] Consequently, revisions in the Antidumping Agreement that could lower dumping margins have been major focus of submissions to the Rules Committee.

Some proposals that have drawn broad support include a ban on "zeroing," a mandatory "lesser duty" rule, and increased use of "price undertakings." These proposed changes would affect primarily ITA administrative rules for calculating dumping margins, but may also require some modification to U.S. law.

Ban on Zeroing

In U.S. law, AD orders imposed on targeted merchandise must be equal to the dumping margin or "the amount by which the normal value exceeds the export price or constructed export price of the subject merchandise."[49] The ITA typically calculates the margin by first identifying, to the extent possible, all U.S. transactions, sale prices, and levels of trade for each model or type of targeted merchandise sold by each company in the exporting country. These model types are then aggregated into a subcategories, known as "averaging groups," which are used to calculate the "weighted average export price." The export prices for each subgroup are then compared to the corresponding agency-calculated "weighted average normal value." Finally, the results of all of these comparisons are added up to establish the overall dumping margin of the targeted product.[50]

When authorities add up the dumping margins of each of the subgroups to establish an overall dumping margin for the subject merchandise, they sometimes encounter negative margins in a subgroup, an indicator that the items in that category are not being dumped. However, rather than including the negative margin in their calculations, which might result in a lower overall dumping margin, ITA officials factor in the results of that subgroup as a zero.[51] Officials use a similar practice when re-calculating dumping margins in administrative reviews of AD orders or suspension agreements. One justification for the zeroing practice is that the dumping margin could be skewed if, when determining the weighted average dumping margin, the subgroup that has the negative dumping margin represents a substantial percentage of export sales.

The U.S. practice is currently being challenged in the WTO on a number of fronts. On February 6, 2004, the European Union formally requested the establishment of a dispute settlement panel on zeroing, citing 31 U.S. AD cases targeting products of the EU. The EU claims that in these cases the dumping margin would have been minimal, or even negative, if U.S. officials had not used zeroing.

A panel was established on March 19, 2004.[52] In a split decision, in late October 2005, the dispute settlement panel report found for the United States in its use of zeroing in the course of administrative reviews, but against U.S. practice when conducting initial investigations.[53]

In part, the Panel determined that the denial of offsets when calculating the weighted average dumping margin using the "average-to-average" comparison methodology when conducting original investigation was inconsistent with U.S. obligations under Article 2.4.2 of the Antidumping Agreement — an aspect of the ruling that the United States did not appeal. In early March 2006 the International Trade Administration began the process of amending its procedures by soliciting public comments on amended methodology.[54]

On April 18, 2006, the WTO Appellate Body overturned the dispute panel's ruling that "zeroing" methodology was permissible in administrative reviews.[55] While the European Union welcomed the decision, USTR responded that "the Appellate Body's analysis failed to address many of the important issues raised in the appeal, and appears difficult to reconcile with other areas of antidumping."[56]

On November 24, 2004, Japan also requested consultations with the United States on zeroing, citing 15 cases that the practice was used when calculating dumping margins on Japanese merchandise.[57] Mexico requested consultations on zeroing on January 10, 2005, as it related specifically to a dumping determination on stainless steel products.[58] A dispute settlement panel has been established on one other complaint by Mexico, involving U.S. zeroing practices on oil country tubular goods from Mexico.[59]

On December 10, 2004, Thailand also requested WTO consultations on zeroing, challenging use of U.S. practice when establishing provisional duties on shrimp exports.[60]

Since the European Union's practice of zeroing had already been found to violate the Antidumping Agreement in a dispute settlement case brought by India, many observers speculated that any dispute proceeding against the United States on the practice will produce a similar result.[61]

The U.S. practice of zeroing is neither required, nor prohibited, by U.S. law; therefore it is not clear if congressional action would be required if the United States loses one of these disputes or if the DDA changes the rules.[62]

Mandatory Lesser Duty Rule

Article 9.1 of the Antidumping Agreement encourages the imposition of an AD duty lower than the full dumping margin if investigating authorities determine that the lesser amount is sufficient to offset the injury suffered or threatened to the domestic industry. Many WTO members favor amending the Antidumping Agreement to require a *mandatory*, rather than discretionary, "lesser duty rule." Developing countries are especially interested in seeing a mandatory rule applied to exports from their countries, and have proposed this measure as part of a "special and differential treatment" package of trade concessions offered by developed nations to developing countries.[63] There is currently no "lesser duty rule" in U.S. law or practice, and enactment of a mandatory rule might require congressional action.

"Price Undertakings"

Article 8 of the Antidumping Agreement allows the use of "voluntary undertakings from any exporter to revise its prices or to cease exports to the area in question at dumped prices" provided that investigating authorities are satisfied that the injurious effect of the dumping is eliminated. Many WTO members favor increased use of "price undertakings," because they believe that the practice is less damaging to exporters, while also mitigating the injury to domestic producers.[64] Some developing countries favor mandatory use of price undertakings by developed country members in AD cases involving developing countries.

U.S. antidumping law allows for similar alternative arrangements, known in U.S. law as suspension agreements,[65] but in practice, the ITA does not use them very often. At present, there are only six U.S. suspension agreements and one quantitative restriction agreement in place, in comparison to more than 260 active AD orders.[66]

Proposed Changes in Injury Determinations

Another major focus of proposals for amending the Antidumping Agreement is redefining and streamlining the methodology by which administrative authorities determine injury. Some WTO members believe that the guidelines and definitions in the Agreement are too subjective and that procedures lack transparency in many countries.[67] Some proposals in this area involve designing new rules that provide more precise guidance or objective criteria when making injury determinations, while others favor more precise definitions for the terms in Agreement such as "material injury," "material retardation," or "threat of material injury." Some negotiators believe that factors other than dumping are often to blame for industry declines and consequently favor more objective criteria for establishing the existence of a clear and substantial link to dumping before determining injury.[68]

Mandatory Sunset of AD Orders

The current Antidumping Agreement specifies that each antidumping order must be terminated after five years *unless* authorities determine in a review that its expiration would be likely to lead to a recurrence of dumping and subsequent injury to the domestic producer.

Some WTO members are critical of the use of sunset and administrative reviews that determine if relief is still needed. In particular, many have complained that U.S. authorities base sunset review determinations inordinately on submissions by the domestic industry. They claim that, consequently, U.S. AD orders are likely to remain in place as long as the domestic industry opposes their removal.[69]

There seems to be strong support among WTO members for a mandatory termination of AD orders within five years. Other Members favor a more moderate approach that would list specific circumstances or definitive factors that authorities must consider before extending AD orders. Others criticize the length of time that sunset review procedures take to complete and favor a mandatory twelve- month time limit.[70]

Treatment of Developing Countries

Many developing countries complain that antidumping actions on their products, as well as illegal dumping in their countries, affects their economies disproportionately. Article 15 of the Antidumping Agreement recommends that developed countries show "special regard" for the economic situation of least-developed and developing country members, and suggests that "constructive remedies" be used instead of assessing antidumping duties. However, it does not require or specify a particular course of action for antidumping proceedings.

The "Friends of Antidumping" and others have proposed that developing countries should include specific provisions that will provide these countries with "meaningful special and differential treatment" when facing antidumping actions.[71] Some general recommendations for providing special regard have included requiring developed countries to negotiate/accept mandatory price undertakings (suspension agreements) when investigating products of developing countries, and raising the *de minimis* threshold (i.e. the margin at which the amount of dumping is found to be insignificant).

Many developing countries also maintain the cost of initiating an antidumping proceeding under the existing requirements of the Antidumping Agreement is prohibitive. One recommendation calls for standardizing certain investigative procedures in order to make AD action less costly for all countries.[72] Some suggestions in this vein include requiring shorter periods for investigations, mandatory deadlines for reviews, and development of a questionnaire so that all investigators know precisely what information is necessary to extract when investigating a case.[73]

Possible Effects of Changes

Most of the proposed changes in the Antidumping Agreement, if adopted, would further restrict the ability of all WTO members to grant relief to import-competing industries. Import-competing industries in the United States may find it more difficult to obtain relief, could have lower dumping margins assessed on targeted merchandise, or could be authorized to receive relief for a shorter time period. Other countries would face the same restrictions, however, which could benefit U.S. exporters. U.S. consuming industries, and ultimately consumers, might also benefit from lower prices for production inputs and finished goods.

More specifically, proposals to change dumping margin calculations likely would require changes in the way in which the ITA calculates the level of relief that domestic companies will gain from AD action. Most of these changes can be accomplished administratively, via regulations and procedural changes. However, legislation may be necessary to enact some of the proposals, at least for the sake of greater official transparency. Lower dumping margins would, in turn, reduce the amount of CDSOA disbursements that U.S. petitioners and interested parties receive as the result of AD action.

Suggestions for changes in procedures for determining injury could result in fewer changes to U.S. laws and administrative procedures (which already provide considerable quantitative guidance, narrow definitions, and specific timetables) than they would in other WTO member countries. U.S. exporters might benefit from enhanced transparency in AD investigations in receiving markets, while industries seeking AD action in the United States might be only minimally affected. However, since the overall objective of many WTO members seems to be to restrict the ability of domestic industries in the importing countries to receive relief, it is still possible that modifications in this area could lead to changes that could diminish the use and effectiveness of AD actions.

Proposals for modifying the duration of AD orders, such as requiring mandatory sunset after five years, could have a significant effect on U.S. domestic industries. The United States currently has about 190 AD orders[74] that have been in effect longer than five years (the oldest, on polychloroprene rubber from Japan dates from 1973). Statistics on five-year reviews conducted from January 2000 to January 2005 indicate in the 116 reviews initiated during the period, the ITA and ITC decided to revoke 37 AD orders, continued 52 orders, and an additional 27 investigations are still pending.[75] These statistics indicate that a number of U.S. AD orders do continue in place beyond the five-year period. Therefore, adoption of a mandatory five-year revocation of AD orders could have a substantial impact on U.S. trade remedy policy, as well as on industries that have benefitted from the protection of these orders.

CONCLUSION AND OPTIONS FOR CONGRESS

When Congress granted presidential Trade Promotion Authority (TPA) in 2002 (P.L. 107-210), it agreed to consider legislation to implement a trade agreement under special legislative procedures that limit debate and allow no amendment. Therefore, any negotiated WTO agreement must be subject to an "up or down" vote with limited debate in both Houses.

However, Congress also gave itself considerable oversight authority over trade negotiations by requiring the President and other executive agencies (particularly the USTR) to consult with Congress, to provide congressional committees with regular, detailed briefings on the status of negotiations, and to coordinate closely with a Congressional Oversight Group consisting of chairmen, ranking members, and other representatives from the House Ways and Means and Senate Finance committees.[76] Since many members were particularly concerned about modifications to the Antidumping Agreement, the TPA approval legislation required the President to report within 180 days prior to acceptance of a trade agreement if any of the proposals could require amendments to trade remedy laws.[77] The law also provided specific language for a procedural resolution of disapproval to be introduced in either House if Congress determined that the proposed changes to the trade remedy laws in any agreement are inconsistent with U.S. negotiating objectives on trade remedies.[78] Although the disapproval resolution would not be binding on the President or on the USTR, such a resolution, if passed, would send a clear message that Congress resists any modifications to the WTO Agreements that would weaken U.S. trade remedy laws.

It should be noted that TPA expired on June 1, 2005, and continues now under a two-year extension as requested by the President and approved by Congress. Although the President received the extension, some are concerned that DDA negotiations must be concluded before this grant of TPA terminates on June 1, 2007, if any substantive agreement is to be reached.[79]

In addition, since United States was found to be in violation of its WTO obligations with regard to the CDSOA and the usage of zeroing when conducting initial investigations, some observers suggest that it might be advantageous for the United States to concede on these issues in DDA negotiations, especially if by doing so U.S. negotiators can avoid other changes to the Agreement that might adversely affect U.S. trade remedy laws.

Currently, the gap between the U.S. position on antidumping and that of our WTO trading partners appears to be very wide and may be difficult to narrow. However, trade negotiators from all countries must weigh concessions made against gains in other areas in the WTO negotiations.

REFERENCES

[1] World Trade Organization. Doha Work Program. Ministerial Declaration. WT/MN(05)/DEC, December 22, 2005, Annex D, paragraph 2.

[2] Dunn, Alan M. "Antidumping." In Stewart, Terence P., ed., The World Trade Organization: The Multilateral Trade Framework for the 21st Century and U.S. Implementing Legislation, Washington, DC: American Bar Association, 1996, p. 246.

[3] See World Trade Organization, Negotiating Group on Rules, *Compilation of Issues and Proposals Identified by Participants in the Negotiating Group on Rules*, Note by the Chairman, TN/RL/W/143, August 22, 2003.

[4] WTO, Negotiating Group on Rules. Report by the Chairman to the Trade Negotiations Committee. TN/RL/16, March 28, 2006, p. 1.

[5] 19 U.S.C. 1673.

[6] General Agreement on Tariffs and Trade (GATT) 1994, Article VI (1).

[7] World Trade Organization. "Introduction to Antidumping in the WTO," [http://www.wto.org].

[8] 15 U.S.C. 72. The Antidumping Act of 1916 was repealed in the Miscellaneous Tariff and Technical Corrections Act of 2004 (P.L. 108-429). Cases currently pending under the act were permitted to go forward.

[9] 19 U.S.C. 1675c. The CDSOA was repealed in the Deficit Reduction Act of 2005 (P.L. 109-171) but disbursements under the law were permitted to continue, as if the law were not repealed, for all goods entering the United States before October 2007.

[10] 19 U.S.C. 1673. The ITA may also self-initiate an investigation (19 U.S.C. 1673a(a)).

[11] For a more thorough discussion of U.S. antidumping laws and administrative procedures, please see CRS Report RL32371, *Trade Remedies: A Primer*, Vivian C. Jones.

[12] The "dumping margin" is the ITA-calculated percentage difference between the price (or cost) of the good in the foreign market and the price at which it is sold in the U.S. market.

[13] 19 U.S.C. 1675c.

[14] 19 U.S.C. 1673c(b) and (c).

[15] 19 U.S.C. 1673c(a)(2) applies to quantitative restrictions. 19 U.S.C. 1673c(d) applies to other alternative agreements.

[16] 19 U.S.C. 1675(a).

[17] 19 U.S.C. 1675(b).

[18] 19 U.S.C. 1675(b)(2).

[19] 19 U.S.C. 1675(c).

[20] 19 U.S.C. 1675(d).
[21] ITA investigation statistics [http://www.ia.ita.doc.gov/stats/].
[22] World Trade Organization. "Basic Concepts and Principles of the Trade Remedy Rules," Submission of the United States TN/RL/W/27, October 22, 2002.
[23] All AD statistics in this section originate from the following sources, unless otherwise indicated: World Trade Organization. *Report of the Committee on Anti-Dumping Practices to the General Council,* 2003, and *Report of the Committee on Anti-Dumping Practices under Article 16.4 of the Agreement,* various years and countries. Tables reflecting AD activity since 1995 are available at [http://www.wto.org/english/tratop_e/adp_e/adp_e.htm].
[24] World Trade Organization. "WTO Secretariat Reports Significant Decline in New Final Antidumping Measures." Press Release, November 1, 2004, PRESS/387, [http://www.wto.org/english/news_e/pres04_e/pr387_e.htm].
[25] See especially Prusa, Thomas J. "On the Spread and Impact of Antidumping," *Canadian Journal of Economics*, 34:3, August, 2001, p.601.
[26] Includes those AD cases initiated on the European Communities collectively and those pursued against products of individual EU countries.
[27] See CRS Report RL32371, *Trade Remedies: A Primer*, by Vivian C. Jones.
[28] See CRS Report RL32060, The World Trade Organization: The Doha Development Agenda, by Ian Fergusson.
[29] World Trade Organization. Negotiating Group on Rules. Submission from the European Communities Concerning the Agreement on Implementation of Article VI of GATT 1994 (Anti-Dumping Agreement). TN/RL/W/13, July 8, 2002. [http://docsonline.wto.org].
[30] Ibid., p. 3.
[31] World Trade Organization. Ministerial Declaration. WT/MIN(01)/DEC/1, November 14, 2001, paragraph 28.
[32] "USTR Zoellick Says World Has Chosen Path of Hope, Openness, Development, and Growth." Office of the U.S. Trade Representative. Press Release, November 14, 2001. [http://www.ustr.gov/].
[33] Ibid, p. 5.
[34] "Rockefeller Attacks Zoellick for Doha, Failure to Appear at Markup." *Inside U.S. Trade*, December 13, 2001. [http://www.insidetrade.com].
[35] WTO Negotiating Group on Rules. Note by the Chairman. "Compilation of Issues and Proposals Identified by Participants in the Negotiating Group on Rules." TN/RL/W/143, August 22, 2003, p. 1.
[36] See WTO Negotiating Group on Rules. Report by the Chairman to the Trade Negotiations Committee. TN/RL/13, July 19, 2005, p. 2.
[37] Ibid., pp. 1-2.
[38] Ibid.
[39] Ibid., p. 2.
[40] Ibid.
[41] Comments by speakers at Global Business Dialogue event on November 8, 2005.
[42] "Ministerial Declaration, Annex D, paragraph 2.
[43] Ibid, paragraph 10.
[44] Ibid, paragraph 11.

[45] Ibid, p. D-2.
[46] Ibid.
[47] World Trade Organization. Negotiating Group on Rules. *Compilation of Issues and Proposals Identified by Participants in the Negotiating Group on Rules.* Note by the Chairman. August 22, 2003, TN/RL/W/143, [http://docsonline.wto.org].
[48] Prusa, Thomas J. "Anticompetitive Effects of Antidumping." Presentation at American Enterprise Institute, March 18, 2004.
[49] 19 U.S.C. 1677(35)(A).
[50] See Department of Commerce, Import Administration. *Antidumping Manual,* Chapter 6, "Fair Value Comparisons." 1997 edition. [http://ia.ita.doc.gov/admanual/index.html].
[51] 19 U.S.C. 1677f-1(d)(A)(i) and (ii).
[52] World Trade Organization. Dispute Settlement Body. *United States — Laws, Regulations, and Methodology for Calculating Dumping Margins ("Zeroing").* Request for the establishment of a panel by the European Communities, WT/DS294/7, February 6, 2004. Ruling of the Panel distributed October 31, 2005. Available at [http://docsonline.wto.org].
[53] World Trade Organization. Dispute Settlement Body. *United States — Laws, Regulations, and Methodology for Calculating Dumping Margins ("Zeroing").* Report of the Panel. WT/DS294/R, October 31, 2005.
[54] 71 F.R. 11189.
[55] World Trade Organization. Appellate Body. *United States — Laws, Regulations, and Methodology for Calculating Dumping Margins ("Zeroing").* Report of the Appellate Body. WT/DS294/AB/R, April 18, 2006.
[56] "WTO Appellate Body Reverses Panel Decision For U.S. on Zeroing in Administrative Reviews." BNA Daily Report for Executives, April 19, 2006.
[57] World Trade Organization. Dispute Settlement Body. *United States — Measures Relating to Zeroing and Sunset Reviews.* Request for Consultations by Japan, WT/DS322/1, G/L/720, G/ADP/D58/1, November 29, 2004. Dispute panel established, January 2005. The panel has announced that its determination will be delayed at least until March 2006.
[58] World Trade Organization. Dispute Settlement Body. *United States — Anti-dumping Determination Regarding Stainless Steel from Mexico.* Request for Consultations by Mexico, WT/DS325/1, G/L/727, G/ADP/D60/1, January 10, 2005. No dispute settlement panel has been established to date.
[59] World Trade Organization. *United States — Anti-dumping Measures on Oil Country Tubular Goods from Mexico.* Request for the Establishment of a Panel by Mexico. WT/DS282/2, February 26, 2003. World Trade Organization. *United States — Anti-Dumping Determinations Regarding Stainless Steel from Mexico.* Request for Consultations by Mexico WT/DS325/1, January 10, 2005.
[60] World Trade Organization. Dispute Settlement Body. *United States — Provisional Anti-Dumping Measures on Shrimp from Thailand.* WT/DS324/1, G/L/726, G/ADP/D59/1, December 14, 2004.
[61] World Trade Organization. Appellate Body. European Communities — Anti-Dumping Duties on Imports of Cotton-Type Bed Linen from India, WT/DS141/AB/R, March 1, 2001.

[62] See Serampore Industries Pvt. Ltd. v. U.S. Department of Commerce, 696 F. Supp. 665 (1988).
[63] World Trade Organization. Negotiating Group on Rules. Note by the Chairman. Compilation of Issues and Proposals Identified by Participants in the Negotiating Group on Rules, TN/RL/W/143, August 22, 2003, p. 49.
[64] Ibid., page 46.
[65] See 19 U.S.C. 1673c.
[66] ITA statistics [http://www.ia.ita.doc.gov/stats/]. Quantitative restriction agreement is on 15 steel products from Russia. See also CRS Report RL32371, *Trade Remedies: A Primer*, by Vivian C. Jones.
[67] See World Trade Organization. Negotiating Group on Rules. *Compilation of Issues and Proposals Identified by Participants in the Negotiating Group on Rules.* Note by the Chairman. August 22, 2003, TN/RL/W/143, [http://docsonline.wto.org], pp. 15-20.
[68] World Trade Organization. Negotiating Group on Rules. *Antidumping: Illustrative Major Issues.* Submission by Brazil, Chile, Colombia, Costa Rica, Hong Kong, China, Israel, Japan, Korea, Mexico, Norway, Singapore, Switzerland, Thailand, and Turkey. April 26, 2002, p. 3.
[69] One representative example of this view is World Trade Organization. Negotiating Group on Rules. "Proposal on Reviews." Paper from Brazil; Chile; Colombia; Costa Rica; Hong Kong; China; Israel; Japan; Korea; Norway; Singapore; Switzerland; the Separate Customs Territory of Taiwan, Penghu, Kinmen and Matsu; and Thailand. TN/RL/W/83, April 25, 2003 [http://docsonline.wto.org].
[70] World Trade Organization. Negotiating Group on Rules. *Compilation of Issues and Proposals Identified by Participants in the Negotiating Group on Rules.* Note by the Chairman. August 22, 2003, TN/RL/W/143, pp. 58, 143 [http://docsonline.wto.org].
[71] World Trade Organization. Negotiating Group on Rules. Paper by Brazil; Colombia; Costa Rica; Hong Kong, China; Israel; Korea; Japan; Mexico; Norway; Separate Customs Territory of Taiwan, Penghu, Kinmen and Matsu; Singapore; Switzerland; Thailand and Turkey. TN/RL/W/46, January 24, 2003 [http://docsonline.wto.org].
[72] World Trade Organization. Negotiating Group on Rules. Paper by the European Communities and Japan. TN/RL/W/138, July 17, 2003.
[73] Ibid.
[74] ITC statistics at [http://www.usitc.gov/ trade_remedy/731_ad_701_cvd/index.htm].
[75] Ibid.
[76] 19 U.S.C. 3807. See CRS Report RL31974, Trade Agreements: Requirements for Presidential Consultations, Notices, and Reports to Congress Regarding Negotiations, by Vladimir Pregelj.
[77] 19 U.S.C. 3804 (d)(3)(A).
[78] 19 U.S.C. 3804(d)(3)(C).
[79] Comments by speakers at Global Business Dialogue event on November 8, 2005.

Chapter 7

DISPUTE SETTLEMENT IN THE WORLD TRADE ORGANIZATION: AN OVERVIEW[*]

Jeanne J. Grimmett

ABSTRACT

Dispute resolution in the World Trade Organization (WTO) is carried out under the WTO Dispute Settlement Understanding (DSU), whose rules and procedures apply to virtually all WTO agreements. The DSU provides for consultations between disputing parties, panels and appeals, and possible compensation or retaliation if a defending party does not comply with an adverse WTO decision by a given date. Automatic establishment of panels, adoption of reports, and authorization of requests to retaliate, along with deadlines for various stages of the dispute process and improved multilateral surveillance and enforcement of WTO obligations, are aimed at producing a more expeditious and effective system than that which existed under the GATT. To date, 349 WTO complaints have been filed, slightly more than half of which involve the United States as a complaining party or defendant. Expressing dissatisfaction with WTO dispute settlement results in the trade remedy area, Congress directed the executive branch to address dispute settlement issues in WTO negotiations in its grant of trade promotion authority to the President in 2002 (P.L. 107-210). WTO Members had been negotiating DSU revisions in the now-suspended WTO Doha Round, though a draft agreement was not produced. S. 817 (Stabenow), S. 1542 (Stabenow), S. 2317 (Baucus), and H.R. 4186 (Camp) would each establish a new position in the Office of the United States Trade Representative (USTR) to help the USTR investigate and prosecute WTO disputes. S. 2467 (Grassley) would make the USTR General Counsel a confirmable position expressly responsible for WTO dispute settlement. H.R. 4733 (Rangel) and H.R. 5043 (Cardin) would create new congressional entities with functions related to WTO disputes.

---

[*] Excerpted from CRS Report RS20088, dated September 14, 2006.

BACKGROUND

From its inception, the General Agreement on Tariffs and Trade (GATT) has provided for consultations and dispute resolution among GATT Contracting Parties, allowing a party to invoke GATT dispute articles if it believes that another's measure, whether violative of the GATT or not, has caused it trade injury. Because the GATT does not set out a dispute procedure with great specificity, GATT Parties over time developed a more detailed process including ad hoc panels and other practices. The procedure was perceived to have certain deficiencies, however, among them a lack of deadlines, the use of consensus decision-making (thus allowing a Party to block the establishment of panels and adoption of panel reports), and laxity in surveillance and implementation of dispute settlement results. Congress made reform of the GATT dispute process a principal U.S. goal in the Uruguay Round of Multilateral Trade Negotiations.

WTO DISPUTE SETTLEMENT UNDERSTANDING

The Uruguay Round Understanding on Rules and Procedures Governing the Settlement of Disputes (DSU), which went into effect January 1, 1995, continues past GATT dispute practice, but also contains several features aimed at strengthening the prior system.[1] A Dispute Settlement Body (DSB), consisting of representatives of all WTO Members, administers dispute proceedings. While the DSB ordinarily operates by consensus (i.e., without formal objection of any Member present), the DSU reverses past consensus practice at fundamental stages of the process. Thus, unless it decides by consensus *not* to do so, the DSB is to establish panels; adopt panel and appellate reports; and, where WTO rulings have not been implemented and if requested by a prevailing party, authorize the party to impose a retaliatory measure. The DSU also sets forth deadlines for various stages of the proceedings and improves multilateral monitoring of the implementation of adopted rulings. Given that panel reports are to be adopted automatically, WTO Members have a right to appeal a panel report on issues of law. The DSU created a standing Appellate Body to carry out this new appellate function; the Body has seven members, three of whom serve on any one case.

The DSU provides for integrated dispute settlement — that is, the same rules apply to disputes under virtually all WTO agreements unless a specific agreement provides otherwise. If a dispute reaches the retaliatory stage, this approach allows a Member to impose a countermeasure in a sector or under an agreement other than the one at issue ("cross-retaliate"). The preferred outcome of the dispute mechanism is "a solution mutually acceptable to the parties and consistent with the covered agreements"; absent such a solution, the primary objective of the process is withdrawal of a violative measure, with compensation and retaliation being avenues of last resort. The DSU has proved popular, with 349 complaints filed from January 1, 1995, to date; slightly more than half involve the United States as either a complaining party or a defendant. The United States Trade Representative (USTR) represents the United States in WTO disputes.

The DSU was scrutinized by Members pursuant to an Uruguay Round Declaration, which called for completion of a review within four years after the WTO Agreement entered into force (i.e., by January 1, 1999). Members did not agree on any revisions in this review, and although negotiations on dispute settlement issues had continued during the currently suspended Doha Round, a draft agreement on dispute settlement was not produced.[2] Discussions have addressed, inter alia, "remand, sequencing, post-retaliation, third-party rights, flexibility and Member control, panel composition, time-savings, and transparency."[3] The United States has proposed greater Member control over the dispute settlement process, guidelines for WTO adjudicative bodies, and increased transparency (e.g., through open meetings and timely access to submissions and final reports).[4]

STEPS IN A WTO DISPUTE PROCEEDING

Consultations (Art. 4)

If a WTO Member requests consultations with another Member under a WTO agreement, the latter must generally respond within 10 days and enter into consultations within 30 days. If the dispute is not resolved within 60 days after receipt of the request to consult, the complaining party may request a panel. The complainant may request a panel earlier if the defending Member has failed to enter into consultations or if the disputants agree that consultations have been unsuccessful.

Establishing a Dispute Panel (Arts. 6, 8)

If a panel is requested, the DSB must establish it at the second DSB meeting at which the request appears as an agenda item, unless it decides by consensus not to do so. The panel is generally composed of three persons. The Secretariat proposes the names of panelists to the disputants, who may not oppose them except for "compelling reasons." If there is no agreement on panelists within 20 days from the date the panel is established, either disputing party may request the WTO Director-General to appoint the panelists.

Panel Proceedings (Arts. 12, 15)

After considering written and oral arguments, the panel issues the descriptive part of its report (facts and argument) to the disputing parties. After considering any comments, the panel submits this portion along with its findings and conclusions to the disputants as an interim report. Absent further comments, the interim report is considered to be the final report and is circulated promptly to WTO Members. A panel must generally circulate its report to the disputants within six months after the panel is composed, but may take longer if needed. The period from panel establishment to circulation of the report to all Members should not exceed nine months. In practice, panels have increasingly failed to meet the six-month deadline.[5]

Adoption of Panel Reports/Appellate Review (Arts. 16, 17, 20)

Within 60 days after a panel report is circulated to WTO Members, the report is to be adopted at a DSB meeting unless a disputing party appeals it or the DSB decides by consensus not to adopt it. Within 60 days of being notified of an appeal (extendable to 90 days), the Appellate Body (AB) must issue a report that upholds, reverses, or modifies the panel report. The AB report is to be adopted by the DSB, and unconditionally accepted by the disputing parties, unless the DSB decides by consensus not to adopt it within 30 days after circulation to Members. The period of time from the date the panel is established to the date the DSB considers the panel report for adoption is not to exceed nine months (12 months where the report is appealed) unless otherwise agreed by the disputing parties.

Implementation of Panel and Appellate Body Reports (Art. 21)

Thirty days after the panel and any AB reports are adopted, the Member must inform the DSB how it will implement the WTO ruling. If it is "impracticable" to comply immediately, the Member will have a "reasonable period of time" to do so. The period will be: (1) that proposed by the Member and approved by the DSB; (2) absent approval, the period mutually agreed by the disputing parties within 45 days after the date of adoption of the report or reports; or (3) failing agreement, the period determined by binding arbitration. Arbitration is to be completed within 90 days after the reports are adopted. To aid the arbitrator in determining a compliance period, the DSU provides a non-binding guideline of 15 months from the date of adoption; awards have ranged from six months to 15 months, one week. The DSU envisions a time period of no more than 18 months from the date a panel is established until the reasonable period of time is established. Where there is disagreement as to whether a Member has complied in a case, a panel may be convened to resolve the dispute (Article 21.5); the compliance panel has 90 days to issue its report, which may be appealed.

Compensation and Suspension of Concessions (Art. 22)

If defending party fails to comply with the WTO recommendations and rulings within the compliance period, the party must, upon request, enter into negotiations with the prevailing party on a compensation agreement within 20 days after the expiration of this period; if negotiations fail, the prevailing party may request authorization from the DSB to retaliate. If requested, the DSB is to grant the authorization within 30 days after the compliance period expires unless it decides by consensus not to do so. The defending Member may request arbitration on the level of retaliation or whether the prevailing Member has followed DSU rules in formulating a proposal for cross-retaliation; the arbitration is to be completed within 60 days after the compliance period expires. Once a retaliatory measure is imposed, it may remain in effect only until the violative measure is removed or the disputing parties otherwise resolve the dispute.

Compliance Issues

While many WTO rulings have been satisfactorily implemented, a number of difficult cases have tested the implementation articles of the DSU, highlighting some deficiencies in the system and prompting suggestions for reform.[6] For example, gaps in the DSU have resulted in the problem of "sequencing," an issue that first manifested itself during the compliance phase of the U.S.-EC dispute over the EC's banana import regime. Article 22 of the DSU allows a prevailing party to request authorization to retaliate within 30 days after a compliance period ends if the defending party has not complied. Article 21.5 provides that disagreements over the adequacy of compliance measures are to be decided using WTO dispute procedures, "including whenever possible resort to the original panel"; the compliance panel's report is due within 90 days and may be appealed. The DSU does not integrate Article 21.5 into Article 22 processes, nor does it expressly state how compliance is to be determined so that a prevailing party may pursue action under Article 22.

Sequencing has been discussed but not resolved in the current WTO dispute settlement negotiations. Multilateral action is needed to revise WTO rules in this area given the January 2001 adoption of a WTO appellate report which in effect concluded that a panel convened to arbitrate the level of trade retaliation under Article 22.6 does not have a mandate to decide initially if a WTO Member is in compliance with WTO rulings, and further stated that rules regarding sequencing must be decided by WTO Members as a whole (Appellate Body Report, *United States — Import Measures on Certain Products from the European Communities*, WT/DS165/AB/R (Dec. 11, 2000)). In the meantime, disputing parties have filled the gap in the DSU through bilateral procedural agreements.

WTO Dispute Settlement and U.S. Law

Adoption of panel and appellate reports finding that a U.S. measure violates a WTO agreement does not give the reports direct legal effect in this country. Thus, federal law would not be affected until Congress or the Executive Branch, as the case may be, changed the law or administrative measure at issue.[7] Procedures for Executive Branch compliance with adverse WTO decisions are set out in §§ 123 and 129 of the Uruguay Round Agreements Act (URAA). The DSU generally applies to disputes involving state and local measures covered by WTO agreements and Members are obligated to ensure compliance at this level (DSU, Art. 22.9 and n.17). Only the federal government may bring suit against a state or locality to declare its law invalid because of inconsistency with a WTO agreement; private remedies based on WTO obligations are also precluded by statute (URAA, § 102(b),(c)).

Sections 301-310 of the Trade Act of 1974 provide a means for private parties to petition the United States Trade Representative (USTR) to take action regarding harmful foreign trade practices. If the USTR decides to initiate an investigation, whether by petition or on its own accord, regarding an allegedly WTO-inconsistent measure, he or she must invoke the WTO dispute process to seek resolution of the problem. The USTR may impose retaliatory measures to remedy an uncorrected foreign practice, some of which may involve suspending a WTO obligation (e.g., a tariff increase in excess of negotiated rates). The USTR may terminate a Section 301 case if the dispute is settled, but under § 306 must monitor foreign compliance and may take further retaliatory action if compliance measures are unsatisfactory.

A "carousel" provision added to § 306 in P.L. 106-200 directs the USTR periodically to revise the list of imports subject to Section 301 retaliation unless the USTR finds that implementation of WTO obligations is imminent or the USTR and the Section 301 petitioner agree that revision is unnecessary.

Article 23 of the DSU requires WTO Members to use DSU procedures in disputes involving WTO agreements and to act in accord with the DSU when determining if a violation has occurred, determining a compliance period, and taking any retaliatory action. Section 301 may be generally be used consistently with the DSU, though some U.S. trading partners continued to complain that the statute allows unilateral action and forces negotiations through its threat of sanctions. The EC challenged Section 301 in the WTO in 1998, with the dispute panel finding that the language of § 304, which requires a USTR determination as to the legality of a foreign practice by a given date, is prima facie inconsistent with Article 23 because in some cases it mandates a determination and statutorily reserves the right for the determination to be one of inconsistency with WTO obligations before the exhaustion of DSU procedures. The panel also found, however, that the serious threat of violative determinations and consequently the *prima facie* inconsistency was removed because of U.S. undertakings, as set forth in the Uruguay Round Statement of Administrative Action (H.Doc. 103-316) and made before the panel, that the USTR would use its statutory discretion to implement Section 301 in conformity with WTO obligations. Moreover, the panel could not find that the DSU was violated by § 306, which directs USTR to make a determination as to imposing retaliatory measures by a given date, given differing good faith interpretations of the "sequencing" ambiguities in the DSU. See Panel Report, *United States — Sections 301-310 of the Trade Act of 1974*, WT/DS152/R (Dec. 22, 1999)(*adopted* Jan. 27, 2000). The EC has also challenged the "carousel" statute described above, but the case remains in consultations (WT/DS200). The issue has also been raised in Doha dispute settlement negotiations.

Recent Legislation Related to WTO Dispute Settlement

In its grant of trade promotion authority to the President in 2002 (P.L. 107-210), Congress directed the Executive Branch to address dispute settlement issues in WTO negotiations, particularly to seek the adherence of panels to previously-agreed standards of review, and provisions encouraging the early identification and settlement of disputes. Three 109th Congress bills — S. 817 (Stabenow), S. 1542 (Stabenow), and H.R. 4186 (Camp) — would create a Chief Trade Prosecutor in the Office of the USTR who would, among other things, assist the USTR in investigating and prosecuting disputes before the WTO. S.2317 (Baucus) would create a Chief Trade Enforcement Officer in the Office of the USTR to do the same. S. 2467 (Grassley) would make the USTR General Counsel a confirmable position and assign to the position functions related to, among other things, WTO dispute settlement. H.R. 4733 (Rangel) would create an Office of the Congressional Trade Enforcer. H.R 5043 (Cardin) would create a Congressional Advisory Commission on WTO Dispute Settlement and allow certain private U.S. persons to participate in WTO dispute consultations and panel proceedings. S. 2467 has been placed on the Senate Legislative Calendar; no other action has been taken to date on these bills.

REFERENCES

[1] The text of the DSU, panel and Appellate Body reports, and information on the WTO dispute process is available at [http://www.wto.org/english/tratop_e/ dispu_e/ dispu_e.htm]. WTO disputes are listed and summarized by the WTO Secretariat in its "Update of WTO Dispute Settlement Cases," available at the WTO website, above. A summary of U.S. dispute settlement activity is provided by the Office of the United States Trade Representative (USTR) in its "Snapshot of WTO Cases Involving the United States," at [http://www.ustr.gov] (search under Trade Agreements, Monitoring and Enforcement). U.S. written submissions to WTO dispute panels are also available at the USTR website. For statistical information on cases involving the United States, see CRS Report RS21763, *WTO Dispute Settlement: Stages and Pending U.S. Activity Before the Dispute Settlement Body*, by Todd B. Tatelman. For the status of current cases in which the United States has been successfully challenged, see CRS Report RL32014, WTO Dispute Settlement: Status of U.S. Compliance in Pending Cases, by Jeanne J. Grimmett.

[2] *DSU Review: Members Continue to Discuss Revised Contributions*, Bridges Weekly Trade News Digest, April 26, 2006, at [http://www.ictsd.org/weekly /06-04-26/wtoinbrief.htm]. In light of the ongoing suspension of the Doha Round, the chairman of the dispute settlement negotiations is currently consulting with WTO Members to determine whether to proceed with negotiations or to await further developments with respect to the Round. Telephone conversation with USTR staff, Sept. 13, 2006.

[3] Special Session of the Dispute Settlement Body, *Report by the Chairman, Ambassador David Spencer, to the Trade Negotiations Committee*, TN/DS/14 (Nov. 25, 2005). For a discussion of proposals, see International Centre for Trade and Sustainable Development, *Review of the Dispute Settlement Understanding*, Doha Round Briefing Series, Nov. 2005, at [http://www.ictsd.org/pubs/dohabriefings/index.htm].

[4] See, e.g., WTO documents TN/DS/W/79 (July 13, 2005), TN/DS/W/82 (Oct. 24, 2005), and TN/DS/W/82/Add.1 (Oct. 25, 2005), as corrected. Recently, at the request of the disputing parties, certain WTO panel proceedings have been open to the public through closed-circuit TV broadcast at the WTO. See *WTO opens panel proceeding to public for the first time*, WTO news item, Sept. 12, 2005; *Registration begins for public hearings of "US/Canada — Continued suspension of obligations in the EC-hormones dispute" (complainant EC) panels on 27-28 September and 2-3 October 2006 in Geneva*, WTO news item, June 26, 2006, at [http://www.wto.org/english/news_e/ news_e.htm].

[5] See European Commission, "DSB Special Session: Non-paper on Panel Composition," December 9, 2003, Ref. 575/03, at 5, at [http://trade-info.cec.eu.int/doclib/html/ 115445.htm].

[6] Some of these issues are discussed in CRS Report RL31860, *U.S.-European Union Disputes in the World Trade Organization*, by Raymond J. Ahearn and Jeanne J. Grimmett.

[7] See Uruguay Round Agreements Act (URAA) Statement of Administrative Action, H.Doc. 103-316, vol. 1, at 1032-33. Implementing legislation states that "[n]o

provision of any of the Uruguay Round Agreements, nor the application of any such provision to any person or circumstance, that is inconsistent with any law of the United States shall have effect." URAA, § 102(a)(1); see also H.Rept. 103-826, Pt. I, at 25. Note that federal courts have held that WTO reports are not binding on the judiciary. For example, *Corus Staal BV v. Department of Commerce*, 395 F.3d 1343 (Fed. Cir. 2005). See generally CRS Report RS22154, *WTO Decisions and Their Effect in U.S. Law*, by Jeanne J. Grimmett.

Chapter 8

TRADE PREFERENCES FOR DEVELOPING COUNTRIES AND THE WTO[*]

Jeanne J. Grimmett

ABSTRACT

World Trade Organization (WTO) Members must grant immediate and unconditional most-favored-nation (MFN) treatment to the products of other Members with respect to tariffs and other trade-related measures. Programs such as the Generalized System of Preferences (GSP), under which developed countries grant preferential tariff rates to developing country products, are facially inconsistent with this obligation because they accord goods of some countries more favorable tariff treatment than that accorded to goods of other WTO Members. Because such programs have been viewed as trade-expanding, however, Contracting Parties to the General Agreement on Tariffs and Trade (GATT) provided a legal basis for one-way tariff preferences and certain other preferential arrangements in a 1979 decision known as the Enabling Clause. In 2004, the WTO Appellate Body ruled that the Clause allows developed countries to offer different treatment to developing countries, but only if identical treatment is available to all similarly situated GSP beneficiaries. Where WTO Members' preference programs have provided expanded benefits, the WTO has on occasion waived Members' WTO obligations. A number of trade preference bills have been introduced in the 109th Congress, including proposed extensions of the GSP and Andean preference programs, each of which is set to expire in 2006. Among these are H.R. 5070, which would extend the GSP and Andean preferences for one year and expand and extend textile benefits under the African Growth and Opportunity Act (AGOA); H.R. 6076 and S. 3904, which would extend until 2008 the GSP, Andean preferences, and a third-country fabric provision for lesser-developed beneficiaries expiring in 2007; and H.R. 6142, which would extend the GSP and the AGOA third-country fabric provision until 2008 and expand textile and apparel benefits for Haiti.

---

[*] Excerpted from CRS RS22183, dated September 25, 2006.

Trade Preferences and GATT MFN Requirements

As parties to the General Agreement on Tariffs and Trade (GATT) 1994, World Trade Organization (WTO) Members must under Article I:1 of the GATT grant immediate and unconditional most-favored-nation (MFN) treatment to the products of other Members with respect to customs duties and import charges, internal taxes and regulations, and other trade-related matters. Thus, whenever a WTO Member accords a benefit to a product of one country, whether it is a WTO Member or not, the Member must accord the same treatment to the like product of all other WTO Members.[1] Tariff preference programs for developing countries are facially inconsistent with this obligation as the favorable treatment provided by the granting country to the goods of a specific group of countries is not extended to all WTO Members. Since preference programs have been viewed as vehicles of trade liberalization and economic development for developing countries, however, GATT Parties have accommodated them in a series of joint actions.

In 1965, the GATT Parties added Part IV to the General Agreement, an amendment that recognizes the special economic needs of developing countries and asserts the principle of nonreciprocity. Under this principle, developed countries forego the receipt of reciprocal benefits for their negotiated commitments to reduce or eliminate tariffs and restrictions on the trade of less developed contracting parties.[2] Because of the underlying MFN issue, GATT Parties in 1971 adopted a waiver of Article I for the Generalized System of Preferences (GSP), which allowed developed contracting parties to accord more favorable tariff treatment to the products of developing countries for 10 years.[3] The GSP was described in the decision as a "system of generalized, nonreciprocal and nondiscriminatory preferences beneficial to the developing countries."

At the end of the GATT Tokyo Round in 1979, developing countries secured adoption of the Enabling Clause, a permanent deviation from MFN by joint decision of the GATT Contracting Parties. The Clause states that notwithstanding GATT Article I, "contracting parties may accord differential and more favourable treatment to developing countries, without according such treatment to other contracting parties" and applies this exception to: (1) preferential tariff treatment in accordance with the GSP; (2) multilateral nontariff preferences negotiated under GATT auspices; (3) multilateral arrangements among less developed countries; and (4) special treatment of the least-developed countries "in the context of any general or specific measures in favour of developing countries."[4] To describe the GSP, the Clause refers to the above-quoted description in the 1971 waiver. The Enabling Clause has since been incorporated into the GATT 1994.[5]

WTO Waivers for Preferential Trade Agreements

The European Union had argued in the GATT that it could further deviate from Article I:1 MFN requirements for nonreciprocal free trade with developing countries under GATT Part IV, discussed above, as well as Article XXIV, which provides an MFN exception for customs unions and free trade areas meeting specified conditions. At issue was the Lomé IV Convention, a preferential, nonreciprocal trade arrangement between the EEC and African, Caribbean and Pacific (ACP) countries. The Convention extended beneficial tariff and quota treatment to ACP imports as well as development assistance to ACP countries. GATT panels concluded in unadopted 1993 and 1994 panel reports that such a deviation was not justified under either provision.[6] Regarding the Article XXIV claim, the 1994 report concluded that because the Lomé Convention involved non-GATT Parties, the Article did not cover the agreement and thus could not be used to justify the inconsistency with Article I of trade preferences for bananas imported from ACP countries.[7] The European Communities (EC) subsequently obtained a temporary waiver of GATT Article I:1 for the Lomé agreement; a waiver was later granted for the successor ACP-EC Partnership (Cotonou) Agreement until December 31, 2007.[8]

WTO WAIVERS FOR U.S. PREFERENCE PROGRAMS[9]

The United States holds a waiver of Article I:1 obligations for tariff preferences accorded the former Trust Territories of the Pacific Island (TTPI); the waiver expires December 31, 2006.[10] U.S. waivers for tariff preferences under the Caribbean Basin Economic Recovery Act (CBERA) and the Andean Trade Preference Act (ATPA), each of which pertained solely to GATT Article I:1 obligations, expired December 31, 2005, and December 4, 2001, respectively.[11] The United States does not hold a waiver for preferences authorized in the African Growth and Opportunity Act (AGOA), which are available to sub-Saharan African countries through September 30, 2015.[12]

In February 2005, the United States submitted requests for new GATT waivers for the following preferential tariff programs through their current expiration dates: (1) CBERA, as amended by the United States-Caribbean Trade Partnership Act (through September 30, 2008); (2) ATPA, as amended by the Andean Trade Promotion and Drug Eradication Act (through December 31, 2006); and (3) AGOA (through September 30, 2015).[13] These programs extend duty-free treatment that in some cases is subject to quantitative restrictions and, consequently, the requests seek waivers not only of GATT Article I:1 but also of GATT Article XIII, paragraphs 1 and 2, which require nondiscrimination in administering quotas. The waivers are still pending, with questions on the programs having been raised by Brazil, China, India, Pakistan, and Paraguay[14]

WTO-LEGALITY OF NON-TRADE CONDITIONS IN PREFERENCE PROGRAMS

In *European Communities - Conditions for the Granting of Tariff Preferences to Developing Countries*, the WTO Appellate Body (AB) explained how developed country WTO members may design preferential-tariff programs within the requirements of the Enabling Clause.[15] The dispute between India and the European Communities (EC) stemmed from an EC Regulation which awarded tariff preferences to a closed group of 12 beneficiary countries on the condition that they combat illicit drug production (the Drug Arrangements). India brought the claim alleging that the Drug Arrangements were inconsistent with GATT Article I:1 and unjustified by the Enabling Clause.

The initial dispute panel, in a report issued on December 1, 2003, concluded that the EC was in violation of its WTO obligations, with one panelist dissenting on procedural grounds.[16] Addressing the nature of the Enabling Clause and its procedural implications, a two member majority first concluded that the Enabling Clause functions as an exception to the GATT Article I:1 MFN obligation and that, consequently, the burden of proof rests on the party that invokes the Enabling Clause as a defense (7.53). The lone dissenter argued that the MFN obligation does not apply to the Enabling Clause and that India did not properly bring the claim under the Clause (9.15, 9.21). Employing a broad reading of the term "non-discriminatory" in the Clause's description of the GSP, the panel concluded that developed countries were required to provide "identical tariff preferences" under GSP schemes to "all developing countries" (7.161). Applying this standard, the panel then ruled that the Drug Arrangements were inconsistent with GATT Article I:1 and could not be justified under the Clause (7.177). The European Communities appealed.

The Appellate Body report, issued on April 7, 2004, first addressed the relationship between GATT Article I:1 and the Enabling Clause. The AB upheld the panel's findings that the Enabling Clause is an exception to GATT Article I:1 and that the Clause does not exclude the applicability of Article I:1 (99-103). The AB explained that the Enabling Clause is to be read together with Article I:1 in the procedural sense, since a challenged measure, such as the Drug Arrangements, is "submitted successively to the test of compatibility with the two provisions." In other words, when the Enabling Clause is implicated, the dispute panel first examines whether a measure is consistent with Article I:1, "as the general rule," and, if it is found not to be so, the panel then examines whether the measure may be justified under the Clause (101-102).

Noting the "vital role" played by the Enabling Clause "in promoting trade as a means of stimulating economic growth and development" and the intent of WTO Members through the Clause to encourage the adoption of preference schemes, the AB found that the Clause was not a typical GATT exception or defense (106, 114). Thus, the AB modified the panel's finding and held that, unlike the ordinary practice with respect to GATT exceptions, under which exceptions are invoked only by the responding party, "it was incumbent upon [complainant] India to *raise* the Enabling Clause in making its claim of inconsistency with Article I:1 of the GATT 1994" and to identify specific provisions of the Clause which it believed were violated by the respondent's measure (115, 123)(emphasis in original). At the same time, the burden of justifying GSP schemes under the cited Enabling Clause provisions still rests on a respondent (125). In application, the AB found that India sufficiently raised the issue, thereby placing the burden on the EC to justify the Drug Arrangements under the Clause.

Most importantly, the AB reversed the panel's substantive decision regarding the breadth of acceptable preference programs under the Enabling Clause. The AB found instead that developed countries can grant preferences beyond those provided in their GSP to developing countries with particular needs, but only if identical treatment is available to all similarly situated GSP beneficiaries (173). The AB elaborated that similarly situated GSP beneficiaries are all GSP beneficiaries that have the "development, financial, and trade needs" to which the treatment is intended to respond (173). In reaching this conclusion, the AB reversed the panel's reading of the term "non-discriminatory" as used to define the GSP in the Enabling Clause. Even under the more expansive view of the Enabling Clause, however, the AB upheld the Panel's ruling that the EC failed to prove the Drug Arrangements were in fact "nondiscriminatory" (189). Two factors led the AB to its conclusion: (1) the closed list of beneficiary countries in the Drug Arrangements could not ensure that the preferences would be available to all GSP beneficiaries suffering from illicit drug production and trafficking, and (2) the Drug Arrangements did not set out objective criteria that distinguished beneficiaries under the Drug Arrangements from other GSP beneficiaries (187, 188).

Before the WTO Dispute Settlement Body adopted the ruling, the U.S. WTO representative stated, according to meeting minutes, that the United States was pleased that the Appellate Body had "reversed the Panel's finding that the Enabling Clause required developed countries under their GSP programs to provide *identical* preferences to *all* developing countries" and that the AB's decision "would help maintain the viability of GSP programs."[17] The United States raised concerns, however, about the AB's finding that complainant India needed to raise the Clause, but that the EC bore the burden of proving that the Drug Arrangements were consistent with the Clause. The United States questioned the legal basis for this "hybrid approach" suggesting that difficulties might ensue in allowing the complaining party to set the burden of proof for the respondent.

TRADE PREFERENCE LEGISLATION IN THE 109TH CONGRESS

S. 191 (Smith) and H.R. 886 (Kolbe) would offer preferential market access for goods produced in certain least-developed countries.[18] The eligible duty-free goods would include textiles, even though they are excluded from the GSP. The pending bills also incorporate the criteria for eligibility in AGOA. H.R. 3175 (McDermott) would extend through September 30, 2015, an AGOA provision that authorizes duty-free treatment of apparel assembled in lesser-developed AGOA beneficiaries regardless of the origin of the fabric. The provision, under which preferential treatment is granted in annually decreasing amounts, is set to expire September 30, 2007 (19 U.S.C.A. § 3721(b)(3)(B)(i)). The bill would also authorize duty-free treatment of over-quota agricultural products from AGOA beneficiary countries, but with a formula for the possible imposition of a safeguard tariff in the event the unit import price of a good is lower than an annual trigger price. S. 1937 (DeWine) and H.R. 4211 (Meek) would amend the CBERA to accord duty-free treatment to certain textiles from Haiti, provided the President certifies that Haiti meets a variety of eligibility requirements, including eliminating barriers to U.S. trade and investment, combating corruption, and protecting internationally recognized worker and human rights.[19] H.R. 5070 (Rangel) would, inter alia, extend the GSP and the Andean trade preference programs for one year, and extend until December 31, 2007, the AGOA third-country fabric provision for lesser-developed African countries. H.R. 6076 (Rangel) and S. 3904 (Baucus) would extend the GSP and Andean preferences, as well as the above-described AGOA benefit, until 2008. H.R. 6142 (Thomas) would also extend the GSP until 2008, with tightened rules for competitive need limitations waivers; extend the AGOA third-country fabric provision until 2008, with an amended rule of origin thereafter; and expand textile and apparel benefits for Haiti. The GSP and Andean programs are set to expire on December 31, 2006.[20]

REFERENCES

[1] While the WTO uses the term "most-favored-nation" to describe nondiscriminatory trade treatment, U.S. law has since 1998 referred to this treatment as "normal trade relations" (NTR) status. See P.L. 105-206, § 5003. This report uses the WTO terminology.

[2] Edmond McGovern, International Trade Regulation 9.212 (updated 1999)[hereinafter McGovern]. Part IV is generally viewed as nonbinding, though some have argued otherwise with regard to certain of its provisions. *Id.*; John H. Jackson, William J. Davey and Alan O. Sykes, Jr., Legal Problems of International Economic Relations 1171 (4th ed. 2002).

[3] GATT, Generalized System of Preferences; Decision of 25 June 1971, L/3545 (June 28, 1971).

[4] GATT, Differential and More Favourable Treatment, Reciprocity and Fuller Participation of Developing Countries; Decision of 28 November 1979, L/4903 (Dec. 3, 1979). In 1999, the WTO General Council waived GATT Article I:1 until June 30, 2009, to allow developing country Members to provide preferential tariff treatment to products of least-developed countries, without being required to do so for like products of other Members. Preferential Tariff Treatment for Least-Developed Countries; Decision on Waiver, WT/L/304 (June 17, 1999).

[5] Agreement Establishing the World Trade Organization, Annex 1A, General Agreement on Tariffs and Trade 1994, 1(b)(iv); *see* WTO Appellate Body Report, *infra* note 15, at 90.3.

[6] McGovern, *supra* note 2, 9.212.

[7] Panel Report, *EEC — Import Regime for Bananas*, 156-164, DS38/R (1994), *as reprinted in* 34 Int'l Legal Materials 180 (1995).

[8] GATT, L/7604 (December 19, 1994); WTO, WT/L/436 (December 7, 2001).

[9] For further information on current U.S. trade preference programs, *see* CRS Report 97-389, *Generalized System of Preferences*, by Vivian C. Jones; CRS Report RL32895, *Textile Exports to Trade Preference Regions*, by Bernard A. Gelb; CRS Report RS21772, *AGOA III: Amendment to the African Growth and Opportunity Act*, by Danielle Langton.

[10] United States — Former Trust Territory of the Pacific Islands; Decision of 14 October 1996, WT/L/183 (Oct. 18, 1996). The waiver covers the Republic of the Marshall Islands, the Federated States of Micronesia, the Commonwealth of the Northern Mariana Islands, and the Republic of Palau.

[11] Council for Trade in Goods, Caribbean Basin Economic Recovery Act; Draft Decision, G/C/W/21/Rev.1 (Oct. 23, 1995); Council for Trade in Goods, Andean Trade Preference Act; Draft Decision, G/C/W/54 (Sept. 4, 1996); World Trade Organization, WTO Analytical Index; Guide to WTO Law and Practice 87 (1st ed. 2003).

[12] African Growth and Opportunity Act, P.L. 106-200, Title I, 19 U.S.C. §§ 3701 *et seq.*, as amended by § 3108 of the Trade Act of 2002 (P.L. 107-210), the AGOA Acceleration Act of 2004 (P.L. 108-274), and the Miscellaneous Trade and Technical Corrections Act of 2004 (P.L. 108-429).

[13] *See* Request for a Waiver; Caribbean Basin Economic Recovery Act , G/C/W/508 (Jan. 3, 2005); Request for a Waiver; Andean Trade Preferences Act, G/C/W/510 (Jan. 3, 2005) and G/C/W/510/Add.1 (Mar. 15, 2005); and Request for a Waiver; African Growth and Opportunity Act (AGOA), G/C/W/509 (Jan. 3, 2005).

[14] See *Minutes of the Meeting of the Council for Trade in Goods*, May 9, 2006, at 3-11, G/C/M/84 (June 29, 2006); Mar. 10, 2006, at 3-13, G/C/M/83 (May 1, 2006); Nov. 10, 2005, at 9-12, G/C/M/82 (Nov. 28, 2005).

[15] Appellate Body Report, European Communities — Conditions for the Granting of Tariff Preferences to Developing Countries, WT/DS246/AB/R (Apr. 7, 2004).

[16] Panel Report, European Communities — Conditions for the Granting of Tariff Preferences to Developing Countries, WT/DS246/R (Dec. 1, 2003).

[17] Dispute Settlement Body, *Minutes of Meeting*, Apr. 20, 2004, 58-59, WT/DSB/M/167 (May 27, 2004)(emphasis in original).

[18] Countries that could be designated as beneficiaries include Afghanistan, Bangladesh, Bhutan, Cambodia, Kiribati, Lao People's Democratic Republic, Maldives, Nepal, Samoa, Solomon Islands, Timor-Leste (East Timor), Tuvalu, Vanuatu, Yemen, and Sri Lanka.

[19] For further information, *see* CRS Report RS21839, *Haitian Textile Industry: Impact of Proposed Trade Assistance*, by Bernard A. Gelb.

[20] Current beneficiaries of the Andean trade preference program, 19 U.S.C.A. §§ 3201 *et seq.*, are Bolivia, Colombia, Ecuador, and Peru. All but Bolivia have been engaged in free trade agreement (FTA) negotiations with the United States, with negotiations having been concluded with Colombia and Peru. It has been U.S. policy to remove a beneficiary country from a tariff preference program once it becomes a party to a U.S. FTA.

INDEX

A

access, viii, x, xi, 2, 3, 4, 6, 7, 9, 11, 12, 14, 15, 16, 18, 20, 21, 25, 28, 29, 30, 32, 39, 40, 73, 82, 87, 88, 89, 90, 92, 93, 94, 96, 97, 99, 100, 101, 102, 103, 105, 107, 108, 109, 111, 112, 114, 129, 130, 145, 156, 161, 162, 175, 185
accounting, 109, 134, 138, 145
achievement, 162
ADA, 162
adjustment, 19, 20, 147
ADP, 171
Afghanistan, 187
Africa, 6, 75, 105, 115, 160
African Growth and Opportunity Act (AGOA), xiii, 181, 183, 185, 186, 187
age, 143
agricultural exports, 61, 110, 111
agricultural market, viii, 6, 11, 12, 14, 32, 39, 87, 92, 99, 103, 162
agricultural sector, 39, 97
agriculture, viii, ix, 2, 4, 6, 7, 8, 9, 10, 12, 14, 15, 16, 17, 18, 19, 20, 21, 22, 23, 24, 25, 29, 30, 32, 64, 80, 84, 87, 88, 90, 92, 93, 102, 103, 104, 105, 112, 115, 117, 127, 134, 137, 139, 140, 146, 148, 161
airlines, 142
alternative(s), 27, 66, 108, 157, 166, 169
aluminum, 145, 148
ambiguity, 161
amendments, 24, 104, 168
annual review, 157
antidumping, xi, xii, 4, 9, 12, 17, 25, 30, 100, 136, 145, 153, 154, 155, 157, 158, 160, 161, 162, 163, 164, 165, 166, 167, 169
Antidumping Agreement, xi, xii, 153, 154, 155, 156, 158, 161, 163, 164, 165, 166, 167, 168
apparel, xiii, 181, 185

Appellate Body, ix, xiii, 36, 42, 47, 64, 121, 122, 156, 161, 165, 171, 174, 176, 177, 179, 181, 183, 184, 185, 186, 187
appendix, 67
appetite, 158
arbitration, ix, 37, 63, 121, 124, 125, 176
Argentina, 6, 19, 71, 75, 115, 140, 160
argument, 45, 175
Armenia, 131, 135
Asian countries, 115
assessment, 23, 24, 106
assets, 135
assumptions, 32, 73, 112
auditing, 3, 29
Australia, viii, 6, 20, 28, 32, 71, 72, 87, 88, 90, 112, 115, 140, 160
Austria, 6
authority, ix, xii, 16, 18, 29, 46, 87, 89, 90, 104, 125, 145, 168, 173, 178
autonomy, 132
availability, 15, 56, 79
average costs, 70
averaging, 71, 164
avian influenza, 140
awareness, 18
Azerbaijan, 135

B

background information, xii, 28, 36, 149, 154, 155
balance of payments, 134
Bangladesh, 187
banking, 135, 141, 147
banks, 123, 141, 151
bargaining, 13, 23, 93
barley, 49, 54, 68, 113
barriers, x, 2, 4, 5, 6, 7, 9, 17, 18, 19, 68, 103, 105, 108, 129, 130, 131, 133, 148, 185

BD, 99
beef, xi, 51, 68, 72, 100, 112, 113, 114, 130, 140
behavior, viii, 33, 65, 69
Belgium, 3, 6
benchmarks, 7, 22
benign, 39
beverages, 136, 143
Bhutan, 187
binding, 7, 23, 24, 26, 38, 40, 147, 168, 176, 180
blame, 166
Bolivia, 6, 115, 187
borrowers, 141
bounds, 73, 94, 107, 110, 116
Brazil, viii, ix, 6, 11, 12, 15, 19, 20, 21, 22, 28, 30, 31, 35, 36, 37, 40, 42, 44, 46, 63, 64, 72, 83, 87, 88, 90, 91, 92, 99, 100, 103, 105, 115, 118, 121, 122, 123, 124, 125, 126, 127, 160, 161, 172, 183
Bretton Woods conference, 133
Britain, 22, 115
Bulgaria, 6, 115
bureaucracy, 135, 148
Burkina Faso, 6, 28, 31, 102, 115, 119
Bush Administration, x, 130

C

Cambodia, 187
Canada, 36, 37, 71, 81, 115, 117, 140, 160, 179
CAP, 84
capacity building, 16, 19, 29, 101
capital account, 134
Caribbean, 2, 6, 13, 28, 31, 71, 115, 182, 183, 186, 187
categorization, 65
category a, 69, 164
category b, 46
cattle, 83, 113
causal relationship, vii, viii, 33
causality, viii, 33, 67
Census, 144, 151
central planning, 133, 135, 136
certainty, 93
certificate, 47, 49, 53, 57, 63, 141
certification, 140
Chad, 6, 28, 31, 66, 67, 82, 84, 102, 115, 119
chicken, 141
children, 48
Chile, 6, 115, 161, 172
China, vii, 1, 3, 5, 6, 19, 21, 71, 90, 102, 103, 105, 115, 131, 134, 146, 149, 160, 161, 172, 183
circulation, 175, 176
civil society, 3
classes, 49, 68, 71

Cold War, 144, 145, 146
collaboration, 124
Colombia, 115, 161, 172, 187
commerce, 5, 29, 132
commodity(ies), vii, viii, 15, 19, 25, 32, 33, 34, 35, 36, 37, 39, 40, 41, 42, 43, 44, 45, 46, 47, 48, 49, 52, 54, 55, 56, 57, 61, 63, 65, 66, 68, 71, 72, 73, 74, 76, 78, 83, 92, 95, 96, 98, 107, 110, 111, 112, 113, 114, 122, 123, 134, 136
commodity markets, 37, 39, 54, 110
communist countries, 133, 145
community, x, 130, 144, 147, 148, 149, 155
comparative advantage, 138
compatibility, 184
compensation, xii, 40, 64, 65, 72, 173, 174, 176
competition, viii, xi, 6, 11, 14, 21, 30, 87, 90, 91, 93, 94, 99, 101, 103, 105, 114, 116, 134, 141, 142, 143, 147, 148, 153, 155
competition policy, 30, 103
competitive advantage, 12, 138
competitive markets, 110
competitive need limitations, 185
competitiveness, 134, 142
competitor, 71, 72, 122
compilation, 162
complexity, 31
compliance, vii, viii, ix, 24, 29, 33, 34, 35, 36, 37, 38, 39, 41, 42, 44, 46, 63, 110, 121, 122, 125, 126, 138, 145, 176, 177, 178
components, 92
composition, 95, 134, 175
computer software, 139
concrete, 2, 13, 14, 18, 20, 91
confidence, 69, 142
confidence interval, 69
conformity, 31, 106, 178
confusion, 7, 136, 143
Congress, viii, x, xi, xii, xiii, 10, 13, 18, 21, 22, 23, 24, 26, 29, 33, 35, 37, 52, 83, 87, 88, 89, 90, 104, 124, 126, 127, 129, 130, 139, 145, 151, 153, 154, 155, 156, 162, 163, 168, 172, 173, 174, 177, 178, 181, 185
Congressional Budget Office, 117, 119
consensus, 2, 5, 12, 14, 15, 21, 63, 133, 149, 154, 162, 163, 174, 175, 176
conservation, 46, 48, 64, 65, 81
constraints, 17, 21, 22, 68
construction, 155
consulting, 40, 179
consumers, 39, 79, 135, 139, 167
consumption, 73, 97, 112
control, 68, 135, 136, 142, 175
convergence, 15

corn, 36, 37, 49, 52, 54, 57, 68, 70, 71, 73, 74, 75, 112, 113
corporate governance, 135
corporations, 156
corruption, 185
Costa Rica, 69, 75, 115, 161, 172
costs, vii, 19, 26, 31, 33, 35, 40, 45, 50, 54, 55, 56, 57, 62, 63, 64, 65, 70, 81, 124, 136, 162, 163
costs of production, 45, 54, 70
Cotonou Agreement, 6
cotton, viii, ix, 6, 10, 14, 15, 31, 32, 33, 35, 36, 37, 40, 41, 42, 43, 45, 46, 47, 48, 49, 54, 57, 61, 63, 65, 69, 70, 71, 72, 73, 74, 75, 89, 90, 92, 101, 102, 103, 110, 112, 113, 115, 116, 118, 119, 121, 122, 123, 124, 125, 126
coupling, 71
coverage, 16, 26, 57, 65, 131, 146, 149
covering, vii, 12, 33, 42, 54, 64
credibility, 26
credit, 14, 37, 40, 43, 48, 51, 66, 69, 91, 94, 106, 110, 116, 122, 123, 124, 126, 145
criticism, xi, 11, 99, 153
crop production, 49
crops, viii, 33, 37, 45, 46, 47, 48, 49, 52, 54, 57, 63, 64, 65, 69, 71, 72, 73, 74, 75, 85, 108, 113, 123
CRP, 48
crude oil, 134
Cuba, 6, 115, 133
currency, 137
current account, 134
current account surplus, 134
current prices, 65
customers, 137, 143
CVD, 34, 38, 41, 42
Cyprus, 6, 151
Czech Republic, 6, 135

D

dairy products, 49, 72
danger, 25
data set, 55
database, 51, 53, 55, 84, 119
dating, 5
debt, 29, 78
decisions, vii, 1, 2, 4, 8, 9, 13, 27, 47, 102, 156, 177
decoupling, viii, 33, 64, 66, 73, 74
defense, 142, 184
deficiency, 46, 47, 48, 49, 51, 53, 63, 111
definition, 5, 32, 73, 123
delivery, 19, 142, 143
demand, 18, 69, 71, 113, 114, 135, 141, 142, 145
democracy, 146

denial, 165
Denmark, 6
Department of Agriculture, 28, 30, 34
Department of Commerce, 144, 145, 151, 157, 171, 172, 180
dependent variable, 68
deposits, 141
depreciation, 134, 136, 145
depression, 44, 78, 134
desire, 17
developed countries, xii, 3, 4, 5, 6, 10, 12, 15, 16, 20, 25, 29, 30, 31, 89, 90, 92, 93, 97, 100, 101, 102, 103, 104, 105, 108, 110, 115, 140, 167, 181, 182, 184, 185, 186
developed nations, xi, 153, 161, 165
developing countries, xiii, 5, 7, 10, 12, 13, 15, 16, 17, 19, 20, 23, 25, 26, 30, 31, 32, 35, 74, 81, 88, 89, 91, 92, 93, 97, 99, 100, 101, 102, 103, 104, 105, 107, 108, 110, 115, 116, 118, 125, 132, 150, 158, 160, 161, 165, 166, 167, 181, 182, 184, 185
developing nations, 21, 154, 161
development assistance, 183
deviation, 92, 97, 182, 183
differential treatment, 9, 29, 30, 92, 104, 105, 161, 165, 167
direct investment, 134, 145, 151
disaster, 48, 52, 53, 65
discipline, 35, 37, 91
discrimination, 72
displacement, 21, 44, 45, 67, 69, 71, 72, 74, 78, 91, 99, 106, 143
Dispute Settlement Body (DSB), ix, 34, 37, 42, 63, 64, 83, 121, 125, 171, 174, 175, 176, 179, 185, 187
Dispute Settlement Understanding (DSU), xii, 34, 38, 39, 41, 42, 43, 44, 63, 82, 83, 173, 174, 176, 177, 178, 179
dissatisfaction, xii, 173
distortions, viii, 35, 37, 87
distribution, 134
divergence, 45
division, 133
division of labor, 133
Doha, v, vii, viii, ix, xi, xii, 1, 2, 3, 4, 5, 6, 7, 8, 9, 11, 13, 14, 15, 16, 18, 19, 20, 21, 22, 23, 24, 25, 26, 27, 28, 29, 30, 31, 32, 33, 35, 42, 64, 72, 74, 87, 88, 89, 90, 92, 93, 96, 102, 103, 104, 107, 109, 110, 111, 114, 115, 117, 118, 119, 125, 140, 153, 154, 161, 169, 170, 173, 175, 178, 179
domestic economy, 133
domestic industry, 41, 74, 77, 149, 156, 157, 164, 165, 166
domestic policy, 39, 94

Dominican Republic, 10, 21
donations, 111
donors, 110
draft, xii, 5, 13, 17, 23, 24, 30, 90, 92, 93, 105, 119, 137, 155, 163, 173, 175
dual exchange rate, 136
due process, 12
Duma, 148, 151
dumping, 37, 42, 103, 104, 145, 155, 156, 157, 158, 163, 164, 165, 166, 167, 169, 171
duplication, 65
duration, 38, 91, 163, 168
duties, xii, 40, 42, 76, 103, 145, 147, 154, 156, 157, 158, 164, 165, 167, 182
duty-free access, 97
duty-free treatment, 183, 185

E

ears, 42, 123
East Timor, 187
Eastern Europe, 142
economic development, 3, 5, 115, 131, 182
economic growth, ix, x, 18, 129, 130, 134, 135, 136, 141, 145, 148, 150, 184
economic institutions, 148
economic policy, 133, 136, 144
economic problem, 134, 135
economic reform(s), xi, 131, 133, 134, 135, 136, 146
economic theory, 147
economics, 48, 68
Ecuador, 75, 115, 187
education, 111, 139
eggs, 83
Egypt, 6, 115
El Salvador, 69, 75, 115
election, 21, 136
electricity, x, 129, 137
emerging issues, 42
emigration, 145, 146
energy, x, 129, 134, 135, 137, 138, 146, 148
engagement, 154, 163
environment, 5, 18, 27, 29, 74, 131, 163
equilibrium, 45, 69
equipment, 139, 142
equity, 73, 76
erosion, 25, 101, 140, 142
estimating, 109
Estonia, 6
Europe, 12, 142
European Commission, 20, 84, 117, 179
European Union (EU), viii, x, 2, 6, 7, 10, 11, 12, 13, 14, 15, 16, 18, 19, 20, 21, 22, 25, 26, 28, 30, 31,
32, 34, 40, 63, 66, 67, 74, 84, 87, 88, 89, 90, 91, 93, 94, 95, 96, 97, 99, 100, 102, 103, 105, 106, 111, 114, 115, 118, 119, 129, 130, 137, 138, 140, 141, 142, 143, 146, 160, 161, 165, 170, 179, 182
eexchange rates, 136
exclusion, 42, 48, 64, 65, 72
expenditures, 57, 142
expertise, 141
export promotion, 40
export subsidies, viii, 4, 11, 14, 15, 31, 39, 40, 41, 42, 43, 62, 68, 73, 76, 87, 88, 89, 90, 91, 92, 93, 94, 99, 101, 102, 103, 104, 105, 106, 108, 109, 110, 112, 113, 119, 122, 123, 139
exporter, 71, 74, 100, 122, 123, 157, 160, 166
exports, ix, 15, 25, 37, 40, 43, 44, 45, 61, 63, 69, 71, 72, 78, 79, 89, 91, 92, 110, 111, 112, 113, 121, 122, 123, 126, 134, 136, 137, 138, 140, 144, 146, 157, 165, 166
exposure, viii, 33

F

fabric, xiii, 181, 185
failure, 2, 4, 13, 25, 26, 79, 125, 154
faith, 178
farm land, 114
farmers, 6, 15, 19, 21, 32, 47, 65, 126
farms, 54, 139
FAS, 118
federal courts, 180
federal government, 53, 139, 140, 177
federal law, 177
fertilizers, x, 129
films, 139
finance, 29, 115
financial crisis, 136
financial sector, 136
financial support, 15, 137
financing, 40, 91, 99, 106, 123
Finland, 6
firms, xi, 3, 79, 142, 144, 153, 155
fish, 12
fisheries, 42, 163
fishing, 163
flex, 96
flexibility, 12, 15, 17, 20, 48, 96, 101, 108, 175
float, 136
focusing, xi, 8, 12, 22, 130
food, 6, 10, 14, 15, 32, 46, 48, 52, 91, 92, 94, 99, 101, 102, 106, 108, 110, 123, 139
food products, 123
foreign aid, 46
foreign banks, 123

foreign direct investment, 134, 145, 151
foreign investment, x, 129, 130, 132, 136, 141, 143, 147
foreign policy, 144
forgiveness, 78
France, 6, 11, 21, 22, 99, 115
free goods, 185
free trade, 21, 26, 89, 182, 187
free trade agreement, 21, 26, 89, 187
free trade area, 182
freedom, 12, 145, 146, 156
fruits, 43, 47, 52, 65, 100
fuel, 134, 145
funding, 58, 77
funds, 76, 89
furniture, 148

G

G-6, viii, 2, 6, 87, 88, 115
GDP, 109, 134, 139
General Agreement on Tariffs and Trade (GATT), ix, x, xi, xii, 2, 5, 29, 34, 37, 38, 41, 44, 75, 76, 77, 82, 103, 129, 130, 131, 133, 142, 144, 149, 154, 156, 161, 169, 170, 173, 174, 181, 182, 183, 184, 186
General Agreement on Trade in Services (GATS), 123, 131, 142, 149
general knowledge, 38
Generalized System of Preferences, xii, 136, 139, 143, 181, 182, 186
generation, vii, 1, 27
Georgia, 146
Germany, 6, 115
gestures, 7
global competition, 134, 155
global markets, 120
global trade, vii, ix, 1, 5, 7, 17, 18, 19, 27, 88, 90, 109, 119
goals, 4, 6, 9, 10, 11, 16, 17, 27, 29, 39, 73, 148
goods and services, vii, 12, 131, 132, 134, 135
governance, 135
government, 3, 21, 28, 29, 40, 43, 49, 52, 53, 54, 55, 66, 70, 72, 74, 75, 76, 77, 78, 79, 81, 91, 103, 106, 112, 114, 122, 123, 131, 135, 136, 137, 138, 139, 140, 141, 142, 143, 144, 145, 146, 147, 148, 177
Government Accountability Office, v, 1
government procurement, 29, 103, 131
grading, 48
grains, 32, 49, 83
grants, 76, 78
grazing, 48, 72

Greece, 6
greed, 38, 40, 103
groups, ix, 3, 5, 6, 12, 17, 18, 19, 21, 24, 25, 28, 74, 88, 93, 124, 134, 164
growth, ix, x, 18, 49, 129, 130, 134, 135, 136, 141, 145, 148, 150, 184
Guatemala, 6, 75, 115
guidance, 4, 7, 166, 167
guidelines, xii, 153, 156, 163, 166, 175
Guyana, 75

H

Haiti, xiii, 75, 181, 185
hands, 21, 135
hard currency, 137
harm, 163
harmonization, viii, 87, 93, 107
harmony, 163
health, 134, 140, 141
health insurance, 141
heat, 71, 137
heating, 137
hip, ix, x, 7, 68, 129, 130, 147, 148
hogs, 113
Honduras, 75
Hong Kong, v, vii, ix, xii, 1, 2, 3, 4, 5, 7, 8, 9, 10, 13, 14, 15, 16, 17, 18, 20, 22, 23, 27, 28, 31, 32, 88, 89, 90, 91, 93, 100, 101, 102, 103, 114, 118, 119, 153, 154, 161, 162, 172
host, 22
House, 18, 24, 93, 103, 119, 127, 139, 168
housing, 135, 139
human rights, 185
Hungary, 6, 135, 149
hybrid, 185

I

identification, 112, 178
images, 3
IMF, 31, 133
immigrants, 21
immunity, 99
implementation, 23, 29, 31, 38, 46, 75, 92, 97, 99, 104, 106, 107, 108, 116, 127, 136, 137, 143, 158, 163, 174, 177, 178
import restrictions, 40, 55, 57, 143
import substitution, 41, 122
imports, 11, 12, 16, 21, 40, 44, 63, 68, 72, 78, 79, 92, 97, 103, 108, 111, 112, 131, 132, 133, 134, 136,

139, 140, 143, 144, 145, 146, 148, 150, 154, 155, 156, 157, 178, 183
in transition, 149
incentives, 70, 76
incidence, 85
inclusion, 46, 47, 65, 70, 73, 82
income, ix, 19, 29, 43, 49, 57, 65, 68, 77, 80, 81, 88, 102, 109, 112, 113, 134
income distribution, 134
income effects, 109
income support, 43
increased competition, 148
independent variable, 68, 69
India, viii, 6, 11, 12, 13, 19, 20, 22, 31, 75, 87, 88, 90, 93, 100, 102, 103, 105, 115, 160, 161, 165, 171, 183, 184, 185
indication, 18, 73
indicators, 138
Indonesia, 6, 115
industrialized countries, 133, 150
industry, 24, 41, 74, 77, 78, 124, 125, 126, 134, 137, 138, 141, 142, 143, 148, 149, 155, 156, 157, 164, 165, 166
infant industries, 141
infants, 48
infrastructure, 77, 111
initiation, 160
inspections, 141
inspectors, xi, 130
institutions, 31, 148
instruments, 161
insurance, 48, 49, 50, 52, 53, 55, 56, 57, 64, 65, 69, 72, 84, 91, 106, 141, 147, 151
intellectual property, x, 29, 129, 131, 132, 137, 138, 139, 145, 146, 148
intellectual property rights, x, 29, 129, 131, 132, 137, 138, 139, 145, 146, 148
intensity, 65
intentions, 125
interaction, 29
interdependence, 133
interest groups, 134
interest rates, 106
intermediaries, 141
international division of labor, 133
International Monetary Fund, 31, 133, 148
international standards, 145
international trade, viii, 5, 37, 64, 87, 104, 114, 126, 138, 147, 158
interval, 69
intervention, 22, 52

investment, x, 30, 35, 103, 105, 107, 129, 130, 131, 132, 134, 135, 136, 141, 143, 144, 145, 146, 147, 148, 185
investors, 144, 145, 146, 148, 151
Ireland, 6
Israel, 6, 115, 161, 172
Italy, 6, 115

J

Japan, viii, 6, 15, 16, 20, 28, 40, 71, 87, 88, 90, 91, 94, 95, 101, 106, 111, 114, 115, 146, 160, 161, 165, 168, 171, 172
jobs, 21, 147
joint-stock companies, 137
judiciary, 180
jurisdiction, 24
justification, 164

K

Kazakhstan, 135
Kenya, 75
Korea, 6, 26, 89, 114, 115, 160, 161, 172
Kyrgyzstan, 146

L

labor, 157
land, 48, 68, 72, 114, 135
language, 26, 64, 82, 161, 168, 178
Latin America, 31, 71
Latvia, 6
laws, 12, 24, 96, 131, 135, 136, 138, 141, 145, 147, 154, 155, 156, 160, 161, 162, 163, 164, 167, 168, 169
LDCs, 5, 6, 13, 16, 29, 92, 95, 100, 101, 103, 108, 109, 115
leadership, ix, x, 7, 10, 25, 124, 129, 130, 147, 148
legal protection, 145
legality, 38, 178
legislation, viii, xi, 18, 21, 23, 29, 32, 34, 35, 37, 43, 89, 104, 122, 126, 133, 135, 153, 167, 168, 179
lending, 89
liberalization, 7, 11, 12, 17, 18, 19, 20, 21, 22, 25, 26, 27, 31, 32, 36, 81, 100, 103, 104, 105, 109, 110, 115, 119, 147, 155, 182
licenses, 143
likelihood, viii, 34, 35, 36, 66
linkage, viii, 23, 33, 37, 45, 52, 64, 65, 67, 68, 71, 73
listening, 114
Lithuania, 6

litigation, ix, 35, 64, 88, 89, 93, 94
livestock, 39, 48, 52, 65, 80, 113, 139
living standard, 147
loans, 48, 52, 76
local government, 140
location, 28
long distance, 142
long run, 135, 147
longevity, 140
lower prices, 126, 167

M

Macedonia, 131
major cities, 134
major decisions, 2, 4, 13
Malaysia, 89, 115, 118
mandates, 178
manufacturing, 21, 134, 155, 160, 162
market, viii, 2, 3, 4, 6, 7, 9, 10, 11, 12, 14, 15, 16, 18, 19, 20, 21, 28, 29, 30, 32, 33, 35, 37, 38, 39, 40, 43, 44, 45, 46, 47, 48, 49, 50, 52, 53, 54, 56, 57, 61, 62, 63, 64, 65, 67, 68, 69, 70, 71, 72, 73, 74, 75, 78, 79, 82, 83, 87, 88, 90, 91, 92, 93, 94, 97, 99, 100, 101, 102, 103, 104, 108, 109, 111, 112, 114, 115, 122, 123, 133, 135, 139, 140, 141, 142, 144, 145, 146, 147, 154, 155, 156, 161, 162, 169, 185
market access, viii, 2, 3, 4, 6, 7, 9, 10, 11, 12, 14, 15, 16, 18, 20, 21, 28, 29, 30, 32, 39, 40, 73, 82, 87, 88, 90, 92, 93, 94, 97, 99, 100, 101, 102, 103, 104, 108, 109, 111, 114, 156, 161, 162, 185
market economy, 135, 139, 141, 144, 146
market opening, 11, 19, 88
market share, 44, 45, 64, 67, 68, 69, 78, 79, 155
market value, 154
market-based economy, 133
marketing, 39, 42, 44, 47, 48, 49, 52, 53, 57, 62, 63, 66, 69, 72, 73, 76, 111, 122, 123, 126
markets, vii, viii, x, xi, 4, 7, 9, 11, 15, 16, 21, 33, 37, 39, 40, 45, 46, 54, 68, 71, 72, 75, 79, 87, 110, 113, 114, 120, 129, 130, 133, 134, 147, 155, 167
Marshall Islands, 186
Mauritius, 6, 28, 115
measurement, 51
measures, xii, 9, 12, 13, 30, 31, 35, 36, 40, 41, 42, 44, 75, 76, 78, 79, 91, 94, 103, 104, 106, 107, 109, 123, 132, 136, 147, 155, 156, 158, 161, 177, 178, 181, 182
meat, 48, 83, 113, 139, 140
media, 28
mediation, 48

membership, viii, x, xi, 5, 26, 38, 87, 122, 130, 131, 132, 140, 149
merchandise, 155, 157, 164, 165, 167
metals, 136, 143, 145
Mexico, 6, 8, 71, 75, 105, 115, 146, 161, 165, 171, 172
Middle East, 71
military, 135, 137
milk, 49, 52, 57, 61, 68, 72, 73, 83, 110, 113
minority, 135, 141
modeling, 45, 68, 70
models, 68
modernization, 142
momentum, 20
monopoly, 79, 91, 136, 141, 142
monopoly power, 91
motion, 37
motivation, 133
movement, 12, 18, 20, 21, 93, 132
multinational corporations, 156

N

narcotic, 108
nation, xii, 26, 131, 138, 142, 144, 156, 181, 182, 186
national income, 29
natural disasters, 15, 48, 79, 81
natural gas, x, 129, 134, 137, 138
natural resources, 134
negative consequences, 35
negative relation, 68
negotiating, ix, xi, xii, 2, 4, 5, 6, 7, 8, 9, 11, 12, 13, 20, 21, 22, 24, 27, 28, 29, 30, 42, 88, 89, 90, 93, 94, 102, 103, 104, 105, 112, 119, 140, 153, 154, 155, 161, 163, 168, 173
negotiation, 11, 18, 19, 22, 29
Nepal, 187
Netherlands, 6, 151
New Zealand, 72, 115, 140, 160
Nicaragua, 69
Nigeria, 6, 115
nontariff barriers, 131
Norway, 6, 101, 115, 161, 172
nuts, 52

O

objective criteria, 166, 185
objectivity, 74
obligation, xii, 177, 181, 182, 184
observations, 71

Index

Office of Management and Budget, 27
Office of the United States Trade Representative, xii, 3, 29, 173, 179
oil(s), x, 83, 129, 134, 136, 137, 144, 165
oilseed, 48, 112
open economy, 133, 135
openness, 132, 148
organization, vii, ix, x, 6, 74, 129, 130
Organization for Economic Cooperation and Development (OECD), 19, 28, 34, 67, 68, 150
organizations, 3, 21, 28, 106, 133
Overseas Private Investment Corporation, 144
oversight, xi, 93, 153, 168
ownership, 48, 135, 137, 142

P

Pacific, 2, 6, 13, 28, 31, 182, 183, 186
Pakistan, 6, 75, 115, 183
Paraguay, 6, 75, 115, 183
partnership, 6, 28
patents, 138
pegged exchange rate, 136
penalties, 156
permit, 45, 73, 99, 125, 140
Peru, 75, 115, 187
pharmaceuticals, 136, 143
Philippines, 6, 115
piracy, 139
planning, 133, 135, 136
plants, 140
Poland, 6, 135, 145, 149
policy makers, 25
policy reform, viii, 33, 38, 39, 42, 46, 66, 72, 73, 74, 87, 94, 104, 110, 112, 116
policymakers, 35, 145
political leaders, ix, x, 7, 129, 130, 146, 147, 148
polychloroprene, 168
poor, 3, 102, 134, 135, 145, 148
population, 134
pork, xi, 114, 130, 140
ports, 143
Portugal, 6
posture, 101
poultry, 48, 52, 83, 100, 113, 139, 140
poverty, 19, 29, 134
poverty rate, 134
power, 21, 135
predictability, x, 7, 31, 93, 129, 130, 132, 138
preference, xiii, 71, 101, 181, 182, 184, 185, 186, 187
preferential treatment, 185

prejudice, vii, 33, 36, 37, 41, 43, 44, 45, 64, 66, 69, 70, 71, 74, 77, 78, 79, 123, 124
premiums, 55, 56, 57, 99
president, 7, 18, 22, 23, 24, 29, 31
Putin, President Vladimir, ix, x, 129, 130, 130, 133, 135, 136, 147, 148, 151
press conferences, 28
pressure, ix, 20, 87, 89, 99, 140, 158
price changes, 68, 75
prices, x, 15, 19, 32, 39, 45, 47, 48, 49, 52, 57, 62, 63, 65, 67, 68, 71, 73, 75, 76, 78, 79, 80, 85, 99, 102, 108, 112, 113, 114, 123, 126, 129, 134, 136, 137, 138, 139, 144, 148, 154, 164, 166, 167
pricing policies, x, 129, 138
primary data, 56
private banks, 142
private sector, 3, 24, 135
privatization, 135, 137, 139
producers, vii, x, 21, 31, 32, 37, 39, 45, 48, 49, 50, 63, 65, 72, 79, 80, 102, 112, 114, 124, 129, 134, 135, 138, 139, 140, 143, 145, 147, 148, 155, 166
product market, 68
production, vii, 15, 33, 39, 45, 46, 47, 48, 49, 51, 52, 54, 56, 57, 61, 63, 64, 65, 66, 69, 70, 71, 72, 73, 74, 75, 79, 80, 81, 94, 99, 107, 111, 116, 125, 135, 138, 139, 140, 142, 145, 148, 167, 183, 185
production costs, vii, 33, 55, 64
production quota, 66
profit, 150
profitability, 114
program, viii, ix, 6, 27, 29, 33, 34, 35, 36, 37, 39, 42, 43, 44, 45, 46, 47, 48, 49, 51, 52, 54, 56, 57, 58, 63, 64, 65, 66, 69, 70, 72, 73, 74, 75, 79, 81, 82, 83, 84, 85, 92, 105, 110, 112, 113, 120, 121, 122, 123, 124, 125, 126, 136, 139, 142, 143, 144, 150, 187
proliferation, 26
property rights, x, 29, 129, 131, 132, 137, 138, 139, 145, 146, 148
proposition, 21, 26, 70
public health, 140
public interest, 157
PVP, 107

Q

qualifications, 65
questionnaires, 18
quota free, 89, 92, 100
quotas, 52, 66, 92, 97, 99, 103, 109, 111, 112, 132, 140, 147, 183

R

rain, 49
range, viii, 2, 3, 4, 13, 17, 21, 24, 28, 30, 32, 46, 87, 99, 100, 101, 108, 136, 137, 141
raw materials, 134, 144, 156
reading, 184
real estate, 114
recession, 134
reciprocity, 25
reconcile, 105, 165
reconciliation, 92
recurrence, 157, 166
reduction, 11, 12, 23, 39, 51, 69, 72, 73, 74, 79, 80, 83, 89, 91, 92, 93, 97, 101, 102, 105, 108, 112, 113, 114
reforms, xi, 20, 38, 94, 107, 111, 113, 131, 133, 136, 146, 154, 155
regional, 9, 12, 19, 26, 30, 89, 108, 136, 139, 140, 148
regression, 45, 68, 69
regression analysis, 45
regulations, 7, 23, 131, 132, 137, 138, 141, 143, 147, 148, 167, 182
regulatory requirements, 79
rejection, 21
relationship, vii, viii, xi, 30, 33, 68, 69, 130, 144, 184
relationships, 45
relevance, vii, 33, 82
reproduction, 139
reserves, 178
resistance, 42
resolution, xii, 137, 141, 145, 149, 168, 173, 174, 177
resources, 134, 139, 140
restaurants, 141
restructuring, 133, 135, 139
retaliation, ix, xii, 7, 37, 63, 64, 121, 124, 125, 156, 173, 174, 175, 176, 177, 178
retardation, 166
returns, vii, 33, 54, 63, 69, 70, 74, 112, 113, 114
revenue, 24, 39, 45, 48, 49, 54, 56, 63, 64, 65, 70, 72, 76, 79, 80, 84, 114
rewards, 65
rice, 32, 37, 43, 44, 47, 49, 52, 54, 57, 61, 63, 65, 68, 70, 71, 73, 74, 75, 78, 83, 112, 113, 114, 123, 137
risk, 13, 18, 19, 29, 35, 43, 124, 127
Romania, 149
rubber, 168
rule of origin, 185
rural development, 46, 92, 102, 108

Russia, ix, x, xi, 115, 129, 130, 133, 134, 135, 136, 137, 138, 139, 140, 141, 142, 143, 144, 145, 146, 147, 148, 149, 150, 151, 172

S

safety, 65, 131, 140
sales, 44, 45, 71, 78, 91, 155, 157, 164
Samoa, 187
sanctions, 123, 124, 178
Saudi Arabia, 69
savings, 141, 175
scaling, 155
school, 48
search, 179
securities, 141
security, 48, 92, 102, 108, 139
seed, 49, 54
Senate, 10, 24, 93, 112, 118, 126, 139, 168, 178
sequencing, 175, 177, 178
series, vii, 1, 3, 4, 5, 7, 18, 23, 24, 38, 68, 74, 137, 182
shaping, 147
shares, 44, 54, 78, 79, 134
sharing, 49, 53
short run, 147
shrimp, 165
sign, 25, 47, 142, 148
signals, 63
signs, 12
simulation, 69, 72, 75, 85
Singapore, 103, 161, 172
social problems, 78
society, 3
software, 139
South Africa, 6, 75, 105, 115, 160
South Korea, 6, 114, 115
Soviet Union, xi, 130, 132, 133, 134, 135, 137, 139, 141, 142, 146, 149
soybean, 75
soybeans, 49, 54, 57, 62, 70, 73, 112, 113
Spain, 6
specialty crop, 52
specificity, 94, 112, 174
speech, 147
speed, 12, 18
Sri Lanka, 187
St. Petersburg, x, xi, 129, 130, 134, 146, 148
stability, x, 97, 129, 130, 142, 148, 149
stages, xii, 108, 137, 156, 173, 174
stakeholders, 22, 155, 156
standards, 3, 29, 45, 79, 131, 140, 145, 178
statistics, 30, 45, 158, 160, 168, 170, 172

steel, x, 129, 145, 148, 155, 160, 165, 172
stimulus, 161
stock, 73, 112, 137, 139
storage, 48, 141
strain, 26
stress, 7, 24
strikes, 79
structural adjustment, 20
structural changes, 132
structuring, 92
subgroups, 164
sub-Saharan Africa, 183
subsidization, 37, 40, 45, 78, 91
subsidy, vii, viii, x, 1, 7, 9, 11, 15, 33, 34, 35, 36, 37, 38, 40, 41, 42, 43, 44, 52, 54, 55, 56, 57, 63, 64, 65, 68, 69, 70, 71, 73, 74, 76, 77, 78, 83, 84, 89, 93, 103, 105, 106, 110, 122, 123, 124, 125, 126, 129, 138
substitution, 41, 122, 134
suffering, 64, 185
sugar, 31, 49, 52, 55, 57, 66, 72, 73, 75, 89, 100, 112, 113, 136, 143
sugar beet, 52
summer, 9
supply, 69, 71, 135, 139
suppression, 37, 44, 45, 67, 71, 74, 78
surplus, 49, 63, 134
surveillance, xii, 173, 174
sustainable economic growth, 148
Sweden, 6
Switzerland, 3, 5, 6, 9, 30, 31, 101, 115, 161, 172

T

Taiwan, 71, 131, 160, 172
tanks, 3, 28
Tanzania, 6
targets, 12, 65, 73, 90, 100, 102, 105, 138, 160
tariff, xii, 1, 7, 9, 11, 12, 15, 16, 17, 18, 20, 23, 24, 25, 30, 31, 32, 38, 40, 73, 76, 88, 92, 93, 94, 96, 97, 99, 100, 101, 102, 103, 105, 108, 109, 110, 111, 112, 123, 131, 136, 140, 142, 143, 144, 146, 150, 177, 181, 182, 183, 184, 185, 186, 187
tariff rates, xii, 30, 40, 102, 109, 136, 181
tax credit, 76
tax reform, 135
taxation, 145
technical assistance, 16, 144
technical change, 163
technology, 29
telecommunications, 142, 148
telephone, 142
temporary protection, 143

tension, 2, 17, 27
territory, 76, 132
textiles, 31, 185
Thailand, 6, 19, 75, 89, 99, 115, 161, 165, 171, 172
theory, 147
third-country fabric, xiii, 181, 185
threat, 25, 36, 76, 157, 166, 178
threshold, vii, 33, 41, 42, 44, 72, 110, 163, 167
thresholds, 7, 22, 92, 96, 149
time, x, xi, 2, 4, 9, 10, 13, 15, 17, 18, 21, 22, 23, 24, 26, 27, 29, 30, 31, 35, 42, 47, 56, 63, 78, 89, 90, 92, 93, 94, 104, 122, 126, 129, 130, 131, 132, 133, 134, 136, 138, 140, 145, 147, 149, 155, 157, 158, 160, 166, 167, 174, 175, 176, 179, 184
time frame, 17, 27, 31, 63, 104, 122
timing, 20, 27
tobacco, 48, 53, 66
total costs, 45, 54, 62
total product, 56, 72, 73, 99, 116, 156
total revenue, 54
TPA, vii, viii, 1, 2, 3, 4, 7, 17, 18, 22, 23, 24, 25, 26, 27, 29, 31, 87, 89, 90, 104, 168
trade, vii, viii, ix, x, xi, xii, 1, 3, 4, 5, 6, 7, 8, 9, 10, 12, 13, 14, 15, 16, 17, 18, 19, 21, 22, 24, 25, 26, 27, 28, 29, 30, 31, 33, 35, 37, 41, 42, 43, 44, 45, 46, 48, 54, 61, 64, 65, 68, 69, 70, 71, 72, 73, 74, 75, 78, 79, 81, 87, 88, 89, 90, 91, 92, 93, 94, 97, 98, 100, 101, 102, 103, 104, 105, 106, 107, 108, 109, 110, 114, 115, 116, 117, 118, 119, 122, 123, 124, 125, 126, 129, 130, 131, 132, 133, 134, 136, 137, 138, 139, 140, 142, 143, 144, 145, 146, 147, 148, 149, 153, 154, 155, 156, 158, 161, 162, 163, 164, 165, 168, 169, 172, 173, 174, 177, 178, 179, 181, 182, 184, 185, 186, 187
trade agreement, xi, 7, 9, 12, 13, 21, 24, 26, 30, 88, 89, 104, 108, 109, 126, 146, 153, 168, 187
trade deficit, 21, 144
trade liberalization, 17, 18, 19, 21, 31, 100, 104, 105, 109, 110, 115, 119, 147, 155, 182
trade policies, 132
trade policy, 3, 21, 109, 110, 145
trade preference, xiii, 108, 144, 181, 183, 185, 186, 187
trademarks, 100, 138
trade-off, 4, 7, 17, 19, 25, 162, 163
trading, vii, x, 5, 7, 10, 14, 20, 22, 26, 40, 79, 89, 90, 104, 125, 129, 130, 138, 147, 149, 155, 158, 162, 169, 178
trading partners, x, 10, 20, 89, 90, 129, 130, 138, 147, 149, 155, 169, 178
transactions, 157, 164
transformation, 156
transition, 10, 53, 135, 139, 141, 149

transition period, 135
transitions, 147
transparency, 7, 12, 29, 31, 65, 103, 149, 162, 163, 166, 167, 175
transport, 79, 99
transportation, 135, 145
trend, 44, 78, 134, 149, 158
triggers, 92
Trinidad and Tobago, 69
trust, 99
Turkey, 115, 160, 161, 172
Tuvalu, 187

U

U.S. economy, 23, 24
U.S. Export-Import Bank, 144
uncertainty, 21, 22, 26
unemployment, 139, 147
unemployment insurance, 147
uniform, 73
unions, 182
United Kingdom, 21
United Nations, 29, 115
United States, vii, viii, ix, x, xi, xii, 1, 3, 4, 5, 6, 7, 10, 11, 12, 14, 15, 16, 18, 19, 20, 21, 22, 23, 24, 25, 28, 29, 30, 31, 34, 35, 36, 37, 40, 42, 43, 44, 45, 46, 47, 49, 51, 62, 63, 66, 70, 71, 74, 83, 87, 88, 89, 90, 91, 92, 93, 94, 96, 97, 99, 103, 105, 106, 110, 111, 112, 121, 122, 123, 124, 125, 127, 129, 130, 132, 133, 137, 138, 140, 141, 142, 143, 144, 145, 146, 148, 149, 153, 155, 156, 157, 160, 161, 163, 165, 167, 168, 169, 170, 171, 173, 174, 175, 177, 178, 179, 180, 183, 185, 186, 187
universities, 68
Uruguay, 5, 6, 7, 23, 31, 36, 37, 51, 52, 71, 75, 81, 88, 89, 97, 99, 103, 104, 114, 115, 116, 131, 133, 140, 142, 154, 174, 177, 178, 179
Uruguay Round, 23, 31, 36, 37, 51, 52, 81, 88, 89, 97, 99, 103, 104, 114, 116, 131, 133, 140, 142, 154, 174, 177, 178, 179
USDA, 34, 35, 46, 47, 48, 51, 52, 53, 54, 55, 56, 57, 58, 62, 70, 73, 81, 82, 83, 84, 98, 114, 118, 119, 124, 127, 150
users, 12, 41, 122, 156, 158, 160

V

values, 78, 82, 114

Vanuatu, 187
variable, 40, 68, 69
variables, 68
variation, 57
vegetable oil, 83
vegetables, 43, 47, 52, 65, 100
vehicles, 143, 182
vein, 167
Venezuela, 6, 75, 115
veterinarians, 141
vision, 27
voice, 139, 147
vulnerability, viii, 34, 35, 36, 43, 45, 46, 66, 70, 71

W

wealth, 134
web, 117
welfare, 26, 75, 110
well-being, 147
West Africa, 6
wheat, 32, 49, 54, 57, 62, 68, 70, 71, 75, 83, 113
wine, 97
winter, 71
withdrawal, 174
women, 48
wool, 49
workers, xi, 153, 154, 155
World Bank, 5, 19, 28, 31, 110, 117, 133, 148, 149, 150
World Trade Organization, vii, ix, x, xi, xii, 1, 3, 6, 27, 29, 31, 33, 34, 35, 67, 81, 82, 88, 114, 117, 118, 119, 129, 130, 150, 153, 154, 161, 169, 170, 171, 172, 173, 179, 181, 182, 186
world trading system, 104
World War I, 133
writing, 46

Y

Yemen, 187
yield, 3, 20, 49, 56, 65, 162
Yugoslavia, 145

Z

Zimbabwe, 6